READING AND WRITING

the WORLD with MATHEMATICS

ONE WEEK LOAN

The *Critical Social Thought* Series

Edited by Michael W. Apple, University of Wisconsin—Madison

READING AND WRITING
the WORLD with
MATHEMATICS

Toward a Pedagogy
for Social Justice

ERIC GUTSTEIN

Routledge
Taylor & Francis Group

New York   London

Published in 2006 by
Routledge
Taylor & Francis Group
270 Madison Avenue
New York, NY 10016

Published in Great Britain by
Routledge
Taylor & Francis Group
2 Park Square
Milton Park, Abingdon
Oxon OX14 4RN

Printed in the United States of America on acid-free paper
10 9 8 7 6 5 4 3

International Standard Book Number-10: 0-415-95083-X (Hardcover) 0-415-95084-8 (Softcover)
International Standard Book Number-13: 978-0-415-95083-1 (Hardcover) 978-0-415-95084-8 (Softcover)
Library of Congress Card Number 2005014291

Library of Congress Cataloging-in-Publication Data

Gutstein, Eric.
   Reading and writing the world with mathematics : toward a pedagogy for social justice/ Eric Gutstein.
         p. cm. -- (Critical social thought)
   Includes bibliographical references.
   ISBN 0-415-95083-X (alk. paper) -- ISBN 0-415-95084-8 (pbk. : alk. paper)
   1. Mathematics--Social aspects--United States. 2. Mathematical readiness. 3. Problem solving--United States. 4. Mathematics--Study and teaching (Elementary)--United States. I. Title. II. Series.

QA10.7.G88 2005
510--dc22
                                                                                          2005014291

Taylor & Francis Group
is the Academic Division of Informa plc.

Visit the Taylor & Francis Web site at
http://www.taylorandfrancis.com

and the Routledge Web site at
http://www.routledge-ny.com

To the people of the Morningside community

Contents

Series Editor's Introduction

Over the past three decades, the broad and diverse area of critical educational studies has made major gains in helping educators understand the complex relationships between education and differential power. The intersecting dynamics of class, race, gender, and sexuality, and how they are represented and struggled over in schools and the curricula, teaching, and evaluative practices that go on in them, have been interrogated in powerful ways. Yet for all of the gains that have been made, many of these materials too often have been "from the balcony." They are often not sufficiently linked to the concrete realities of teachers' and students' lives and to the pedagogic and political agendas of teachers, for example, who take the critical perspectives being produced and who daily attempt to create a practice based on them.

In courses at universities and in activist forums throughout the United States and elsewhere, there is a good deal of attention paid to the politics of curriculum and teaching. There are serious discussions about whose knowledge counts as "official knowledge" and whose knowledge and culture get labeled as being merely "popular" and, hence, are not seen as legitimate in schools. These discussions are often heated and powerful, with voices heard from various groups involved in the public struggles over what we should teach our children (see Apple, 2000, 2001).

In the larger society, members of both dominant and subaltern groups weigh in on these issues in the public arena. People such as E. D. Hirsch, Jr., representing the neoliberal and neoconservative politics of culture now increasingly dominant, claim to have found the one best "common" culture and the one best teaching method (see Hirsch, 2005; Apple, 2005). Yet this claim to have found the universal answer that will supposedly help all children is constantly contested by voices of marginalized groups who call for forms of curricula, teaching, and evaluation that do not instill a culture of dominance (Apple & Buras, in press).

For many people, the issues involved in the struggles over whose knowledge is considered legitimate are clear in areas such as history or reading. After all, there is a long tradition of public battles over these subjects. The "math wars" notwithstanding (Cohen & Hill, 2001), however, it seems to be harder for many politically progressive educators and for the general public to picture how the content and pedagogy of other areas such as mathematics fit into these debates. After all, isn't mathematics simply a technical computational field? Granted, there's an aesthetic component to mathematics, one that speaks to the importance of imagination and intuition; but could it possibly be political? The book you are about to read provides compelling reasons for answering this question with a resounding "Yes."

Rico Gutstein draws his inspiration from Paulo Freire (Freire, 1970). But this book is not simply a re-statement of Freire's crucial work. While it takes its principles from the tradition of critical pedagogy in which Freire was so influential, Gutstein does not stop there. Indeed, he goes much further. *Reading and Writing the World with Mathematics* provides the best "thick" description of the actual application of such principles in schools in cities in the United States. And it does this in a way that shows the power of mathematics both in helping students understand the communities in which they live and in gaining a better sense of how inequalities are produced and contested in this world. Coupled with the descriptions of the work of progressive educators in *Democratic Schools* (Apple & Beane, 1995), with the voices of critical educators in important journals such as *Rethinking Schools* and especially with the material found in *Rethinking Mathematics* (Gutstein & Peterson 2005), and with the crucial work being done in schools such as those in Porto Alegre in Brazil (Apple, Aasen, Cho et al., 2003), Gutstein's book provides a significant stimulus for radically changing the politics of knowledge and pedagogy in mathematics.

Having said that, however, I actually want to partly correct what I just said. The importance of what Rico Gutstein has accomplished goes well beyond one subject area. It provides a model for efforts throughout the curriculum in areas such as science (see also Roth & Barton, 2004) and so many others.

What Gutstein does here has particular resonance today, since this is a time when the forces of conservatism have put immense pressure on education to make closer connections both to an increasingly unequal paid labor market and to a curriculum based on a return to dominant forms of knowledge (Apple, 2001, 2003). Without a sense of the real possibility of interrupting these conservative policies and practices, educators can either become cynical or have nowhere to turn to for alternative and oppositional practices of teaching and curricula that actually work. Thus, if you have read Pauline Lipman's or Angela Valenzuela's powerful critical analyses of what is actually happening in the name of "reform" in urban schools (Lipman, 2004; Valenzuela, 2005) and wonder what you can do to make a difference inside classrooms, this is the book for you. And if you have read Jean Anyon's compelling case for the importance of progressive social movements in transforming the conditions under which schools operate (Anyon, 2005) and want to know how critical curricula and teaching can assist in this, then once again there is no better place to go than this volume.

Neither Gutstein nor I are romantic about what can be done by one teacher to effect lasting social change in and through education. Yet we both believe that it is important for all of us to remind ourselves that education is not divorced from society; it is a significant *part* of society. Because of this, we need to stress something that is too often forgotten. Struggling in and over education—over its curriculum and pedagogy, over its goals, and over the rights of students to collaborate with others in constructing all of this—*is* struggling in society. Gutstein's reflections on this are important. He also shows how cooperative relations between university educators and schools can be built in ways that make a difference both for people from the university and for real students in real schools. For those of us who believe that a democratic and socially critical education can and must be built, the story he tells and his very honest reflections on it provide a model both for collaborative work and for critical curricula and pedagogy. Let us imagine (no, let us *do* it) what schooling would be like if it were multiplied a thousand fold.

Michael W. Apple

*John Bascom Professor of
Curriculum and Instruction
and
Educational Policy Studies
University of Wisconsin–Madison*

References

Anyon, J. (2005). *Radical possibilities: Public policy, urban education, and a new social movement.* New York: Routledge.
Apple, M. W. (2001). *Educating the "right" way: Markets, standards, god, and inequality.* New York: RoutledgeFalmer.

Apple, M. W. (2005). Reply to E. D. Hirsch, Jr. In D. Ravitch (Ed.), *Brookings papers on education policy* (pp. 186–197). Washington, DC: The Brookings Institution.

Apple, M. W., & Beane, J. A. (Eds.) (1995). *Democratic schools*. Alexandria, VA: Association for Supervision and Curriculum Development.

Apple, M. W., & Buras, K. L. (Eds.). (in press). *The subaltern speak: Curriculum, power, and educational struggles*. New York: Routledge.

Apple, M. W., Aasen, P., Cho, M. K. et al. (2003) *The state and the politics of knowledge*. New York: RoutledgeFalmer.

Cohen, D., & Hill, P. (2001). *Learning policy*. New Haven: Yale University Press.

Freire, P. (1970). *Pedagogy of the oppressed*. New York: Herder and Herder.

Gutstein, E., & Peterson, B. (Eds.) (2005). *Rethinking mathematics: Teaching social justice by the numbers*. Milwaukee, WI: Rethinking Schools, Ltd.

Hirsch, E. D., Jr. (2005). Educational reform and content: The long view. In D. Ravitch (Ed.), *Brookings papers on education policy* (pp. 175–186). Washington, DC: The Brookings Institution.

Lipman, P. (2004). *High stakes education*. New York: RoutledgeFalmer.

Roth, W. M., & Barton, A. C. (2004). *Rethinking scientific literacy*. New York: RoutledgeFalmer.

Valenzuela, A. (Ed.) (2005). *Leaving children behind*. Albany, NY: SUNY Press.

Acknowledgments

I am truly convinced that if you don't have a person who is willing to read your work as closely as she reads her own and then gives you the *real*, no-holds-barred feedback, the writing just won't be very good. In my case, I have my friend, comrade, partner, spouse, and colleague, Pauline Lipman, as that critic. After having had me as the critic for your two books, you got your chance to pay me back ... and did you ever! You pushed the ideas, forced me to clarify "fuzzy thinking," and strengthened this book—a lot. I know I wrote it, but if I had done it without you, it would have been substantially weaker. Thanks.

To my co-authors—Maria Barbosa, Adrián Calderón, Grisel Murillo, and Lizandra Nevárez—I look forward to watching you continue to grow into the *mensches* that you are and to our long-term friendships. You all are very special.

My *very* special thanks to Bill Tate and Tom Romberg—since my graduate school days at Wisconsin, you both have consistently and strongly been in my corner and supported me and my work.

My genuine appreciation to Vicki Trinder for research assistance, translation, and field observations; Lizandra Nevárez, Jesús Rojas, and Oscar Sánchez for translation help; Bill Bigelow, Brian Greer, Sandi Gutstein, Annette Henry, Gloria Ladson-Billings, Bill Schubert, Ole Skovsmose, Signe Waller, and Bill Watkins for feedback and discussion on various chapters/parts of the manuscript; Sandi Jackson for pushing me to write this book; Enora Brown, Marta Civil, Nell Cobb, Stephen Haymes, Lena Licón Khisty, Danny Martin, Swapna Mukhopadhyay, and Kgethi Setati for conversations about education and my teaching and research; Ed Silver for supporting that JRME article and working with me to improve it; Tom

Carpenter and all the CGI folks for letting me work on the project years ago (and paying me no less!), where I learned so much about mathematics education; and Rebeca de los Reyes for your unflagging confidence, trust, and support.

To Marilyn Frankenstein: you blazed some trails that I have been lucky enough to walk in, and without them, we would have had a lot less insight on the way.

My thanks also to Michael Apple for your support and belief that this book was worth writing, and to Catherine Bernard, Brook Cosby, Katy Smith, and all the other staff of Routledge/Taylor & Francis for help in making this real.

To my mom for giving me your *chutzpah* and for refusing to cross that picket line at the Harlem Woolworth's when I was a little boy and wanted that ball so much, then helping me to understand why I couldn't have it—thanks. Thanks also to my dad and my sister for always loving me. And to my family, Sandi, Jesse, Cristina, Malayâ, and Celia, and of course, to you, Pauline, you all are an inspiration and powerful source of love and support—I love you all.

Finally, to all the students, family members, and community members of "Morningside," whom I cannot name—I do not speak for you, in any way, but hopefully with you. I thank you all for allowing me to share the struggles for a better collective future for us all.

Portions of this book will appear in the following publications:

Gutstein, E. (in press-a). "And that's just how it starts": Teaching mathematics to develop student agency. *Teachers College Record.*

Gutstein, E. (in press-d). "The real world as we have seen it": Latino/a parents' voices on mathematics for social justice. *Mathematical Thinking and Learning.*

I thank the publishers for permission to reprint or use the material in revised form.

CHAPTER 1

Social Justice, Equity, and Mathematics Education

> With every single thing about math that I learned came something else. Sometimes I learned more of other things instead of math. I learned to think of fairness, injustices, and so forth everywhere I see numbers distorted in the world. Now my mind is opened to so many new things. I'm more independent and aware. I have learned to be strong in every way you can think of. *(Lupe, 8th grade, May 1999)*[1]

On Wednesday, September 11, 2002, the first anniversary of the World Trade Center attack, I stood in front of my seventh-grade mathematics class at Rivera Elementary (a pseudonym), a Chicago public school located in a Mexican immigrant community. At noon, the assistant principal's voice came over the loudspeaker announcing the time, and the city shut down for three minutes of silence by order of Chicago Mayor Daley. At 12:03 I looked up at the 30 somber students in front of me and asked them to put away their math books. I went to the overhead projector, put a blank transparency on the machine, and sat facing them on my high stool. After a few more seconds of silence, I asked my class, "What questions do you have about September 11?"

This was our third class together, and we had just begun to build real relationships. Given the solemnity of the moment and subject, it was not surprising that students were initially silent. But the questions began to come, slowly at first, and then they came and came. I made no attempt to create discussion or answer their questions but only wrote them on the overhead. Their responses were from the heart, reflecting seventh-graders' fears, lack of knowledge about the situation, and plain good sense. They asked things like, "Where is Bin Laden?", "If the U.S. goes to war with Iraq, who will be the allies?", "Will/Can there be another world war?", and "Why did they choose the U.S.?" Candela asked, "Why does Mr. Rico (my classroom name[2]) want to know our questions?" That question I did answer—I told them that I wanted to know them better and that I wanted them to ask as many questions as possible.

After about 15 minutes as the questions slowed, I asked students what questions they thought that people in other countries asked about September 11. They had fewer replies to this, and after about five minutes, I put on the overhead a photo of a rally held in Islamabad, Pakistan on September 15, 2001. The photo showed several men holding a large banner that read, "Americans, Think! Why You Are Hated All Over the World?" (See Figure 1.1.) I asked students what the photo meant to them. They answered things like "people hate us because we are free," "because of our money," and finally someone said, "because we stick our noses in so many other countries' business."

Figure 1.1 Islamabad, Pakistan, demonstration, September 15, 2001 © AP/Wide World Photos.

During this conversation, someone mentioned bombing Afghanistan. I told students that none of the hijackers were thought to be Afghan. I then shared some history, available to anyone who digs, reads, and remembers, but not widely propagated in mainstream media—the CIA involvement in Afghanistan and its funding of the Taliban and the *mujahedeen* (anti-Soviet resistance[3]) in the amount of well over $4 billion (Galster, 2001). I also told them that then-President Reagan referred to the mujahedeen (including Bin Laden) in 1985 as "freedom fighters" (Ahmad, 2001). Someone made a comment about our tax dollars funding them.

After about 40 minutes, we returned to doing mathematics (we had a double period that day). As students worked on problems, I circulated among them. Moises asked me if I would fight against Iraq or Afghanistan. I told him that I would not because I did not believe in going to war for oil, power, and control. Then Lucia said her brother was in the Navy. I asked why, and she said because he did not know what else to do. I then asked would he have enlisted if he had received a four-year college scholarship with full room and board, books, and fees. She said no.

That Friday, I gave my students the first of what I call *real-world* mathematics projects, titled "The Cost of the B-2 Bomber—Where Do Our Tax Dollars Go?" (see Appendix 1). The essence of the project was to use U.S. Department of Defense data and find the cost for one B-2 bomber, then compare it to a four-year, full scholarship to the University of Wisconsin–Madison, a prestigious out-of-state university. The students had to answer whether the whole graduating class of the neighborhood high school (about 250 students) could receive the four-year, full scholarships for the cost of one bomber. Eventually, they discovered that the cost of one bomber could pay for the full, four-year scholarships for the whole graduating class (assuming constant size and costs) for the next 79 years!

This real-world project was one of many that I gave my students in five different classes at Rivera from 1997 to 2003. These projects formed a core component of what I call *teaching mathematics for social justice*, the subject of this book. Hopefully, this vignette gives a taste of what my classes were like—in which real and potentially controversial issues were explored and discussed; genuine views (including my own) and differences were solicited, accepted, and respected; and mathematics became a key analytical tool with which to investigate, make sense out of, and possibly take action on important social justice issues in the world. As Leandro pointed out on the B-2 bomber project, "This is a good way to understand the world because now we see that mathematics is all around us." The stories of my classes, and my students' and my voice, and even those of their parents, fill these pages.

Before sharing these stories, I give a brief overview of this book. My central argument is this: *Students need to be prepared through their mathematics education to investigate and critique injustice, and to challenge, in words and actions, oppressive structures and acts—that is, to "read and write the world" with mathematics.* I discuss the quoted terms in detail, but essentially to read the world is to understand the sociopolitical, cultural-historical conditions of one's life, community, society, and world; and to write the world is to effect change in it. I contend that mathematics education can serve the larger struggles for human emancipation that Paulo Freire (1970/1998) wrote about in *Pedagogy of the Oppressed.* I also argue that teachers (and not only mathematics teachers) need to conceptualize themselves as "transgressive" (hooks, 1994), see their role as part of larger social movements, and explicitly attempt to create conditions for young people to become active participants in changing society. This idea is not new in general, but as I discuss in the next section, with few exceptions it is rarely discussed in mathematics education.

I also describe who my students were, not as individuals (that occurs through their writing), but how they fit into the world as members of particular racial/ethnic, linguistic, and social class groups. In this chapter, I briefly situate their story within the current sociopolitical context of the United States and the world, one of global contradictions and increasing economic and social polarization. I examine the mathematics experiences of those groups and frame my teaching and students' learning with respect to the goals of mathematics education in the country today. I present the plan of the book and conclude the chapter with an introduction to Rivera Elementary. Along the way, I describe myself and how I understand my roles in this narrative, especially my relation to students and their community.

Sociopolitical Context of Mathematics Education

Mathematics education in the United States today is complex and cannot be fully understood independent of broader forces affecting all areas of education—and society. Apple (2004) succinctly characterized the educational situation:

An unyielding demand—perhaps best represented in George W. Bush's policies found in *No Child Left Behind*—for testing, reductive models of accountability, standardization, and strict control over pedagogy and curricula is now the order of the day in schools throughout the country. In urban schools in particular, these policies have been seen as not one alternative, but as the *only* alternative [emphasis original]. (p. x)

I do not try to fully explain this context, as others have done a far better job than I could (e.g., Apple, 2001; Lipman 2004), but important aspects relate specifically to mathematics education. A significant question is: What constitutes mathematical literacy, how does it relate to political economy, and how do different conceptions of it relate to the ways school educate students? Mathematical literacy is important because how one understands it strongly influences mathematics education programs, policies, and practices, and has implications for what students learn in school.

Mathematical Literacy

I examine here the meaning of *functional* and *critical* literacy as they relate to mathematical literacy, the relationship of mathematical literacy to economic competitiveness, and the meaning of mathematical literacy for different groups of students within society.

Functional and Critical Literacy. Functional literacy refers to the various competencies needed to function appropriately within a given society. All societies need to ensure these competencies. A literacy is functional when it serves the reproductive purposes (i.e., maintaining the status quo) of the dominant interests in society—in the United States, these are the needs of capital. Thus, providing functional literacy for some individuals (e.g., low-paid service workers) could mean a curriculum focusing on low-level basic skills, while for others (e.g., "knowledge workers"[4]), it could mean a curriculum emphasizing communicating, reasoning, and solving novel, ill-formed problems. But both curricula are functional in Giroux's (1983) sense:

> Literacy in this [functional] perspective is geared to make adults more productive workers and citizens within a given society. In spite of its appeal to economic mobility, functional literacy reduces the concept of literacy and the pedagogy in which it is suited to the pragmatic considerations of capital; the notions of critical thinking [as in critical literacy], culture, and power disappear under the imperatives of the labor process and the need for capital accumulation. (pp. 215–216)

In contrast, *critical literacy* means to approach knowledge critically and skeptically, see relationships between ideas, look for underlying explanations for phenomena, and question whose interests are served and who benefits. Being critically literate also means to examine one's own and others' lives in relationship to sociopolitical and cultural-historical contexts. Although critical literacy includes acquiring or constructing knowledge of particular concepts, ideas, skills, and facts, it is also avowedly political—to help people recognize oppressive aspects of society so they can participate in creating a more just world (Macedo, 1994).

In 1989, the National Council of Teachers of Mathematics (NCTM)[5] produced the *Curriculum and Evaluation Standards for School Mathematics* (i.e., the NCTM *Standards*). In a critique of the *Standards*, Apple (1992) argued that there were various social forces involved in creating the *Standards*, as in any consensus document, and these included politically progressive mathematics educators but also individuals advancing neoliberal corporate interests. In the larger contested terrain of education policy, situated within the overall political, economical, and ideological context, he contended that issues of power were at play and that the intentions of the principal writers (mostly mathematics educators) could not guarantee to what ends the document would be put. Apple distinguished between functional and critical literacies: "Whose definition of mathematical literacy is embedded in the *Standards*? Literacy is a slippery term. Its meaning varies in accordance with its use by different groups with different agendas" (p. 423). Apple, citing Lankshear and Lawler (1987), contrasted a domesticating, functional literacy designed to make "less powerful groups ... more moral, more obedient, more effective and efficient workers" versus a critical literacy that would "be part of larger social movements for a more democratic culture, economy, and polity" (p. 423).

To address Apple's question about whose version of mathematical literacy the *Standards* embraced, one can examine the NCTM's (2000) vision of a mathematics classroom from the *Principles and Standards for School Mathematics*, the updated NCTM *Standards*, in which "all students have access to high-quality, engaging mathematics instruction" (p. 3). This is a rich image of mathematical literacy:

> Students confidently engage in complex mathematical tasks.... draw on knowledge from a wide variety of mathematical topics, sometimes approaching the same problem from different mathematical perspectives or representing the mathematics in different ways until they find methods that enable them to make progress. ... are flexible and resourceful problem solvers.... work productively and reflectively ... communicate their ideas and results effectively.... value mathematics and engage actively in learning it. (p. 3)

However, I argue that this vision, which I use as a working definition of *mathematical power* in this book, as meaningful and comprehensive as it is, tends to act as functional—not critical—literacy because of how U.S. schools are presently constituted. To clarify, by functional literacy, I do not mean a basic-skills, rote-memorization curriculum. Rather, I refer to any set of competencies that does not engender the systematic search for the root causes of injustice, but instead leaves unexamined structural inequalities that perpetuate oppression. This notion of functionality applies regardless of one's education, and this approach to literacy "even at the highest level of specialism, functions to domesticate the consciousness via a constant disarticulation between the narrow reductionistic reading of one's field of specialization and the reading of the universe within which one's specialism is situated" (Macedo, 1994, p. 15).

Thus, it is not the quality of the curriculum or some other evaluative criteria that determine whether a given curriculum (in the broad sense) promotes functional or critical literacy, but rather how it serves the larger educational and sociopolitical structures and demands of society. But while I argue that almost all mathematics curricula in the United States today (be they imbued with mathematical power or with mindless, drill-and-kill repetition) develop functional literacy because schooling tends to reproduce dominant social relations, it *is* possible to disrupt this—that is, developing mathematical power can serve critical literacy and emancipation. In fact, I contend that this development is a necessary—but insufficient—component of teaching and learning mathematics for social justice, and I explain that in this book.

The Relationship of Mathematical Literacy to Economic Competitiveness. My starting point for examining, from a social justice perspective, the relationship of economic competitiveness to mathematical literacy is its meaning in the original NCTM *Standards*. The NCTM defined four "new societal goals." The first was for "mathematically literate workers" for economic competitiveness and market preparedness:

> Today, economic survival and growth are dependent on new factories established to produce complex products and services with very short market cycles.... Traditional notions of basic mathematical competence have been outstripped by ever-higher expectations of the skills and knowledge of workers; new methods of production demand a technologically competent workforce.... Businesses no longer seek workers with strong backs, clever hands, and "shopkeeper" arithmetic skills. (p. 3)

The NCTM ended the above section by contending that although mathematics should not be taught solely for work-force preparation, nonetheless, businesses needed highly "flexible" and "adaptable" workers to meet rapidly changing economic conditions.

The NCTM also mentioned mathematical literacy in two of its other new societal goals: "lifelong learning" and "opportunity for all." In both, the document couched mathematical literacy in terms of economic competition. The "lifelong learning" subsection was motivated by the statement that changing economic conditions demand adaptive workers who therefore need a form of "dynamic literacy" (p. 4). The NCTM then presented its position on equity in the subsection on "opportunity for all." Although the NCTM stated that "[t]he social injustices of past schooling practices can no longer be tolerated," the opportunity goal also bound mathematical literacy to economic competition. This subsection ends with, "We cannot afford to have the majority of our population mathematically illiterate. Equity has become an economic necessity" (p. 4). Thus equity itself serves market economics.

From a social justice perspective, there is a significant problem with framing mathematical literacy from the perspective of economic competition. In essence, this positioning places the maximization of corporate profits above all else. This is fundamentally in opposition to a social justice agenda that instead places the material, social, psychological, spiritual, and emotional needs of human beings, as well as other species and the planet, before capital's needs. The NCTM position on mathematical literacy has multiple facets, but this current is strongly represented. Its voice is authoritative and representative of a broad segment of mathematics educators and teachers. Furthermore, the 1989 *Standards* were a significant marker in contemporary mathematics education history and set the stage for the development of state standards, "standards-based" curricula, and advanced the mathematics education reform movement in the United States to a new level. I am not suggesting that the actual authors of the *Standards* themselves advocated mathematical literacy to serve only economic competitiveness. However, the positioning of mathematical literacy in the *Standards* situated it in the larger sociopolitical and economic context of U.S. competitiveness in a global economy and the necessity to maintain market share and dominance.

The Meanings of Mathematical Literacy for Different Social Groups. What world is the mathematics education of Latino/a students preparing them for? The national Latino/a *status dropout rate* (youth between 16–24 with no high school or equivalency diploma) was 28%, a rate higher than any other ethnic group (National Center for Education Statistics, 2003). Rivera's neighborhood high school had 547 ninth graders in November 1998. Approximately 260 of that class graduated in 2002, a completion rate of about 48%. These figures correlate with economic data. A 1999 Chicago study found that the mean per capita income was $29,043 for whites, $15,272 for African Americans, $24,594 for Asian Americans, $16,489 for Native Americans, and $12,680 for Latinos/as (Chicago Metropolis 2020, cited in Human Relations Foundation/Jane Addams Policy Initiative, 2003). The situation is worse for undocumented workers (and many Rivera students and families are undocumented). These workers are generally in non-unionized, low-wage service and laborer occupations, approximately 30% of which are restaurant-related, hand-packing and assembly, and janitorial and cleaning jobs. Undocumented workers' median wage in Chicago was $7.00 an hour in 2001, and only 25% of those employed had health insurance (Mehta, Theodore, Mora, & Wade, 2002).

There is some debate about future educational requirements of the U.S. labor force. Popular conceptions occasionally float about that most if not all jobs will require significant technical skills. However, various data suggest otherwise. Although there is a trend that the percentage of jobs requiring technological skills will increase, that is not the whole story. In 2001 the Bureau of Labor Department reported that millions of low-wage jobs requiring minimal training and little technological expertise will be created in the first decade of the 21st century:

> The largest education and training category, short-term on-the job training [requiring one month or less], with 53 million workers in 2000, accounted for 37 percent of total employment and is projected to account for 35 percent of job growth. It is the fastest growing of the four categories requiring work-related training, and includes large faster-than-average-growing occupations such as security guards, teacher assistants, and combined food preparation and serving workers, including fast food. More than half of the 30 occupations with the largest numerical job growth fall into this category. These workers had the lowest earnings of any education and training group in 2000—60 percent as much as the mean for all wage and salary workers. (Hecker, 2001, pp. 80–81)

The fast food industry, with approximately 3.5 million workers in the United States (Schlosser, 2002) is a particularly clear example of this trend. Three of the largest global, fast food corporations (Burger King, McDonald's, and TriCon) employed 3.7 million people in the world in 1999. When their top executives met that year, they articulated the goal of "zero training" for low-skilled workers (Schlosser, 2002). At a taped session at a 1999 conference, the executives spoke with one voice:

"Make the equipment intuitive, make it so that the job is easier to do right than to do wrong" advised Jerry Sus, the leading systems engineer at McDonald's. "The easier it is for him [the worker] to use, the easier it is for us not to have to train him." (Schlosser, 2002, p. 71)

One industry executive advocated that directions be pictorial as much as possible, and if they had to be written, that they be at a fifth-grade level, and in both Spanish and English.

These data suggest a different story than one of all jobs requiring highly technical skills and mathematical power: Capital does *not* need all workers to have the knowledge supported by the NCTM's vision of school mathematics, because, in fact, the labor market does not have positions for all those highly educated workers (Apple, 1986). What it does need, however, especially in Chicago in an era of transnational capital movement, are specific types of workers (Lipman, 2004). This includes an ever-growing army of low-skilled, compliant, docile, pleasant, obedient service sector workers to mow grass, trim hedges, and tend lawns; cook and serve food and clean up afterwards in the restaurants; change the bedding in corporate and tourist hotel industries; take care of children, run errands, and walk dogs; clean houses, schools, cafeterias, hotels, train and bus stations, business offices, clothes, and cars; and perform myriad other tasks that do not require workers to do mathematics in the same ways as the people they serve. Labor force indicators all suggest that these service sector workers not only do not need the same knowledge, skills, and dispositions that highly technologically trained knowledge workers do, but in addition, they will overwhelmingly be low-income, people of color, immigrants, and often women (Paral, 2002). In fact, my students' families *were* these workers. The conception of (mathematical) literacy that applies to them in a stratified labor force is, from the perspective and desires of fast food industry executives, zero training, pictogram instructions, and as a last resort, Spanish and English writing—at a fifth-grade level. On the other hand, the conception of mathematical literacy for knowledge workers is essentially the NCTM's vision of mathematical power.

Thus, even when one distinguishes between critical and functional literacy within contemporary U.S. mathematics education, one has to further realize the layering *within* functional literacy that has a profound impact on people's lives. That is, a particular way the U.S. mathematics curriculum is functional is that it prepares workers differentially and slots people for particular roles in the labor market. No discussion of mathematical literacy in the current period is adequate without a thorough examination and critique of how it interacts with, and whether it contributes to, unequal relations of power in society.

Thus, in analyzing the sociopolitical context of mathematics education, my contention is that (a) mathematical literacy, as a form of functional literacy distinct from critical literacy, serves the needs of capital accumulation in the United States; (b) the NCTM, as the major organizational voice within the mathematics education community, has framed mathematical literacy largely from the perspective of U.S. economic competitiveness in the global order and has avoided discussion of whose interest is served; and (c) mathematical literacy for various groups of students in a stratified labor market, unfortunately, has divergent meanings for different social groups. A reconceptualization of the purpose of mathematics education is needed—one that includes envisioning mathematical literacy as critical literacy for the purpose of transforming society, in its entirety, from the bottom up toward equity and justice, for all students whether from dominant or oppressed groups.

The Mathematics Education of Students of Color and Low-Income Students

Few disagree that mathematics education for certain groups in the United States, primarily Latinos/as and African Americans and some Asian groups of students (e.g., Hmong, Cambodians, and some Asian Pacific Islanders) (Pang, Kiang, & Pak, 2004), is dramatically different from that for white students (Secada, 1992; Tate, 1997). The same is true for low-income students compared to wealthy ones (Anyon, 1980; Knapp & Woolverton, 2004). On every major assessment, at any grade level, Latinos/as and African Americans score well below whites in mathematics, whether one examines the National Assessment of Educational Progress (NAEP) data on fourth and eighth graders or ACT and SAT (FairTest, 2004a, 2004b; NAEP, 2004). This pattern holds true for Chicago Public Schools (CPS) as well (Rosenkranz, 2002). And the gaps are hardly narrowing (NAEP, 2004), although there is evidence that students in the United States overall are learning more mathematics (Tate, 1997).[6] There are some data that students of color are learning more and narrowing achievement gaps on various assessments, but most of those gains may reflect low-level computational skills, rather than deeper, conceptual areas of mathematical power (W. Secada, 1992; personal communication, December 9, 2004). There is also, of course, the problematic nature of trying to assess student learning by examining standardized test scores.

What we do know, in general, is that large disparities between whites and students of color, and between well-off and low-income students exist in course-taking patterns; membership in mathematical (and scientific) fields; and various measures of achievement and learning. Some may argue about the size of, and trends in, the gaps, but the travesty of unequal experiences, opportunities, and outcomes between rich and poor and between whites and students of color is unarguable—equity is not here.

There are certainly examples of mathematical excellence and outstanding learning among low-income students of color, such as *Project Seed* (Phillips & Ebrahimi, 1993; W. F. Tate, personal communication, October 20, 2004), the *Algebra Project* (Moses & Cobb, 2001), *Project IMPACT* (Campbell, 1996), and *QUASAR* (Silver & Stein, 1996), to name but a few, as well as the work of renowned African American mathematician Abdulalim Shabazz (Hilliard, 1991). Hilliard pointed out that Dr. Shabazz, who taught at two historically Black universities, Clark Atlanta University and Tuskegee University, "directly or indirectly, is linked to the production of more than half of the African American holders of the Ph.D. in mathematics" (p. 31).[7]

However, one should pose the question: Why is this excellence not the norm, and why are many surprised and consider it an anomaly when it happens? Furthermore, when individual students of color do succeed, despite educational and (often) economic obstacles strewn in their paths, the meritocracy ideology of individual achievement works to pit people against each other (MacLeod, 1995). Conforti (1992) pointed out that "each instance of success by individual black people undermines racial discrimination as an explanation of the lack of success on the part of other black individuals" (p. 235). This ideology can lead to a blaming of self and others, because if success is individual, then so is failure. An analysis of systemic factors is avoided, and collective solidarities erode. So even "successful" mathematics programs for students of color can get positioned within the larger sociopolitical context in ways that undermine the common benefit of marginalized communities.

Mathematics Education Reform, Social Justice, and Equity

Given this dismal picture of the mathematics "mis-education" of low-income students and students of color (Woodson, 1933/1990), what have educators done? Advocates of equity in mathematics education have addressed these issues for years in many ways. These include, in addition to the ones above, programs focused on gender equity (*EUREKA*, Campbell & Shackford, 1990; *EQUALS*, Mayfield & Whitlow, 1983), those that build on the *funds of knowledge* ("the knowledge base that underlies the productive and exchange activities of households," Moll & González, 2004, p. 700) of working-class communities (Civil, 2002, in press), culturally relevant mathematics teaching (Gutstein, Lipman, Hernández, & de los Reyes, 1997; Ladson-Billings, 1995a; Tate, 1995), community-centered initiatives grounded in students' lived experiences (such as the previously mentioned *Algebra Project*, Moses & Cobb, 2001), as well as research that helps us understand how teachers of bilingual students can use students' home languages as resources (Gutiérrez, 2002; Khisty, 1995; Moschkovich, 2002).

The above projects, and many others, collectively have placed equity closer to the center of the mathematics reform movement. This includes the NCTM agenda, even though, as I explain above, NCTM overshadowed equity's moral imperative by strongly emphasizing economic considerations in the 1989 *Standards*. In the updated version of the *Standards*, *Principles, and Standards for School Mathematics* (NCTM, 2000), the NCTM made equity the first of its six core principles, perhaps to highlight its importance. Overall, the NCTM has been important in bringing equity issues to the awareness of some teachers who may not have considered its relationship to teaching and learning mathematics.

However, the equity framework within mathematics education in the United States is still relatively narrow. The NCTM (2000) still discussed equity mainly from the perspective of ensuring appropriate opportunities to learn, with appropriate supports, but did not critique any societal inequities behind the lack of those opportunities. Nor did the document provide direction as to how one might take steps to rectify the obvious inequities. Missing from discussions within the NCTM circles, and unfortunately from much of those within mathematics education, is that we need fundamental political and economical change in society if we are to even approach equity—and mathematics can play a significant role. Although there are notable exceptions (discussed in chapter 2), mathematics education and educators tend to focus on classroom processes, teaching, and learning, and equity advocates generally seek ways to increase equity *within* mathematics education (e.g., Campbell, 1996; Carey, Fennema, Carpenter, & Franke, 1995). While essential, this is in contrast to the position that society must be thoroughly restructured and that mathematics is a vehicle *through* which to accomplish this change.

The goal of increasing equity within mathematics education does not explicitly position teachers and students as having the transformative power to rectify fundamental structural inequalities through their participation in civil society, both within and outside of educational arenas. In this sense, it does not connect schooling to the larger sociopolitical context of society. And there is little discussion in mathematics education about how teachers can concretely create conditions for students to use mathematics as an analytical tool to understand and begin to work against unjust social conditions. In contrast, I argue that teaching mathematics as such a tool is an essential component in the education of all students, and especially for students of color and low-income students. Not only do these latter students not receive adequate opportunities, resources, teachers, and curricula to learn rich mathematics (Oakes, Joseph, & Muir, 2004; Secada, 1992; Tate, 1997)—but at least as important in my view—even when they do, it is often in settings that do not necessarily prepare them for, nor engage them in, struggles for their own emancipation. A crucial aspect of teaching mathematics for social justice is what students do with the mathematics that they learn. Freire (Freire & Macedo, 1987) explained that

> subordinate students ... can use the dominant knowledge effectively in their struggle to change the material and historical conditions that have enslaved them.... The dominant curriculum must gradually become dominated by the subordinate students so as to help them in their struggle for social equity and justice. (p. 128)

Although the perspective on mathematics education that I critique here is the mainstream one within the United States, outside of mathematics education many view education through more political lenses. Within some literature in critical pedagogy (McLaren, 1998; Darder, 2002; Freire, 1970/1998; Giroux, 1983), critical sociology of education (Apple, 2004; Lipman, 2004), critical multiculturalism (May, 1999; Sleeter & McLaren, 1995), and critical race theory (Ladson-Billings & Tate, 1995; Parker, Deyhle, & Villenas, 1999), global capitalism, political transformation of societies, and liberation from oppression, racism, and sexism are explicitly on the agenda. As Darder (2002) says, "A revolutionary pedagogy discards the uncritical acceptance of the prevailing social order and its structures of capitalist exploitation, and embraces the empowerment of dispossessed populations as the primary purpose of schooling" (p. 57). And even within mathematics education, there are broader views that explicitly connect mathematics, education, and broader sociopolitical contexts, both within and outside the United States. I discuss these in chapter 2.

What This Book Covers

In chapter 2, I present a framework toward teaching mathematics for social justice. I start with Freire's philosophy and general approach to liberatory education and explain how I use his ideas both to guide my teaching practice and as a researcher to analyze it. I then explore the history of African American educational struggles and describe how that history influences this work. I conclude the chapter by discussing strengths and limitations of critical approaches to education, including mathematics education, and what I hope this book will contribute.

In chapters 3, 4, and 5, I describe in depth how the process of teaching mathematics for social justice unfolded in my classroom. Chapter 3 is about how I attempted to create conditions for students to read the world with mathematics and develop sociopolitical consciousness. It begins with a brief overview of my class, pedagogy, and curriculum. I discuss and analyze several real-world projects my students completed. I demonstrate that most students came to view mathematics differently, in various ways, including realizing that it could help them understand and analyze social injustice. I also present how students saw their own development. In chapter 4, I examine more of the real-world projects and how students began to write the world with mathematics and develop a sense of social agency. Chapter 5 is about the development of students' mathematical power, and I consider evidence of their mathematical growth. I also examine the relationship of teaching for social justice to a conceptually based mathematics curriculum—Mathematics in Context (MiC) (NCRMSE & FI, 1997–8). MiC is a *reform* mathematics curriculum[8] and was created for students to develop mathematical power.

In chapter 6, I describe how students and I co-created a classroom environment that facilitated using mathematics to read and write the world, in particular, how we went "beyond the mathematics" to create such a climate. I discuss the support for students' cultural and social identities and the complexities of teaching across race, class, gender, language, and cultural differences. I examine conditions that supported this work as well as those that made it difficult, and I analyze my relative "successful" and "nonsuccessful" efforts.

Chapters 7 and 8 focus on students and parents. Chapter 7 is written by four of my former students with a short introduction by me. The chapter is about how students themselves interpreted their experiences. These students have been involved with me in studying our class since they were in seventh grade (I taught their class for most of their seventh grade and all of their eighth grade, in 1997–8 and 1998–9). As of this writing (April 2005), they are 20 years old.

In chapter 8, I examine parents' views on teaching mathematics for social justice based on a series of interviews I conducted with some of my students' parents. I did these interviews after there was a principal change at Rivera, and the temporary replacement, not liking the political nature of my work, forced me to leave. That action set off a community struggle, involving parents, to reinstate me as a teacher. The struggle then shifted, successfully and appropriately, to removing the temporary principal. I tell that story and examine why parents supported this specific mathematics curriculum for their children.

In chapter 9, I summarize my principal arguments; synthesize aspects of the theoretical framework; and draw out implications for teachers, researchers, teacher educators, and curriculum developers. I return to mathematical literacy and argue why it is now more important than ever to teach for social justice due to the current national and global political climate. Finally, I include a methodological appendix and an appendix containing seven real-world projects my students completed.

As I tell this story and present my analysis, I want to clarify several things. First, like Fecho (2004), this narrative is not about "saving" students from dire fates, their neighborhoods, cultures, or anything else. Second, the more I read, study, and discuss, the more I learn that various educators have been doing, and writing about, the things in this book. Perhaps it has been in different circumstances or contexts, but there is clearly a rich history of education for liberation, both internationally and in the United States, from many people's traditions. With this book, I hope to contribute something to this accumulated knowledge and history of struggle. Third, like all teachers, I have strengths and weaknesses and cannot be honest and ignore them here. My teaching, like most, had some powerful flops as well as what I believe to be genuine impact. I do not gloss over the weaknesses, but I try to understand and analyze them in a broader sociopolitical context.

This story is complicated for several reasons. It is an examination of the process of teaching for change in an urban, public school classroom within larger institutional constraints, unequal relations of power, and a racist and sexist society that mitigates against such change. While there are theoretical frameworks and a few powerful models (e.g., Christensen, 2000), there are no blueprints for critical pedagogy. Much of what I did as a teacher was to follow my instincts, experience, and intuitions, and work with my students to co-construct a classroom environment that supported this type of teaching and learning. We made the road by walking it, and the research that I did, with their assistance, was an attempt to capture the process as it unfolded organically.

This story is also complicated because of race, language, culture, national origin, social class, age, religion, and, for the girls, gender differences between myself and my students. I was engaged in a process of social change with people who were different from me across those dimensions. I am a white, monolingual, male professional, a lower-middle-class Jew raised on the edge of Harlem (New York City), and I grew up in a different time period. I graduated high school in 1970, was much affected and radicalized by the social movements of the 1960s and 1970s, mostly the struggles of African Americans and Puerto Ricans and against the Vietnam War, and have been actively involved in social and political movements since then. My students were all young, bilingual Latinos/as from immigrant, working-class families, almost all from Mexico. In many ways, our lives were different, although we did have some things in common which I address in the book. But in a racist and sexist society in which power and status flows from these attributes, there was a genuine power differential, more so than just teacher–student. While this particular dynamic is common in today's U.S. schools (white teacher, of either gender, and working-class students of color), trying to renegotiate coercive relations of power (Cummins, 1989) across these lines while attempting to build solidarities toward sociopolitical change is complicated and an essential part of this story.

Rivera Elementary School, the "Morningside" Community, and Chicago Public Schools

Rivera is a neighborhood, K–8 school of about 800 students, almost all Mexican or Mexican American, with a few other Latino/a and African American students. In the Rivera community (which I call "Morningside"), people usually call themselves *Mexican* even if they were born in the United States, and few use the term "Chicano." Following neighborhood practice, I use the term "Mexican" throughout, although I recognize the complexity of bicultural, binational fluid identities. The community is transnational, that is, people relate to Mexico and often travel back and forth. Many families visit over winter break or summer, and there are regular buses to and from Mexico. It is common to see passengers lined up with bags waiting for buses on designated corners in Morningside. Despite ensuing gentrification that is slowly but surely bringing *güeros* (whites), often students and artists, Morningside is still very much an intact Mexican community—so intact, in fact, that its strength as a supportive, culturally rich community can sometimes make it insular. I know many parents who have lived in Morningside for 20 or more years and still speak little English. This has much to do with their social, political, and economic exclusion, because they work in low-wage sweatshop factories or service jobs with other Latinos/as (mainly Mexicans), and as is true in many large immigrant communities, one can exist there and only speak one's home language.

Rivera has three educational programs: a monolingual English program, a "transitional" bilingual (Spanish-English) program, and a bilingual honors program. Rivera's tracking is important to the story because, in general, students in the different programs responded differently to me and my efforts to enact a social justice curriculum. However, no apartheid-like division exists at Rivera with white, upper middle-class students inhabiting advanced programs while low-income students of color find themselves in low-track ones. I taught in all of Rivera's programs and worked with many hundreds of students over the past 10 years. The tiny handful of middle-class parents I have known had children in the bilingual honors and monolingual program, but virtually *all* students at Rivera are similar demographically—98% to 99% of the students qualify for free lunch. However, the school socialization and education experiences of Rivera students in the different tracks are vastly different.

I worked at Rivera from fall of 1994 until June 2004, except for two semesters, in many capacities. I coordinated the adoption of MiC and provided professional development to teachers; co-facilitated whole-school discussions on race and culture; participated in a two-year, whole-school self-study team; wrote grants and raised funds for the school; helped teachers align curriculum, assessments, and district frameworks; studied culturally relevant mathematics (and science) pedagogy collaboratively with teachers; worked in many teachers' classrooms as a co-teacher or with students individually and in small groups; organized after-school and Saturday tutoring sessions to help students pass the gatekeeping standardized tests; functioned as a mentor to students and as a confidant to the principal; worked with community organizations; and built substantive, long-term relationships with youth and adults in the larger school community.

I also taught my own mathematics class a number of times. I taught a seventh-grade class in the bilingual program during spring of 1997; then in the fall of 1997, I taught a general-track, seventh-grade monolingual class. In November 1997, I switched to a seventh-grade class in the bilingual honors track and remained with that class through their eighth-grade graduation in June 1999. I refer to them as my "two-year class." I next taught a regular-track, seventh-grade, monolingual class in the 2000–2001 school year, and another seventh-grade class in the bilingual honors track for half of the 2002–2003 school year. While teaching, I had full responsibility for my students' mathematics education, including assessment, grading, parent contact, counseling, high school preparation, and standardized test preparation, although I was never a fulltime classroom teacher.

In Chicago, the Iowa Test of Basic Skills (ITBS) is the test that matters when you are in elementary school. On some level, nothing else counts as much. A student simply cannot get to high school without a sufficiently high score on the "Iowa" (as everyone calls it). Although the system was recently pressured legally by a parent advocacy group to consider additional promotion criteria due to the disproportionate number of students of color failing the test, students still live and die by the eighth-grade Iowa. Their test scores determine whether they graduate, go to summer school, repeat the grade, or, if over age, attend a *transitional school*.[9] To say that the Iowa impacts the lives of students, teachers, parents, administrators, and communities in Chicago is an understatement, and this was certainly true for Rivera. From my research (and that of others), in general, in Chicago, the testing system narrows the curriculum; drives out committed teachers and their efforts to teach in ways that connect to students' lives, cultures, and languages; and prevents teachers from providing students opportunities to think deeply about the conditions of their communities and develop their own questions about their lives (Gutstein, 2003b; Lipman, 2004; Lipman & Gutstein, 2004). During the years I taught at Rivera, CPS ramped up its accountability structures, increased its emphasis on testing, centralized its administration, placed hundreds of schools on probation and other strictures, and generally intruded into the classroom in a multitude of ways to prevent teachers from enacting liberatory pedagogies (Lipman, 2004). All these factors had implications for what was possible in my classroom.

CHAPTER 2

Education for Liberation
Toward a Framework for Teaching Mathematics for Social Justice

Before [liberation], we did not know that we knew. Now we know that we knew. Because we today know that we knew, we can know even more. (A farmer from liberated, postcolonial Guinea-Bissau; Freire & Macedo, 1987, p. 114)

Rico,

Well this past week, as you know, you told me about what things we go under or what kind of "educational system" we're under. That made me think a lot. It now makes a lot of sense, like why you teach us math the way you do. Another thing that I realize now, that you said long time ago, was why they call the U.S. America, if there's North and South America. I guess what I'm trying to tell you is that there's a lot of (excuse me but) B.S. things that exist today that people know it's false, but they still teach it. Like why is there a national holiday for "Columbus Day" if they know that the Native Americans were there first? Why did the U.S. history start there and just forget about the Native Americans? Well, thanks for telling me that and I'm glad I asked you. Now I realize a lot of things. *(Angel's math journal, 8th grade, 12/13/98)*

21

In this chapter, I draw together several ideas to outline a broad framework for teaching mathematics for social justice. My framework is based on a number of educational traditions and emerged as I reflected on my teaching practice and attempted to theorize about what was happening in my class. I started developing the framework in 1997 while teaching, although its roots were in an earlier collaborative project with Rivera teachers on culturally relevant mathematics teaching (Gutstein, Lipman, Hernández, & de los Reyes, 1997). I needed to understand and situate my teaching and students' learning, as well as develop the language to describe them. I turned most of all to Paulo Freire's work and to literature on culturally relevant pedagogy and African American liberatory education. I recognize that some have critiqued Freire's views as inadequate in certain areas, specifically race (Haymes, 2002; Ladson-Billings, 1997) and gender (Ellsworth, 1989; Weiler, 1991). In fact, I turned to others beyond Freire because he did not deal substantively with race or teaching other people's children. However, I find much value in his theories, philosophies, and practices to guide and interpret my work.

I view the idea of liberation from oppression as the fundamental purpose of teaching for social justice. Freire was quite explicit about this goal. In 1964, after a military coup d'état in his native Brazil, he was imprisoned for 70 days and then exiled, supposedly for radical activities. He went to Chile, then a hotbed of Latin American revolutionary practice and thought, and was active in education movements. In the late 1960s, influenced by revolutionary movements in Africa, Southeast Asia, China, and Latin America, including the strong social movements that brought Salvador Allende to power in Chile in 1970, Freire wrote *Pedagogy of the Oppressed* (1970/1998) and clearly stated his goals: liberation from oppression and for the (re)humanization of people.

For Freire (1994), liberation and education were inextricably connected:

> There neither is, nor has ever been, an educational practice in zero space-time—neutral in the sense of being committed only to preponderantly abstract, intangible ideas. To try to get people to believe that there is such a thing as this, and to convince or try to convince the incautious that this is the truth, is indisputably a political practice, whereby an effort is made to soften any possible rebelliousness on the part of those to whom injustice is being done. It is as political as the other practice, which does not conceal—in fact, which proclaims—its own political character. (pp. 77–78)

Using mathematics—in school, as an educational practice to analyze and affect society—is clearly political and consistent with a Freirean perspective.

Other educational traditions also embrace liberation as fundamental. Within the long history of African American education, dating to early slavery days, there is a strong tradition of education for liberation (Anderson, 1988; Bond, 1934/1966; Du Bois, 1935; Perry, 2003; Provenzo, 2002; Woodson, 1933/1990).[1] More recently, Ladson-Billings (1995b) developed a theory of culturally relevant pedagogy for African American students and suggested that a liberatory pedagogy needed to do three things: "produce students who can achieve academically, produce students who demonstrate cultural competence, and develop students who can both understand and critique the existing social order" (p. 474). Similarly, Murrell (1997), in describing an emancipatory pedagogy for African American students, stated, "[t]he essence of a liberatory education project is the *cultivation of a consciousness* and the development of children's identities, as well as academic proficiencies" (p. 28). This historical tradition informs my perspectives, and my framework on teaching mathematics for social justice is similar to Ladson-Billings' and Murrell's conceptualizations.

Teaching Mathematics for Social Justice

Teaching mathematics for social justice flows from the broader notion of liberatory education and has two sets of pedagogical goals: one focused on social justice and the other on mathematics (Figure 2.1). However, both

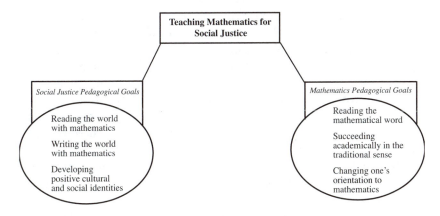

Figure 2.1 Teaching mathematics for social justice.

are necessary in dialectical relationship. The three social justice pedagogical goals are (1) reading the world with mathematics, (2) writing the world with mathematics, and (3) developing positive cultural and social identities. The three mathematics pedagogical goals are (1) reading the mathematical word, (2) succeeding academically in the traditional sense, and (3) changing one's orientation to mathematics.

Social Justice Pedagogical Goals

The three social justice pedagogical goals are important and stand alone in that certain principles apply no matter what one teaches. However, how one actualizes them depends on the discipline. Thus, the goals are simultaneously independent of, and interdependent with, subject matter goals.

Reading the World with Mathematics. *Reading the world* is a term coined by Freire (Freire & Macedo, 1987), and, as I mention in chapter 1, it means, briefly, understanding the sociopolitical, cultural-historical conditions of one's life, community, society, and world. Freire linked it to textual literacy, or learning to read the *word.* He was involved in adult literacy campaigns in Brazil and several other countries, particularly ones emerging from centuries of colonialism. Freire advocated that reading the world should precede reading the word, and that to learn to read, people should first reflect on their lives through political lenses. In Freirean literacy campaigns, field researchers first studied local popular language and selected *generative words* based on their phonemic richness, phonetic difficulty (starting with less difficult ones), and pragmatic tone "which implies a greater engagement of the word in a given social, cultural, and political reality" (Freire, 1973, p. 51). Literacy workers then created *codifications* ("representations of typical existential situations of the group with which one is working," p. 51) in which the generative words were embedded, and then the groups (*culture circles*) examined the codifications. The codifications "function as challenges, as coded situation-problems containing elements to be decoded by the groups.... Discussion of these codifications will lead the groups toward a more critical consciousness at the same time that they begin to learn to read and write" (p. 51). The circle leader focused attention on the generative word only after the circle thoroughly deconstructed the codification, then encouraged participants to visualize the word, and finally presented the word in writing separate from the codification. In this way, the symbols (letters) were tied to ideas generated by circle members who first read their world before reading the particular word.[2] For Freire, reading the world and the word had to happen together: "Not a reading of the word alone, nor a reading only of the world, but both together, in dialectical solidarity" (Freire, 1994, p. 105).

Freire wrote that learning to read the word was always a political act in which one learned to read by reading one's world. However, the two types of "reading" were distinct, and he was well aware of the fallacies of teaching reading disconnected from the process of developing sociopolitical consciousness:

> From the beginning, we rejected the hypothesis of a purely mechanistic literacy program and considered the problem of teaching adults how to read in relation to the awakening of their consciousness.... We wanted a literacy program which would be an introduction to the democratization of culture, a program with men [sic] as its Subjects rather than as patient recipients. (Freire, 1973, p. 43)

Reading the world and the word facilitate each other's acquisition, in that one reason people learn to read is to "read to learn" more about the conditions of their lives and society. This in turn deepens their understanding of society which leads to engagement in social movements, at whatever level people are capable of participating given the daily struggles for survival.

The quotes at the beginning of this chapter, from the farmer in Guinea-Bissau and from Angel, my student, exemplify reading the world. They show the awakening of political consciousness. The farmer reflected on how he and others, collectively, could know more in the present by realizing that they really had valid knowledge in the past, although they did not realize it at the time. Understanding one's own and one's people's development, looking back and appreciating that one has always had knowledge but that fact has been hidden, and being self-empowered to know more through this realization—are all represented in his statement. Angel shows how he had been mulling over certain ideas for a while, rethinking past beliefs and teachings, and coming to new awareness about education, history, pedagogy, nationalism, and politics. His words imply that he was starting to connect various phenomena and beginning to develop a broader analysis. Although mathematics had nothing ostensibly to do with Angel's quote, note that he related to teaching and learning mathematics by saying, "It now makes a lot of sense why you teach us math the way you do."

The idea of reading the world also applies to mathematics. For me, reading the world *with mathematics* means

> to use mathematics to understand relations of power, resource inequities, and disparate opportunities between different social groups and to understand explicit discrimination based on race,

class, gender, language, and other differences. Further, it means to dissect and deconstruct media and other forms of representation. It means to use mathematics to examine these various phenomena both in one's immediate life and in the broader social world and to identify relationships and make connections between them. (Gutstein, 2003c, p. 45)

When students realized that one B-2 bomber equals the cost of providing four-year college scholarships for all the students in the next 79 graduating classes at their neighborhood high school, they were *beginning* to read the world with mathematics. The data and the project functioned as codifications embodying students' futures and the question of allocation of public resources. As they "decoded" the data, they raised questions about the interconnections of these issues and deepened their understanding of how society functions in relation to their own lives. One can know abstractly that a B-2 costs about $2.1 billion, but it can become meaningful and real when one sees oneself and one's future in the numbers. Until then, it may remain just a large number with little connection to one's life.

There are differences in reading the world with mathematics, as my students did, and Freirean literacy campaigns. There are obvious, situational distinctions—mathematics versus reading, youth versus adults, "captives" (i.e., youth who had to attend school) versus volunteers, high-stakes assessments versus no external assessments, relatively fixed "outsider" curriculum versus learner-generated curriculum, the United States versus economically developing and/or newly independent countries, and in-school settings versus community-based situations. But a more conceptual distinction is that in Freirean literacy programs, learners did not actually learn to read in the decodification (i.e., discussion) phase itself,[3] while in my situation, students actually used (and sometimes developed) mathematical tools as part of the decodification. In some settings, they mainly applied mathematics they already knew to new contexts, while in others, they constructed novel mathematical ideas, but in both cases, this is slightly different from a Freirean literacy model. The distinction may be minor but has implications for reading the mathematical word (learning mathematics; see chapter 5).

Writing the World with Mathematics. Freire had a bias toward action. For him, *writing* the world—or changing it—was equally fundamental and could not be separated from reading the world:

Reading the world always precedes reading the word, and reading the word implies continually reading the world.... In a way, however, we can go further and say that reading the word is not preceded merely by reading the world, but by a certain form of *writing* it, or *rewriting* [emphases original] it, that is, of transforming it by means of conscious, practical work. (Freire & Macedo, 1987, p. 35)

Writing the world with mathematics means using mathematics to change the world. An excellent example is Tate's (1995) description of a middle school class in an African American community. The students presented data-based arguments to their city council to confront the problem of a disproportionate number of liquor stores in their neighborhood. Unfortunately, Tate's story is a relatively rare example of younger students actually using mathematics to impact society (see also Turner & Font Strawhun, 2005). Thus, I view writing the world with mathematics as a developmental process, of beginning to see oneself capable of making change, and I refer to writing the world for youth as developing a *sense of social agency*. A "sense" of social agency captures the gradual nature of students' growth—it is not an all-or-nothing proposition. How people perceive and believe in themselves and the actions they actually take is dialectically related. Freire (1970/1998) described this:

Students, as they are increasingly posed with problems related to themselves in the world and with the world, will feel increasingly challenged and obliged to respond to that challenge.... Their response to the challenge evokes new challenges, followed by new understandings; and gradually the students come to regard themselves as committed. (p. 62)

Students (like others) will come to take action over time. Along the way, they change the way they define themselves in relation to the world and their actions on it.

I refer to agency here as *social* rather than individual to clarify that I do not mean primarily psychological or motivational factors such as a student's sense of self efficacy, individual achievement/attainment, or effort optimism —all of which are important and integral to agency—but rather a belief that they are capable of contributing to historical processes. This is related to how one understands history. If one sees it as destiny or as made only by the rich and powerful (as certain "master narratives" of U.S. history suggest) (Takaki, 1993), then one is unlikely to see oneself as an historical actor. Conversely, a grounded understanding of people as the motive force of history (Zinn, 2003) puts one in the position of understanding the potential, including one's own, to contribute meaningfully to social change.

The relationship between reading and writing the world is encapsulated in Freire's notion of *praxis*, the connection of reflection and action. Praxis entails a unity of opposites. So people read the world (develop sociopolitical consciousness) and write the world (develop a sense of social agency) as distinct processes but in the larger movements of social transformation, they occur interdependently. The line between individuals understanding their social reality and the actions they take is not always clearly distinguishable. People deepen their comprehension of the world through engaging in struggles to change their lives, and at the same time, they are more able to change society because they understand it better through actively participating in social change.

Developing Positive Cultural and Social Identities. The final social justice goal is *developing positive cultural and social identities*. By positive cultural identities, I mean that students are strongly rooted in their home languages, cultures, and communities, but at the same time, can appropriate what they need to survive and thrive in the dominant culture (Darder, 1991; Delpit, 1988; Ladson-Billings, 1995b; Murrell, 1997). Ladson-Billings (1995b) named this "cultural competence," in that students are able to "maintain their cultural integrity while succeeding academically" (p. 476). Murrell stated that keeping one's culture included learning to "read the world without losing sight of their cultural community as a source of knowing, understanding, and taking action" (p. 38).

To what extent can educators support the development of students' cultural identities when we are outsiders to their communities, cultures, and languages? In particular, as a white educator, teaching Latino/a students whose cultural backgrounds differed markedly from mine, I had to confront this question. Ladson-Billings (1994) provided examples of three white teachers successfully teaching African American students in culturally relevant ways. She assigned to each teacher a "culture of reference" (p. 28; i.e., with whom did they most affiliate and identify). The culture of reference for one white teacher was white, for one was African American, and for the third was bicultural. Ladson-Billings found that the teacher's ideology and philosophy, and not simply their culture, determined whether the teacher successfully taught the students. Darder (1997) warned of "the trap of essentialist arguments proclaiming that only teachers of color can effectively educate students of color" and added that "the teacher's cultural background, espoused ideology, and academic preparation embody equally important areas of concern in our efforts to create conditions that are conducive to a culturally democratic life in the classroom" (p. 345). However, Murrell (1997) cautioned that

[b]ecause "whiteness" has been constructed in oppositional contrast to "blackness," it is difficult for those who do not already share the cultural motifs of blackness to establish the intersubjectivity needed between learners and teachers in a Freirean literacy learning framework. Two things stand in the way of this intersubjectivity. One is the necessity of white people to critically interrogate and deconstruct their own racial identity in relation to practices of racial oppression and cultural hegemony. The other is to develop the cultural optic of African Americans one needs to "dig again the family wells"—the process of recovering narratives and motifs that are the "dangerous memories" to racial oppression, cultural hegemony, and socioeconomic domination. (p. 37)

Though Murrell and Ladson-Billings referred to African American contexts, the issues are similar for white teachers in Latino/a schools. How I attempted to deal with these complexities had much to do with my own cultural identity, ideology, and life experiences, as well as my understanding of those of my students and their community. I discuss these issues in chapter 6.

I also considered the development of students' social identities, as distinct from cultural identities (though related), to be a social justice pedagogical goal. I mean here that students have the self-confidence, perseverance, and courage to act on their sense of social agency. A caveat is that "to act" for middle school students (indeed for anyone) is always contextualized by one's experiences and level of readiness—and middle schoolers are constrained from acting autonomously by their age, living arrangements, and general societal constraints on youth. People act in ways that are appropriate for them at particular stages of their lives. I discuss students' social identities also in chapter 6.

Mathematics Pedagogical Goals

The mathematics pedagogical goals are more directly about learning mathematics, although I reiterate that both sets of goals—social justice and mathematics—are dialectically interrelated. In the larger framework of teaching mathematics for social justice, each set is necessary, and neither is sufficient by itself.

Reading the Mathematical Word. *Reading the mathematical word* is equivalent to developing mathematical power. Its importance should not be understated in relationship to the social justice goals for several reasons (see chapter 5). First, limited mathematical understanding can prevent students from more fully grasping important political ideas—that is, if one has trouble reading the mathematical word, one may have difficulty reading the world with mathematics (Gutstein, in press-c). Second, issues of academic achievement are concrete, and the barriers are real. Students of color and working class and low-income students are, in general, most impacted by educational underachievement, and their life circumstances suffer most. Economic survival is not an academic discussion for many. To the extent that mathematical power correlates with achievement—which it does not always do—this first goal is crucial. Third, the broader issues of opportunity to learn, access, and equity all demand that marginalized students get the chance to develop mathematical power. And finally, students need specific tools to successfully transform society; mathematical power is such a tool.

Succeeding Academically in the Traditional Sense. Succeeding academically in the traditional sense means that students achieve on standardized tests, pass high school, succeed in college, have access to advanced mathematics courses, and pursue (if they choose) mathematics-related careers. That students achieve "success" in the traditional academic sense is important because of the marginalization and exclusion I detail in chapter 1 and the above point about economic survival. Although having mathematical power suggests that students should achieve traditional success, unfortunately that is not always the case; too many conceptually strong mathematics students do not achieve well on various tests.

My advocacy for traditional success should not be read as a "pipeline" argument (to get more of certain students through the pipeline) but rather as one connected component of a larger, comprehensive set of goals. Some argue that it is important that more students of color, women, and working-class students get access to mathematical courses and life trajectories. I definitely concur but argue against a presumption that more of these students in advanced mathematics classes and careers will necessarily change inequitable relations of power. I disagree with the position that urges increased access to mathematics opportunities, but that simultaneously leaves unchallenged the very structures that created the injustices.

Changing One's Orientation to Mathematics. The third goal is that students fundamentally change their orientation toward mathematics from seeing it as a series of disconnected, rote rules to be memorized and regurgitated, to a powerful and relevant tool for understanding complicated, real-world phenomena. Researchers have documented that many students perceive mathematics as not having meaning and being irrelevant to their lives (Hiebert, Carpenter, Fennema et al., 2003). Some may consider this orientation change central to developing mathematical power. I agree in general, but the distinction between what I discuss in this book and, for example, reform mathematics curricula, is *which* real-world contexts students explore. Reform curricula often are situated in generic real-world settings about daily life, such as shopping, traveling, working, and building. Though important, I distinguish between using mathematics in such settings from those that explicitly ask students to investigate (in)justice. The change in orientation I seek is not just that students believe mathematics is utilitarian, but that they also view it as a tool with which to read the world.

Pedagogical Practices Supporting Social Justice

Teachers can actualize the above social pedagogical goals through various means. Freire (1970/1998) elaborated several pedagogical practices that support education for liberation. Among these are *problem-posing pedagogies* (as distinct from problem-*solving* ones) constituting an education that "involves a constant unveiling of reality.... [that] strives for the *emergence* of consciousness and *critical intervention* in reality [emphases original]" (p. 62). From this perspective, people not only shape history, they also come to understand their power to transcend the fatalism and passivity bred by what Freire termed *banking* systems of education (i.e., "depositing" inert facts into passive recipients). For Freire, problem-posing education poses to students their life conditions not as immutable but merely as challenges or "limit situations" upon which people can act and change. Thus, the starting point for problem-posing pedagogies "must be the present, existential, concrete situation, reflecting the aspirations of the people" (p. 76). He argued, "only by starting from this situation ... can they begin to move. To do this authentically they must perceive their state not as fated and unalterable, but merely as limiting—and therefore challenging" (p. 66). Problem-posing pedagogies are inherently dangerous to the status quo because they prepare students to ask fundamental questions stemming from the concrete analysis of their lives and begin to "unveil reality." Freire pointed out, "Problem-posing education does not and cannot serve the interests of the oppressor. No oppressive order could permit the oppressed to begin to question: Why?" (p. 67). When teachers engage students in reading and writing the world, regardless of the subject, they are enacting problem-posing pedagogies.

In Chicago public schools, navigating between, on the one hand, creating problem-posing pedagogies, and, on the other hand, ensuring that students acquire the social, cultural, and linguistic capital to pass their courses, have real opportunities, and potentially become agents of social change is extremely complex. To resolve this contradiction, teachers may need to provide explicitly students the opportunity to understand the political nature of their educational context. This is important to problem-solving pedagogies, and I give an example in chapter 6.

Another pedagogical practice Freire advocated was for teachers to connect their subject areas to fundamental questions about society:

> And let it not be said that, if I am a biology teacher, I must not "go off into other considerations"—that I must *only* teach biology, as if the phenomenon of life could be understood apart from its historico-social, cultural, and political framework.... If I am a biology teacher, obviously I must teach biology. But in doing so, I must not cut it off from the framework of the whole [emphasis original]. (1994, p. 78)

When teachers ask students to analyze the relationships of school to larger sociopolitical issues, teachers face the thorny question of how to share their own views and analyses, while simultaneously creating space for students to develop their own voices. Freire (Freire & Faundez, 1992) believed that teachers have to both expose students to contrarian views and help them develop their own:

> I have never begun from the authoritarian conviction that I have a truth to impose, the indisputable truth. On the other hand, I have never said, or even suggested, that not having a truth to impose implies that you don't have anything to propose, no ideas to put forward. If we have nothing to put forward, or if we simply refuse to do it, we really have nothing to do with the practice of education.... Educators cannot refrain from putting forward ideas, nor can they refrain either from engaging in discussion with their students on the ideas they have put forward. Basically, this has to do with the near mystery of the praxis of educators who live out their democratic insights: they must affirm themselves without thereby disaffirming their students. (p. 34)

The difficulty of simultaneously affirming oneself as a critical educator —sharing honestly one's views on significant questions—while also affirming one's students is real and a genuine tension I experienced while teaching at Rivera. There is a risk of not doing this well and unduly influencing students to accept the teacher's view without becoming sufficiently independent themselves. But here I again subscribe to Freire's (1994) view: "Is there a risk of influencing the students? It is impossible to live, let alone exist, without risks. The important thing is to prepare ourselves to be able to run them well" (p. 79). I address this dilemma throughout the book, and I discuss how parents perceived it in chapter 8.

Students and teachers need to work together to create a classroom environment in which teachers can actualize the above practices and in which both students and teacher can raise questions, challenges, differences, and problems while conducting political analyses of society. As anyone who has taught middle schoolers can attest, one cannot impose such a classroom culture on them. This co-construction is itself a pedagogical practice supporting education for liberation and relies on meaningful collaboration between students and teachers (Freire, 1970/1998). I discuss in detail this co-construction in chapter 6, and four of my ex-students lend their own voices in chapter 7.

African American Education for Liberation

Many others besides Freire advocated that students and teachers need to be genuine partners in emancipatory education. The strong, well-documented tradition within African American history attests that teachers saw the collective future of their people bound up in their students (Anderson, 1988; Bond, 1934/1966; Foster, 1997; Perry, 2003; Siddle Walker, 1996). hooks (1994) described the "lived pedagogy of the many black teachers of my girlhood [in the rural segregated South] who saw themselves as having a liberatory mission to educate us in a manner that would prepare us to effectively resist racism and white supremacy" (p. 52). Anderson (1988) documented that African American communities emerging from slavery sacrificed whatever was needed to ensure the education of their children as a necessary component of collective survival. Bond (1934/1966) reported that in 1931, African American teachers raised approximately $300,000 for education from Black communities in about half of Alabama's counties (p. 270). This enormous sum of money (during the Great Depression!) is equivalent to about $3.6 million in 2004 dollars.[4]

Perry (2003) elaborated an historical African American philosophy of "freedom for literacy and literacy for freedom, racial uplift, citizenship, and leadership" (p. 6) to which Freire's pedagogy of the oppressed is similar in many ways. She argued that this philosophy is grounded in African Americans' experiences in the United States, institutionalized in their schools and communities, and inscribed in their narratives and traditions. In the face of centuries of slavery, racism, and oppression, the existence of this indigenous philosophy speaks to her question: "How have African Americans, over generations, succeeded in maintaining their commitment to education and producing a leadership and intellectual class?" (p. 7). Perry's presentation of the historical purpose of African

American education drew on Malcolm X's life, whom she paraphrased as follows:

> Read and write yourself into freedom! Read and write to assert your identity as a human! Read and write yourself into history! Read and write as an act of resistance, as a political act, for racial uplift, so you can lead your people well in the struggle for liberation! (p. 9)

The purpose of education from a Freirean point of view strongly echoes these themes.

Perry also discussed learning and teaching in a way that addressed how teachers and students need to work in genuine partnership. Her description of the purpose of learning to read during slavery exemplified these relationships:

> While learning to read was an individual achievement, it was fundamentally a communal act. For the slaves, literacy affirmed not only their individual freedom but also the freedom of their people. Becoming literate obliged one to teach others. Learning and teaching were two sides of the same coin, part of the same moment. Literacy was not something you kept for yourself; it was to be passed on to others, to the community. Literacy was something to share. (p. 14)

Perry framed having knowledge as a collective responsibility and positioned "teachers" (i.e., those who learned to read) as having particular roles in the liberation of their people. While she referred to a specific historical period, she demonstrated that the spirit of reaching out and bringing others along is fundamental to African American educational philosophy.

I draw on this history and tradition because I believe they hold significant lessons for teachers committed to liberatory education. As a white teacher, I could not close the door and "get to my people and tell them all the things they need to know" as one of Foster's (1994, p. 233) African American teacher informants recounted about how he prepared his students to face a racist society. However, I can still see a basis for genuine solidarity between myself and my students in the struggles for a better world. My orientation is that when one teaches for social justice, one does it because "injustice anywhere is a threat to justice everywhere," to quote Dr. King (King, 1986, p. 290). The immediacy of the struggle is not the same for people like myself in positions of relative privilege vis-à-vis my students, as it was (or is) for African American teachers who saw (or see) their futures in their students' faces. But nonetheless, we can stand with our students, and I believe that teachers (and others) need to accept the "gift" of which Vincent Harding (1990) spoke:

> [O]ne of the most powerful aspects of our vocation as teachers over this next period [is] to help the entire nation understand that the freedom struggle of its African American citizens has always been a gift of life and truth to the whole society. Always. (p. 108)

Critical Mathematics Education

These ideas of education for liberation are generally absent from discussions of mathematics education. However, there are exceptions, such as Marilyn Frankenstein's basic mathematics teaching to adults over the past 20 years. She has developed a framework for what she calls *critical mathematical literacy* (1990). In many ways, her work has provided me the most specific guidance on teaching mathematics for social justice, and I have adopted and adapted many of her ideas to my work with middle school students. The goals of her curriculum draw on Freire's ideas and include that students understand mathematics and the political nature of knowledge—whose knowledge is, and is not, valued, as well as how mathematics is often used to hide social realities (1998).

Frankenstein's practices include having students analyze statistical knowledge "critically by examining its underlying interests and methods of collection, description, and inference, and by considering historical, philosophical, and other theoretical insights along with statistical knowledge" (1995, p. 192). Her students probe society's structures and underlying ideologies and begin to understand how mathematics can be used to reveal—or hide—injustice. One way she does this is by using statistical examples that draw students' attention to social inequalities such as how poor people pay taxes they cannot afford while the rich use loopholes to avoid them.

However, Frankenstein was also realistic about the difficulties in having students develop awareness of structural inequities. Like others (e.g., Macedo, 1994), she pointed out that schools teach students to accept the status quo, participating in their own silencing. She contended that independent of strong social movements, there is little likelihood that students will profoundly transform, and she was measured in her expectations of what one mathematics class could provide. While she was hopeful and provided evidence that some students "develop the ability to critique and they increase their questioning of the conditions in which they live" (1987,

p. 201), she acknowledged that they do not easily break with dominant ideologies (1995). She reminded us that "[i]t may be that the most critical collective change that a pedagogy of the oppressed can bring about in our circumstances is a subtle shift in climate that will aid in the progress of liberatory social change" (1987, p. 201). She posed to critical educators the challenge of "how to help students feel, at a deep enough level to challenge the American Dream, that things can be different" (1995, p. 185). This is the difficult question of how to create conditions for students to develop a sense of social agency, and following her, I am also circumspect about my expectations.

Besides Frankenstein, several other mathematics educators in the United States have influenced my understanding of social justice mathematics education. Tate (1994, 1995, 1996, 1997; Tate & Rousseau, 2002) argued for mathematics pedagogy in which the "primary purpose is to empower students to critique society and seek changes based on their reflective analysis" (1995, p. 169). He made clear that the goal of mathematics education should be the same as the "goal of critical race theory [which] is to eliminate racial oppression as part of a larger project to eradicate all forms of oppression" (1999, p. 256). Secada (1991a, 1991b, 1992, 1996, 1999–2002; Secada, Fennema, & Adijian, 1995) has consistently advocated for broadening the analyses in mathematics education to consider fundamental issues of justice, equity, and larger sociopolitical contexts. Peterson (1995, 2003) chronicled his own teaching of fifth-grade Milwaukee students to understand mathematically injustice issues and become socially active. His work serves as an excellent model of teaching mathematics for social justice in a public elementary school. Martin (2000, 2004), Civil (2002, in press), and Gutiérrez (2001, 2002) helped me understand the mathematics learning of African American and Latino/a students, how teachers can support that learning, and the role of sociocultural factors. Boaler (writing about the U.K.; 1997), Mukhopadhyay (1998; Mukhopadhyay & Greer, 2001), and Walkerdine (also writing about the U.K.; 1998), among others, influenced me to think about gender and how it interrelates with power and social class in mathematics education. And Secada (1996), Setati (writing about South Africa; in press; Setati & Adler, 2001), Moschovich (2002), and Khisty (1995) all helped me consider relations of power when students study mathematics in a language not their first.

Besides Frankenstein's work, the principal source on critical mathematics education is Skovsmose's and colleagues' work. Their research is based in Europe, South Africa, and South America. Skovsmose's book, *Towards a Philosophy of Critical Mathematics Education* (1994), posed important questions about the nature of mathematical knowing, purpose of mathematics education, and the meaning of critical mathematical literacy (or *mathe-macy*). Skovsmose asked,

> Is mathemacy also related to the forms of political and ideological ignorance that function as a refusal to know the limits and political consequences of one's view of the world? Could mathemacy be involved in actively naming and transforming the ideological and social conditions that undermine the possibility for forms of community and public life organised around the imperatives of a radical democracy? (p. 27)

In later writings, Skovsmose and colleagues (Skovsmose, 2004, 2005; Skovsmose & Valero, 2001, 2002) broadened the perspective and asked questions about the relationship of mathematics education to globalization and economical and social polarization between (and within) countries. Their fundamental concerns were whether and how mathematics can support the peoples of the world to empower themselves and push societies to distribute more fairly global resources. This larger view encompassing macro sociopolitical forces in relationship to technological and mathematical developments is important in framing the micro context of individual classrooms as we attempt to teach students to read and write the world with mathematics.

The Need for Practical Guidance and Theoretical Rigor

Although many well-known proponents of critical pedagogy (e.g., Giroux, 1983; Macedo, 1994; McLaren, 1998) shed theoretical light on social justice issues, we need more literature that specifies how teachers might actually practice critical pedagogy and how teacher educators might help pre- and in-service teachers do so. May (1999) made this point in discussing critical education:

> A further long-standing criticism of multicultural and antiracist education has been an inability to link effectively theory, policy and practice. Moreover, this criticism has particular purchase for more critical multicultural/antiracist conceptions.... Too often, the concerns of critical educators have been largely ignored because they have been presented as theory divorced from practice; a concern of radical academics with little immediate relevance to either policy makers or practitioners.... After all, it is one thing to proclaim that the world needs to be changed, it is quite another to provide concrete ways by which we might begin the process. (pp. 4–5)

Sleeter and Delgado Bernal (2004) concurred: "Within the United States it [critical pedagogy] has been developed mainly at a theoretical level, often leaving practitioners unclear about what to do.... There is a need for practical guidance that does not, in the process, sacrifice conceptual grounding" (p. 244).

However, while I agree with these critiques, I believe that it is a mistake to overlook the work of teachers and teacher-researchers who define their work as pro-justice, anti-racist, for the common good, or for the survival of their people. The long history of African American liberatory education suggests that we have much to learn from those experiences. The publisher, Rethinking Schools, probably the single most prolific source for critical teaching ideas in the United States today, has published articles and books such as *Rethinking Our Classrooms* (Bigelow, Christensen, Karp et al., 1994), *Rethinking Columbus* (Bigelow & Peterson, 1998), *Rethinking Globalization* (Bigelow & Peterson, 2002), *Reading, Writing, and Rising Up* (Christensen, 2000), and now *Rethinking Mathematics* (Gutstein & Peterson, 2005), as well as the urban education journal *Rethinking Schools.* These have all contributed to Sleeter's and Delgado Bernal's (2004) call for "practical guidance." They have "provide[d] concrete ways by which we might begin the process" of describing how to change the world, as May (1999, p. 5) rightly states we need. It is true, however, that the literature on teaching for social justice and culturally relevant and critical pedagogy, for the most part, rarely addresses mathematics. I mention some of the exceptions in the first two chapters, but the need exists for more practical guidance and theoretical rigor about teaching and learning mathematics for social justice. Building on what has already been done, I have tried in this book to suggest concrete direction while maintaining conceptual clarity, drawing lessons from the actual practice of teaching mathematics for social justice in an urban, Latino/a school.

CHAPTER 3

Reading the World with Mathematics
Developing Sociopolitical Consciousness

> My views about the world have changed the most. This class has
> helped me understand issues like poverty, hunger, wealth, equal-
> ity, and racism. I mean before I thought people lived in nice
> houses because they worked and others were poor because they
> didn't work. Now I know that sometimes wealth is not distributed
> evenly and that racism sometimes affects economical problems.
> *(Freida, 8th grade, May 1999)*

I live in the Albany Park neighborhood in Chicago, with a lot of brick bun-
galows and two-flats with small yards. Most people there who own houses
mow their own grass, but retirees and some others use garden services.
Every Tuesday for years, I knew it was Tuesday because I would look out
my window and see a crew working on a neighbor's yard. An older white
man sat in a pickup truck, reading the newspaper, while several younger
Latinos scurried around, doing all the work at high speed. Every Tuesday,
the same story. My wife and I would comment on it. Below is my journal
entry from the first week of class in 1998, with the eighth graders in my
two-year class; I taught them most of their seventh grade, so we knew each
other well by then.

Now, was this ever an interesting class. I started out by saying, "everyday racism number one." Then I told the story of the guy sitting in the truck while the gardeners did all the work. Then I asked them what they thought the person sitting looked like and what the workers looked like. They said, "white guy sitting" (Armando), "people of color doing the work" (Alejandra). I should have asked them how they knew that, but I didn't. Instead, I made some comment about that being racism. Then I kind of waited for a minute. Finally, Armando said, "why is that racism?" (9/2/98)

After Armando said that, I responded, "Oh, that's a really good question. Is it racism?" For the next 20 minutes, we had a fascinating discussion. Students argued a variety of positions. Some said that the white man probably owned the company, so I asked, "How do you think he got to own the company?" Someone said that he probably was in the United States longer than the Latinos/as and that when one is here longer, one has more opportunity to own companies (and other things). I then asked them to explain the situation of African Americans in Chicago (with which they were familiar—none of us recalled seeing an African American sitting while others worked). They could not really explain. But Rosa persisted and said that Latinos/as come here as immigrants and expect to start at the bottom and work their way up. Further, she said, and Freida joined in, that one could get to own companies by getting more money by going to better schools and therefore getting higher paying jobs. I asked how might the white man have received the opportunity to go to a better school, and Rosa and Freida argued that his family could have had more money. But when I asked how that might have occurred, the circular reasoning became somewhat apparent, and they reverted to the argument that Latinos/as come here as immigrants.

The conversation segued into the relationship between where one lives, how much one makes, and what kind of school one attends. Since we were discussing race and racism, we talked about who lived in which neighborhoods, in terms of race and social class. The next day, I gave students a project, "Racism in Housing Data?", based on the discussion. The first part was as follows:

This past Tuesday in class, we had a discussion about racism. First we talked about the white man in the truck and the Latino gardeners, then we talked about the major league baseball home run race and who's "American,"[1] then we discussed the 1998 median price of a single-family home in the north shore suburb of Kenilworth (which has the most expensive house prices of any

Chicago suburb—$752,250). I asked you, and we discussed, if racism had anything to do with the Kenilworth housing data.

Write at least two good paragraphs on the following question: "How could you use mathematics to help answer the question of whether racism has anything to do with the house prices in Kenilworth?" Be detailed and specific! Describe:

1. What mathematics you would use to answer that question.

2. How you would use the mathematics.

3. If you would collect any data to answer the question, explain what data you would collect and why you would collect that data.

4. Give examples of data that would cause you to believe that racism is involved in the Kenilworth data, and explain why you reached that conclusion based on the analysis of your sample data.

5. Give examples of data that would cause you to believe that racism is *not* involved in the Kenilworth data, and explain why you reached that conclusion based on the analysis of your sample data.

This was typical of the real-world projects I gave my students. These projects were a central part of my curriculum, in addition to conversations about racism, sexism, social class, immigration, foreign policy, budgetary expenditures, and other topics.

An Overview of My Curriculum and Pedagogy

The real-world projects and related conversations comprised about 15% to 20% of students' time in my classes, although in one class (2000–2001), I spent less time on the projects because I struggled that year trying to get students to take themselves seriously as learners and work together (see chapter 6). I taught the Mathematics in Context (MiC) curriculum the rest (75% to 80%) of the time, although in 2000–2001, I taught the Connected Mathematics Project (CMP) (Lappan, Fey, Fitzgerald et al., 1997) most of the year supplemented by MiC. On average, students completed three to four real-world projects per semester. Occasionally I had students do other open-ended problems or projects for variety, fun, or different types of intellectual challenges (e.g., some open-ended problems from the Interactive Mathematics Program [IMP]) (Fendel, Resek, Alper, & Fraser, 1998).

I generally followed the broad recommendations of the National Council of Teachers of Mathematics (NCTM) (1989, 2000) on teaching mathematics. The two curricula were aligned with the NCTM *Standards*, and my own mathematics education included working closely with MiC project staff and being a staff member as a doctoral student with the "Cognitively Guided Instruction" project (Carpenter, Fennema, Franke et al., 1999), a project that could be said to have influenced the *Standards*. I tried to build on students' informal mathematical knowledge; encouraged students to develop their own strategies; and provided opportunities for them to articulate (in writing and verbally), share, discuss, and critique ideas in a supportive, respectful atmosphere. I emphasized conceptual understanding and viewed skill development as an outgrowth of students solving meaningful mathematical problems. I also was well aware of the dire consequences of standardized tests for my students' lives (Gutstein, 2003b) and had to compromise at times and bypass the thoughtful, reflective processes necessary for deeper comprehension in exchange for the "quick fix" that is sometimes necessary to pass the tests. But overall, I tried to actualize the NCTM content and process standards—and went beyond to teach for social justice. Additional aspects of my pedagogy will become apparent in this and subsequent chapters.

Learning to Read the World with Mathematics

Although my focus in this chapter is on using mathematics to develop sociopolitical awareness, students not only used mathematics, they also read, wrote, talked, listened, saw films, went to public events, and generally learned about many aspects of social reality in multiple ways. That is, they developed other competencies as well, as one would expect. With that introduction, I turn to the specific projects.

Racism in Housing Data?

This project emerged from the story about the "Tuesday gardening crew." Students' central task was to examine data in relationship to the question of whether racism was a factor in housing prices. We did not have real data (besides Kenilworth's median house price), so students had to consider which scenarios suggested racism and which did not. They needed to develop mathematically based arguments from opposing perspectives, one implicating racism and one contradicting it. One reason for this was that multiple perspectives emerged in our class discussion. I wanted students to consider how they could draw different conclusions depending on the data so that they would see concretely how data can "tell a story" about something as important as racism.

Some of their responses were underdeveloped or partial but, as a whole, represented sharp insights. Juanita made a straightforward analysis of race–class interactions.

> There would be racism if the Latinos' average salaries are for example $40,000 a year and the whites' are $250,000 a year or more. And the builders are building more new houses in the Latino area so the Latino taxes go up when people move in, thus making the Latinos move out. Then it would be racism.

Her argument was partially based on occurrences in Morningside at the time—gentrification had started at its fringe, and rising property taxes were forcing out long-time, low-income renters and homeowners.

Rosa had a different view. In one of the more elaborate analyses, she contended:

> For example, if a White has a house that cost him $100,000 but he got it 30 years ago, and a Black just got a house for $200,000 a year ago, that wouldn't be racism. It would be racism if, let's say, a white family got the house 3 months ago and they paid $250,000 and then a Black family paid for a house 3 months ago but they paid $752,000, that would be racism, unless the house of the Black people was 3 times as big. If there was no racism, it would be if the White family paid for the house $250,000 and the Black family paid $250,000, but both bought their houses 3 months ago. I reached my conclusion by looking at what time they bought it and at what price.

She considered housing cost over time as a factor in deciding whether racism was implicated.

Students articulated multiple, competing perspectives. They debated what one could determine by examining prices of similar houses in white neighborhoods and neighborhoods of color. Some students argued that if prices were higher in white communities for similar houses, then racism existed by keeping out people of color, who generally had less money. However, other students argued the exact opposite! They said if prices were *lower* on similar houses in white neighborhoods, then racism was present because this meant that in neighborhoods of color, realtors were raising prices and gouging money from Latinos/as and other people of color.

After the initial part of the project (above), I summarized, reproduced, and returned students' responses (Table 3.1). Their suggestions included

TABLE 3.1 Student Views on Factors That Might Implicate Racism in Kenilworth House Prices

1. Are Latinos treated badly?

2. If the same house is priced differently based on the buyer's race, then it's racism.

3. If realtors say different things to different races of people when house buying, then it's racism.

4. Are there wage differences by race (in Kenilworth and elsewhere)?

5. Compare house price paid by race to the percent of different race people living in Kenilworth.

6. If prices in the people of color part were the same as the white part of Kenilworth (or not).

7. Send a white, Latino, African American in and see if prices change [test out #2 above].

8. Take a survey—if people of color say there's racism, and whites say no, then there's racism because the whites are lying.

9. Examine the race of the seller and the buyer—do whites sell only to whites?

10. Examine races of the people in Kenilworth—all white means racism, otherwise not.

11. Compare house prices in different suburbs and racial makeup of Kenilworth to other suburbs.

12. Examine house prices as compared to living expenses—can people of different races afford the Kenilworth house price?

13. Look at house prices over the years to see if they've changed for different races of people.

14. Compare house cost and house size by race.

15. Look at race of real estate dealers—if all white, then racism.

examining the race and class interrelationships, wages, individual and institutional discrimination, the racial composition of different suburbs, size and age of houses, and several other issues. To continue the project, I asked them to choose two items, justify why those were good data to collect, and answer the question: "How can you use the items you choose to answer whether racism is involved?"

In general, students responded thoughtfully. Ariana wrote that if whites denied on surveys that racism existed, "It means they are lying because whites have never been through racism," suggesting direct experience as a criterion of truth. Rosa, who was skeptical of racism as a factor, finished her response by asking, "Mr. Rico, why do you think there is racism?" Freida, who initially argued similarly to Rosa that immigrants expected to "work their way up," thought deeply during this project and wrote:

> Maybe everything is a cycle. I mean to buy a house you have to see the income of a person. Most Latinos work in factories and have low paying jobs. Then they can't pay for a high level of education which is necessary to get a good job. So if you have a well paying job you can buy an expensive house like the ones in Kenilworth.

By implication, those without high-paid jobs—like Latinos/as—could not afford Kenilworth.

Nor were there simple answers. A number of students felt this complexity, although they believed that they could use mathematics to suggest answers. Yesenia wrote:

> I learned that something that might look like racism, might not be racism. I think that the question "Do they have different prices for people of color?" is a very good one because that way you could really find out. You could send some white, Mexican, African American, and Jewish people so they could all go and look at the house pretending they are interested. They will tell them the prices and with the data we will find out if it is racism or not.... If they all get charged the same, then it is really clear it's not racism.

Most students were satisfied that sending potential buyers of different races could provide evidence of racism if prices changed for different peoples. But not all were convinced that the same prices charged for different race buyers meant that *no* racism existed. They allowed for other possibilities as well. And some students drew out subtle points. Danny suggested examining Kenilworth's racial composition: "If there are only white people or mainly another race then there is possible racism. I say possibly because, for example, no one says there's racism against whites in the mainly Mexican neighborhood of Morningside." Note here that he did not equate all white neighborhoods (in his view, discriminatory) with his virtually all Latino/a one, implying that he understood the unequal power relationships that existed.

Students did not emerge from the project with a full answer to the principal question of whether racism was a factor in Kenilworth's median house price. Furthermore, we did not reach a unified view or fully examine the intricacies involved. For example, we only briefly discussed the distinctions between individual and institutional racism. This was partly because of my pedagogical philosophy—to have students investigate important issues like racism, but not to "master" them (as if one could) and then move on to another. First, this was still a mathematics class, not social studies, and time was limited to discuss issues like racism even when examining them mathematically. Second, racism's complexity, its historical roots, and structural and ideological components make it difficult to fully comprehend. Third, I was aware of the dialectic Freire (1994) discussed between students developing their own views and me expressing mine, while simultaneously providing them the necessary background to understand societal structures like institutional racism. I knew that my explanations of racism (and, for that matter, mathematics) would (and should) not automatically translate into students' understanding, and, in any event, they would develop their own conceptions mediated through prior experiences and world views. I did not want them to accept uncritically my opinions, nor could I have made that happen even if I wanted to. And finally, the class was willing and able to explore, on an ongoing basis, injustice in various forms. This was the "normalization" of politically taboo topics, and I planned to revisit racism and other injustices throughout the year, which we did.

Nonetheless, throughout this project, students mathematically addressed the main question. They generated data and discussed averages, cost of living, appreciation and depreciation, taxes, income, employment, education, race, and social class—all in complicated interaction with mathematics as an integral aspect. This project definitely contributed to their capacity to use mathematics to examine disparate opportunities among different social groups, consider the interconnections of various social phenomena, and raise questions about relations of power—all characteristics of reading the world with mathematics.

Discovering That "We Are Not A Minority"

In December 1998 (three months after the Kenilworth project) I read an article by Marilyn Frankenstein (1997) that contained a photo taken in East Los Angeles. The photo showed a large mural of Che Guevara with the caption, "We Are Not A Minority" (Figure 3.1). I was struck by the implicit mathematics of the statement and how Frankenstein used it with her class, which was to examine the politics of knowledge (e.g., who has the power to label another a "minority") as well as to deal with mathematical issues of fractions, percentages, and decimals. I assigned a project, but rather than have students explicitly do mathematics about the statement, I asked them to write about what they thought mathematics had to do with the picture.

First, four students thought the mural was of a Brown Beret.[2] Second, students' overwhelming responses were of cultural pride in being Latino/a and a resistance to being demeaned. Angel's was typical: "It kind of sends a message like, 'we won't be put down by you.' I mean 'you' as another race, and that makes people proud." Paulina echoed this view, but extended her

Figure 3.1 Mural in East Los Angeles of Che Guevara © 1978 by Mario Torero.

view to include other people of color, expressing cross-racial solidarity, and posed her own questions: "I think that this picture is saying the truth that Mexicans and African Americans have been treated really bad for a long time. Why? I think it's because they (Latinos) don't speak English. African Americans because they are black. Why don't white people go through this?" And Ariana had a typical (for her) biting comment that captured what many students wrote: "I believe it's true we should not be treated less because we are all humans. Just because we have some differences, they think we're aliens. No! Wait, I think they will even treat the alien better."

However, only four students (of the 20 who completed this project) used mathematics in a way that I thought they might, which was to consider the percentage of Latinos/as compared to others. Two students made mathematical connections, but the majority did not answer how mathematics might be involved. I did not presume that many knew that people of color are the majority of people on Earth, but I thought that some might raise the question. Interestingly, just a month earlier, we did a project in which we discovered that Asia was about 61% of the world's population and Africa about 13%, or roughly three-fourths of the world. So whites were clearly the minority on the planet. However, although we discussed many issues in that earlier project, we had not made explicit that people of color were the majority of the world, and no one spontaneously connected the two projects.

We had to do the mathematics for students to be convinced. Despite their strong cultural pride and identification as Latinos/as, and despite their recent analysis of relevant data, only one student independently realized that they, as people of color, were a majority on Earth. In retrospect, several reasons may explain why. My request for them to use mathematics was somewhat buried in other questions (my error). Also, the word *minority* was apparently powerful in influencing students' thinking and self-perceptions. But this also makes clear some difficulties in teaching for social justice. Although I had taught this class for a year at the time of this project, students had apparently not internalized using mathematics to analyze social realities. Even allowing for the confusion I may have created by mixing in the question of how mathematics was used with other questions, if students were really attuned to using mathematics in the world, they should have had little trouble in at least suggesting specific ways mathematics was involved. That they did not, in the absence of concrete directions and guidance, suggests that one does not easily become a "reader" of the world using mathematics.

However, in class, after students responded in writing, they had no trouble in doing the math and understanding that who was a minority depended on one's frame of reference. From a global perspective, knowing that whites were maybe 20% of the planet gave my students something to ponder. Thus, even though they did not independently connect mathematics and the term *minority*, mathematics became a means by which students reframed their view of themselves with respect to, at least, the relative numerical proportions. And after close to two years in my class, almost all students in this class reported themselves capable of using mathematics to better understand the world (see later in this chapter).

Simulating Wealth—World and United States

I adapted this wealth simulation project from Bob Peterson (1995) in *Rethinking Schools* and did it with three different classes. I gave students data on the wealth (GNP) and population of each continent (see Appendix 1). The central task was to divide the class into groups (representing continents) by the percentage of people in each continent and then to distribute wealth (cookies) to each continent according to the continent's share of world wealth. For example, Europe's population (in 2000) was about 727 million people (of the Earth's 6.057 billion, about 12%), and its wealth was $9,606.3 billion of $28,081 billion (about 34.2%). Students then determined how many people in the classroom corresponded to Europe's 12% (in our case three or four). Someone counted the cookies, and students computed how many each continent was to receive. Finally each group representing a continent went to a section of the room and received and shared their cookies to find each person's share. The individual share in cookies represented the average wealth per person for each continent.[3]

In one class, the four people assigned to Africa split one cookie, literally sharing the crumbs, a potent metaphor, while the two in North America shared 28 between them. We computed relative shares, and students saw that the average person in North America was about 56 times wealthier than the average person in Africa. This was indeed powerful. But Marisol went beyond this surface level comparison to point out that this was the average, and that wealth within the continent was not evenly distributed. Her comments impacted others, and several students later wrote about her comments. She wrote:

> And even if some continents have more wealth than others, that doesn't mean that the people in the continent all have the same amount of wealth. Some have no wealth at all, while others can have billions of dollars of wealth. If you look at Africa, there are 763 million people living there and they have 436.6 billion dollars in wealth. For all we know, one person might have 436.6 billion dollars in wealth and everybody else might not have any at all. Of course, we know this isn't so, but it just makes you realize that knowing how much wealth each continent has doesn't really tell you anything about how much wealth the people have on each continent. In the U.S., Bill Gates holds more money than anybody else, but if you divide the wealth by population, Bill would probably have an average amount of money [wealth] and a homeless [person] would have an average amount of wealth.

In his essay, Omar mathematized the issue of relative wealth and connected the project to his life. He compared pro athletes' earnings to those of his parents (both factory workers).

> What Marisol said on Friday was right on the spot. Not all the wealth is distributed equally. You may see some homeless guy looking for food but then the next moment, you see someone driving their brand new Mercedes convertible. For example, even the ones that aren't homeless. Our family makes somewhere in the neighborhood of $40,000. I heard that Michael Jordan makes about $1,000 for every minute he plays. So that means that in 40 minutes he makes our whole family's earnings. While my parents work year round for that money. I really think Marisol hit [it] right on the money. I learned that lesson that plays a huge role in life.

Although it was obvious that Bill Gates had more than average, not all students fully appreciated the subtlety of Marisol's critique of a one-number *measure of central tendency* (i.e., the "middle" of a data set around which the rest of the data are balanced). This is not surprising, because even older students have trouble with this point. As an aside, although this chapter is about students using mathematics to develop sociopolitical consciousness, this example also demonstrates how their mathematical knowledge deepened through examining social justice contexts.

Building on Marisol's point that the data for the continent did not reveal wealth distribution within the continent, a few months later we simulated the financial wealth within the United States. I used data separating the population into the wealthiest 1%, the next 19%, and the bottom 80% (Wolff, 1995) (Table 3.2). I asked students to compare the wealth distribution in the world to that of the United States (and gave them the earlier project's data).

When we shared the cookies, Jasmine (the 1%) received 46, while the 21 students in the bottom 80% had to share 6 between them, less than a third each. We discovered that individuals in the richest 1% were, on average, about 138 times wealthier than those in the bottom 80%. Many in the 80% group were so upset, both with the meager share and the obvious injustice, that they refused their morsels.

Students analyzed the situation in different ways. Javier, whose parents also worked in factories, used the chart itself and showed his understanding of the work distribution in society.

> I don't think any of these two distributions are equal. But the most equal to me is the World distribution because for the U.S. distribution, I think you can tell easier that it's uneven. Like the chart, I think it should be vice versa. This bottom 80% should own 48% of the wealth. The next 19% is o.k., but the top 1% should have only 6.0% of the wealth. I mean the bottom 80% is the group that's doing the real hard work.

TABLE 3.2 U.S. Financial Wealth by Population Group, 1989

Population Group	% of Financial Wealth
Top 1%	48.17%
Next 19%	45.76%
Bottom 80%	6.07%

Data from Wolff, 1995.

Other students argued from the simulation. Magdalena wrote:

> Well the wealth distribution seems to be better in each continent than it is in the United States. Because … the money was distributed a little better among the continents. But the simulation we did with the distribution in the U.S. was more of a bad distribution. We could see when Jasmine got 46 cookies to herself. In the other simulation, Paulina and Ricardo [i.e., the "North Americans"] got 14 cookies so you see the distribution was better in the world.

The data upset the students. The final question I asked was, "How does all this make you feel?" Of the 21 who answered, 19 used words like unfair, angry, mad, shocked, appalled, bad, and disturbed. One person appeared to not understand the simulation, and Sandra, who often resisted in class, wrote, "I don't feel nothing." Rosa, who often argued that opportunities existed for immigrants, was both upset but also "in a way happy because the U.S. is 'rich' because it gives people more opportunity (or at least it seems)." None had known the extent to which U.S. wealth was concentrated (I asked students to guess before I gave them the data), and most reported not being previously interested. For example, Carmen wrote, "I thought very little about the subject and it wasn't very interesting." Omar, who reported being "appalled," wrote, "I would have guessed that the bottom 80% would have had at least 1/3 of the money." Ariana wrote, "At first I really did not pay any attention to it. I did not know anything about it so I had no opinion." But in response to how she felt afterwards, she wrote, "This is a really powerful situation and I feel that everyone who lives in the nation should know of how their money is distributed. Maybe people can stop paying taxes until they make a difference."

I also asked students what they learned and how they used mathematics to provide them opportunities to describe their mathematical work and to see if they would mathematically justify their conclusions. Omar wrote:

> I mean the bottom 80% only have 6% of the wealth. But 2.7 million people [of the 270 million U.S. population at the time] have about 8 times as much as the 216 million.… [in] the bottom 80% each person gets 1/3 of a cookie, yet one person of the 1% gets 46 cookies. That's just not fair.

Rosa added, "Well, I see that all the wealth in the U.S. is mostly the wealth of a couple people, not the whole nation. You could really see the difference with the cookies."

In a different class who did the project, Tita wrote how the wealth simulation worked and how one uses mathematics to determine relative versus absolute wealth. She explained why Africa was relatively poorer (per person) than Oceania/Australia even though Africa had more absolute wealth.

> I think that one of the reasons for the unequal distribution is related to the wealth and population. For example, Africa's wealth is really small and the population is really big compared to the other countries population. Africa is the poorest continent because its wealth is not much and it has to be shared by a large amount of people. Another example is Oceania/Australia. Its wealth is $442.4 [billion] and its population is 31 [million]. Its wealth is a bit smaller than Africa but also its population is way smaller than Africa's and that makes it wealthier.

She also raised several perceptive questions. In response to my question: "After doing the activity, what are your questions and what more do you want/need to know?", she wrote:

> Was the situation ever worse than it is now? Do rich continents get their riches by stealing or taking from the poor? Is it true that Africa is the continent with the most gold and silver? What can we do to help poor continents? I would like to know the whole story of how the poor continents became poor and the rich continents became rich.

The wealth simulations were powerful activities for students to begin to develop sociopolitical consciousness. Like the "We Are Not A Minority" project, the simulations helped students see themselves and their life circumstances in a global context. They learned about wealth inequality both within the United States and abroad, and they also learned, as Marisol pointed out when she went beyond average wealth, that one has to go more deeply into numbers to understand the story they tell. Students also raised their own questions about the genesis of the inequalities, and although we did not fully explore that, their responses suggested that they believed it important to learn about the issues. As Lucia wrote, "And this project is good because it informs us about what is going on in the world," which was a fairly typical comment. Mathematics was the key tool students used to allocate the wealth and compare the discrepancies between continents, and it was also the entry point into deeper analyses of resource disparities.

Driving While Brown/Driving While Black:
Investigating Racial Profiling

Racial profiling is a fact of life for African Americans, Latinos/as, and especially since September 11, for people who appear to be from anywhere remotely near the Middle East. It is so much a national problem in the United States that progressive congresspeople introduced the *End Racial Profiling Act of 2004* into both the House and Senate. The bill would prohibit profiling and enact penalties for it, at all levels of government. Racial profiling is also a mathematical phenomenon because one needs mathematics to describe, understand, and document it. One can only establish it by analyzing the discrepancy between collected data and *theoretical probabilities* with respect to police (or other) practices. For example, if Latinos/as make up 25% of motorists driving a particular road, but 70% of the police *discretionary*[4] stops over time are of Latinos/as, one has a mathematical basis to suspect discriminatory practices. Many rich mathematical topics are embedded in a racial profiling investigation and clearly political issues as well. It was ideal for a real-world project.

In February 2001, I gave my class in the regular-track the project (Gutstein, in press-b; see Appendix 1). I introduced it by asking students about racial profiling. All the students lived in Morningside, and many "hung out" a lot, especially the boys. Tomás, often in trouble and well known to local police, had several personal experiences to relate and a whole analysis to go along. Others shared their knowledge, with the main complaint being police harassment of neighborhood youth, but some students were totally unaware. Nor was everyone convinced that profiling was necessarily bad because of gangs and gang violence. In fact, the city targeted Morningside as a "gang hotspot" and stepped up police presence and surveillance. Some students felt safer because of that. Thus racial profiling was a contested and real-life issue that students could study to learn mathematics and investigate racism.

The project was long and complicated and took several days. We started by reviewing probability concepts, and then students used different colored cubes to conduct a probability simulation of Chicago's population by race. The purpose of this phase was for students to become familiar with probability simulations and understand the *law of large numbers* (i.e., the greater the number of "experimental trials," the closer results should be to theoretical probabilities).

I then gave students data from a racial profiling civil suit that was based on field reports from southern Illinois. I used the actual percentages and created a data set with those percentages for students to use[5]

(Table 3.3). Students found the actual percentages of police stops of Latino/a drivers in the area (21.0%) as well as the percentage of Latino/a motorists (2.8%). Next, students had to set up their own simulation of police stops of Latino/a drivers in that area;[6] this was the most difficult mathematical aspect of the project. After students designed and conducted their simulations and collected data, the class discussed the results.

Our simulated data were far from the actual police data. We ranged from 1% to 7% for stops of "Latinos/as," although the 7% could have been erroneous because it was extremely high for our simulations. Edgar wrote:

> I learned about racial profiling, that's when the cops stop more Latinos than other races. I used division, adding, subtracting, multiplication and percents and fractions. I do think it's a problem because cops stop Latinos most of the times by being racist or just because you have a better car than they do, just because you're Latino, they think you're not rich and maybe you stole the car. I think this project talks about racism and why cops stop Latinos more than any other race.

Alicia added her analysis, which included knowledge of the fact that when whites were stopped, a greater percentage of whites than Latinos/as had contraband in their cars.

> Yes, I think it is racial profiling because more Latinos are getting stopped although it's known that the whites would carry more stuff of the badder type [i.e., drugs] (NO OFFENCE but it's TRUE). What I think should be done about it is it should be stopped. They need to stop discriminating people because of their ethnic background.
>
> The questions that pop in my mind are: WHY ARE THEY DISCRIMINATING? WHY DON'T THEY LIKE US FOR WHAT WE ARE? WHY ARE THEY DOING THIS TO US?

Lydia made her argument from the numbers and connected mathematics to the world.

TABLE 3.3 Racial Profiling Data

DWB Data	All Races	Latinos	Latino %
Motorists	1,000,000	28,000	2.8%
Stops	14,750	3,100	21.0%

I learned that police are probably really being racial because there should be Latino people between a range of 1–5 percent, and no, their data is 21 percent Latino people. And also I learned that mathematics is useful for many things in life, math is not just something you do, it's something you should use in life.

She added, "Yes, I think it's a problem because that shouldn't be like that. People come to the U.S.A. for freedom and better opportunities, not to get stopped by cops for no reason." But not everyone thought racial profiling was a problem and that something needed to done about it. Yesenia wrote:

It's not a problem, well that's what I think. Police are maybe just stopping people because they might look suspicious, drunk, or something. They don't just stop you for anything. I think that this project was not accurate to prove anything. I mean what is it proving, it is not accurate in the cubes.

Although this project engaged students and provided a context for them to mathematize, discuss, and write about difficult issues, I felt that we spent insufficient time discussing some important ideas. For example, Edgar commented that police may have stopped Latinos/as with "better cars," but we did not explore the correlations between race and class that might have shed light on this dispute, since his comment implicitly raises the questions: Do Latino/as typically have worse cars? If so, why? He also wrote that the "project talks about … why cops stop Latinos more than any other race," but we did not try to answer that question well enough. Alicia's heartfelt "WHY ARE THEY DOING THIS TO US?", which she wrote before we discussed the analyses as a whole class, was also insufficiently addressed. Although I generally did not try to have closure on these conversations, as I explain earlier, in this setting, I believe that we needed more discussion because too much was left unanswered. This points out that teachers need to be clear about what ground they wish to cover when examining potent issues like racism (especially if the teacher is white), think carefully about how to create space for adequate discussion, and plan coherently for the long term to be able to return to particular issues and build on previous conversations while ensuring that unanswered questions are not overly disconcerting to students—all this, while being mindful that classroom interactions do not necessarily go as planned and real concerns may surface. This may occur particularly when explorations could cause students to feel helpless or demoralized (see chapter 4).

One could argue that this project was unnecessary because the data themselves were transparent. After all, the contrast between 2.8% for Latino/a motorists, and 21.0% for the stops of Latino/a motorists was dramatic. Why do a whole project to make such a simple comparison? There are several answers besides the obvious rich mathematical learning opportunities. First, this context directly and meaningfully connects to students' lives and provides them the chance to mathematize their experiences. Morningside has a large number of undocumented workers, and the INS occasionally raided local area factories looking for them. We discussed raids on workplaces with primarily Latino/a workers as instances of racial profiling. None of my students reported being unfamiliar with immigration issues, pressures on undocumented workers, and the raids. Thus, even if students themselves had not been picked up by police in unwarranted circumstances, they could relate to INS intrusions into Morningside as examples of racial profiling.

Second, while it is true that the data cry out for further investigation, in general, seventh graders have little experience in school relating numbers to their lives and do not easily apply data to themselves. Conducting the simulations themselves and getting their own results appeared to make a big difference in how they viewed the data, especially when we already established the validity of probability simulations by simulating Chicago's racial makeup. And third, and perhaps most important from the perspective of teaching mathematics for social justice and providing opportunities for students to begin making sense of social reality, the chance to investigate a politically charged and volatile social issue using mathematics as the entry point was a powerful experience.

This class had more difficulty in learning to read the world than my classes in the honors bilingual program (for reasons I explain later), but this project clearly impacted them. When I had them fill out an anonymous survey at the end of the year to give feedback on what they learned, how they felt they changed, and other questions, 21 of 26 students mentioned the racial profiling project or learning about racism. Two of the remaining five mentioned other projects (like the the world wealth simulation or the neighborhood gentrification projects that I describe in chapter 4). This class, in total contrast to the honors classes at Rivera, was often regarded by some teachers and administrators as a "problem" class, the antidote for which was to "give them seat work," according to their home-room teacher (see chapter 6). From talking to their other teachers, observing them in other classes, and examining their tests and assignments in other subjects, it appeared to me that actually using mathematics (or any other academic subject) to explore, learn about, and debate issues of race and racism, rather than being told or spoon-fed discrete pieces of nonrelevant information, was totally novel. Merely "telling them" that the data were discrepant would have aligned with what I understood their other schooling experiences to have been, but it would not have helped them start learning to read the world with mathematics as this project did.

Mortgage Loans—Is Racism a Factor?

In December 2002, I did a project titled "Mortgage Loans—Is Racism a Factor?" (see Appendix 1) with a different seventh-grade class (Gutstein, 2003a; in press-c). Students read a *Chicago Tribune* article that presented data on mortgage rejection rates for African Americans, Latinos/as, and whites in the Chicago area and nationally (Table 3.4) (Manor, 2002). The data showed that mortgage lenders rejected both African Americans and Latinos/as at a higher rate than whites. The article presented contrasting analyses. In it, a representative of a national community-based organization claimed "institutional racism" was at fault, while various bank spokespeople argued that banks made loans to everyone because that was how they made money, and therefore race could not be a factor. The article was confusing, with many numbers and multiple comparisons, and introduced a *disparity ratio*, the ratio of the rejection rates for the different races (Table 3.4). This was a ratio of ratios, since the percentages themselves can be considered ratios, and was difficult to grasp. Students had several challenging mathematical questions to answer, leading up to the final assignment:

> 10. Write a good essay answering the following question (you **must** use data from the article or the quote above [see actual project] to make your argument): Is racism a factor in getting mortgages in the Chicago area?

The 2001 data in the article for the whole United States were that whites were denied 17.2% of the time, Latinos/as 26.2%, and African Americans 39.7%. I asked students:

TABLE 3.4 2001 Chicago Area Data, Percent Denied Mortgages, by Race

Chicago Area Data	Whites	Latinos/as	African Americans
Percent Denied in 2001	6.3%	16.2%	31.7%
Disparity Ratio, Compared to Whites	—	2.6:1	5.0:1

2. In paragraph #1, they say that Latinos and Blacks in Chicago are more likely to be turned down for mortgages than Whites. In paragraph #2, they say that Latinos, Blacks, and Whites have an easier time getting mortgages in Chicago than elsewhere. Isn't this a contradiction? How can both paragraphs be true? **Explain** and use data in your explanation.

To answer this question correctly,[7] students had to understand the various data in the article and argue appropriately, which every group was able to do.

I also asked students to consider the opposing views of the bank officers and the community organization spokespeople. In questions 6 and 7, I asked:

6. The Bank One representative argues that racism is not a factor because banks "want to make loans." Using data from the article/chart, list **two** questions you would ask him that would challenge that position.

7. Pretend, for a moment, that your group members are representatives of Bank One. Write what you think you would or could say to defend the statement in the article, that it was "unlikely that racism was causing lenders to refuse loans to Blacks and Latinos here." In other words, see if you can come up with some other explanations, besides racism, to explain why there is a disparity ratio in the Chicago area.

One goal for these questions (indeed, for the project overall) was for students to understand both the data and the text. Using mathematics to develop sociopolitical awareness of one's life, community, society, and broader world is a complicated undertaking that means different things in various settings. For example, in the world wealth simulation, it was relatively easy to use numbers to understand the misdistribution of resources. When students saw a "North American" with 14 cookies, and an "African" with 1/4, and then computed the ratio of the relative (average) wealth to be 56:1, the disparity was straightforward and graphic. Or, when they discovered that one B-2 bomber costs the same as providing full four-year scholarships to a prestigious out-of-state university for the next 79 graduating classes from their local high school (see chapter 1), there was limited mathematical complexity involved. Teachers should certainly raise questions, if students do not, about, for example, the genesis of wealth inequality or the relative merits of funding bombers as opposed to college scholarships, but both the mathematics and the meaning of the numbers in those projects were significantly simpler than in the mortgage rejection project. In this latter project, reading the world with mathematics meant finding one's way through a murky swamp of confusing and potentially conflicting data (mathematical and textual); searching for clues; evaluating and posing questions from different perspectives; and eventually synthesizing the various positions and wayward data to produce a cohesive, coherent, well-argued essay to address the fundamental question: Is racism a factor, and if so, how?

The project took over 2 1/2 weeks, including much class time, the longest project I ever did. It was also the most difficult. I made almost all students rewrite their essays, at least once, usually because they insufficiently substantiated various claims, and I gave them extensive feedback and raised many questions. After students wrote their initial essays, we sat in a circle for two days, and they read aloud their essays if they chose to (or a friend could read the essay for them, anonymously or not). I framed the discussions as our attempts to deepen our collective understanding, rather than a debate. Several wrote about learning from others and revised their essays based on what they heard. In fact, the discussion moved outside the classroom. Nilda wrote in her journal: "Mr. Rico, After all I've been hearing, I am starting to think that maybe racism is a factor." She added, "So I guess I was wrong and this paper you wrote [my response to her first essay] and questions you asked, plus this week's conversations helped me really understand why racism could be a factor." Aida (and others) wrote that, "Me and some of the girls have been talking about the conversation." And Ivan spoke for many when he expressed in his journal our collective attempt to understand the issues: "Even though we discussed it, the whole class has not yet solved the problem [answered if racism is a factor]. On Monday, for sure, we will solve the problem." Tita added:

> Well about the essay, I have changed my mind. Now I think that there really isn't a way to know if racism is or is not a factor. At first I had two arguments, but they were not very good to support that racism was not a factor; during our discussion at class I heard many arguments from both sides of the story.

Their essays provide evidence of grappling with complex ideas and of attempting to make sense of social reality. Jesse argued that multiple perspectives were necessary.

> I think that it is inconclusive whether or not racism is a factor when it comes to getting a mortgage loan in the Chicago area.

It is a factor because white applicants no matter what their income was they were always denied less times than African Americans and Latinos. And it also is a factor because the ratio of applicants denied between African Americans and whites is 5:1 and between Latinos and whites is almost 3:1. That data shows that racism is a factor.

There are always two sides to a story. Racism is not a factor because we do not know whether or not those people had bad credit or if they were unemployed. It could be possible that a lot of those people could have been in debt. Even though the banks want to make loans they also want to make sure that they get paid.

Manolo also wrote an insightful essay implicating racism because the data demonstrated that income was *not* a factor in the disparities. That is, the disparity ratio actually *increased* as incomes went up. This point was particularly difficult to grasp and explain, including for me initially. He wrote:

Yes it is, it is a bad feeling to admit it. But racism is a key reason why many Latinos are being denied. These reports show lack of money is not the problem. Having money hurts you. The high income Latinos are being denied a lot more compared to [high income] whites than low income Latinos are being denied compared to low income whites. In any way you see it, Latinos and blacks are being denied a lot more compared to whites for no reason at all.... I learned so much, one being Latinos are being discriminated against even by banks. The more successful I may be the more chance that I may be rejected and be a statistic.

This project, the last I taught at Rivera, engaged students more than any other project, despite its length, complexity, and timing (right before winter vacation). I believe there are several possible explanations. First, although I created the project, the issue of home ownership was real for my students. We started the project by discussing whose families owned homes (often in extended family relationships) and whose families wanted to (everyone else). Housing stock in the communities where students lived was old, and, as is common for large immigrant families, often crowded. Home ownership meant stability, security, and some prosperity, and all students expressed preferring it to renting. Many students related their family's troubles in securing mortgages. Second, we continually had in-class discussions in which we mathematically dissected the issues. That contributed to students' rethinking their views, as many explained in their writing. Third, my pushing them to justify arguments mathematically, my continual prodding and questioning their assumptions and making them rewrite their essays, and our group reading of the essays over two days created conditions for students to grapple genuinely for understanding. Fourth, the complexity and uncertainty of the issues, and the intellectual challenges of understanding racism, appeared to intrigue and involve students. This was evidenced by their out-of-class conversations, essays, and journals. Fifth, although they could not fully answer the question of whether racism was a factor, they knew the data were skewed against them and African Americans. Some eventually took the position that we could not really answer the question (most of this group said we needed more data), but 20 of the 30 students argued that racism was a factor. Overall, their collective sense of justice was obvious during the project.

Even with nearly three weeks, we still did not have enough time to unpack some of the historical background necessary to understand fully the issues. Banks loan mortgages based on both income and wealth, and I wanted students to understand how institutional racism was an historical factor in the lack of African American wealth (Oliver & Shapiro, 1997). For example, in 1988, African American median income was 62% of white median income, but African American median net worth was only 8% of white net worth (Oliver & Shapiro, 1997). To understand this, one needs to examine *sedimented inequality*, the advantages passed down through the generations. For example, even immigrant whites, in general, could accumulate property and other assets far more easily than African Americans who had emerged from slavery, segregation, sharecropping, and Jim Crow. But by the time I shared these data, we were almost at winter break. Students were tired, had worked hard, and looked forward to vacation. Trying to walk a line between, on the one hand, letting students interact with each other and develop their own ideas, and, on the one hand, bringing in other important concepts, I had not given enough time to the latter. This was just one of the various pedagogical tensions I faced.

Reflections on the Real-World Projects and Dilemmas in Teaching for Social Justice

All the real-world projects my classes completed had some common features. Each project, ranging from two days to almost three weeks, involved students in using mathematics to investigate significant social issues that mattered to them. These topics included, among others, racism in housing prices, mortgage rejection rates, and police practices; living and working conditions for immigrant farm workers; representations such as maps and photo images; neighborhood gentrification; and changing demographics of the region. The above projects in this chapter are representative (see Gutstein, 2005, for a fuller listing), and my comments below apply to all.

Reflections on the Projects

The projects were part of a Freirean problem-posing pedagogy (which I refer to as a pedagogy of questioning; Gutstein, in press-c) that needs not only to provide students the chance to raise their own questions, but also to make clear that few significant, real-life questions are easily answered. Projects, like several in this chapter and others, supported the orientation to dig deeply for answers. On the mortgages project, Leandro wrote: "It seems that whites are getting discriminated the least and blacks the most. You can't say racism is [necessarily] a problem and we must search more deep and search the truth. Instead of judging we must search, ask questions to find the truth." Tita echoed this view with her final comment, "From this project I learned that you should question everything. Like that to have a better project you should question all your answers. That's what I did." And Vanessa wrote in her essay:

> So one question leads to another question, and then you have to answer four more, and those four questions lead to eight more questions. So I think that [racial disparity in mortgage lending] is not racism, but that leads me to the conclusion that if it was not racism, then why do they pay more money to whites? Is that racism?

I usually asked students what were their additional questions about the issues we investigated. But I did that at other times as well, for example, in the September 11 story with which I begin this book. Also, I consistently asked students questions about their mathematics work and also about their opinions and analyses of current events, social issues, our projects, and many other topics. In summer 2001, when my two-year class was between tenth and eleventh grades, I mailed them a survey. One question was: "If you had to write a letter to a seventh-grade Rivera student telling her or him what to expect in my class, what would you write?" Rosa wrote, "What would I write to a seventh grader in Rivera, mmmm.... Well that you ask a lot of questions, and that you ask a lot of questions, and by the way, you ask a lot of questions!"

Their responses to my questions and to the prompts to raise their own questions suggest that students took seriously the idea that questioning one's own answers, as well as those of others, was an important part of learning. They may have come to believe that, as Freire (Freire & Faundez, 1992) wrote, "It is not simply a matter of introducing a question-and-answer session into the curriculum between nine and ten, for example" (p. 40).

The idea that a problem-posing pedagogy is not just "between nine and ten" speaks to the need to maintain a classroom environment that supports honesty, openness, and critical inspection of controversial topics. In such a setting, the real-world projects were only part of the overall classroom context in which students began to develop consciousness. Conversations like the one about "everyday racism" or having students raise their own questions about September 11 were equally essential. Furthermore, projects emerged organically from a number of these discussions (like the B-2 bomber project I discuss in chapter 1), and conversely, the projects themselves led to many interesting and provocative conversations about various issues, aspects of inequality, and students' life experiences. In this way, we went "beyond the mathematics" and collectively made issues of racism, discrimination, and injustice a normal part of classroom life (see chapter 6).

Furthermore, doing the projects was similar to decoding Freirean codifications because they became sites for students "to reflect on their former interpretation of the world" (Freire & Macedo, 1987, p. 36). This was at least partially because I explicitly designed the projects so that students would consider, question, and critique their previous learning and beliefs. For example, I often asked students what they originally knew about a topic and how their views changed after a project. Of course, students will spontaneously reflect on past thoughts and views, but I wanted to make that process explicit. Counterposing their past understandings with new learning seemed to be important to the development of sociopolitical awareness, like the farmer from Guinea-Bissau I quote in chapter 2 who said, "Before [liberation], we did not know that we knew. Now we know that we knew. Because we today know that we knew, we can know even more" (Freire & Macedo, 1987, p. 114). As Juanita wrote in response to my question, "How have your views about the world changed from being in my class over the past two years? Please be specific."

> A lot. Two years ago I didn't really care at all. I've just noticed that since the past two years, I've been more interested in the world, the way things are (in terms of wealth distribution and population). I've been watching the news ever since and learning more about the world when two years before I used to see cartoons and junk, etc.

Freire (1970/1998, 1973) pointed out that the decodification process should encourage learners to reflectively analyze their lives so that they become aware of their own lack of questioning of the status quo. This was one of my intentions. Developing sociopolitical consciousness is anathema to those with power who would have those without maintain their ignorance, silence, and passivity.

Dilemmas and Tensions

However, when developing a pedagogy of questioning, one has to be aware that students may lapse into a relativist position that nothing is knowable. There was some evidence of that on the mortgage project. I pushed so hard on raising questions and having students rethink their essays that some eventually took the view that we could never know if racism was a factor. For example, Garbina wrote, "With all of the arguments brought up in class I have reached a conclusion that there really isn't a way to show if racism is one of the major factors or not." Although many advocated that we needed more data, some, like Garbina, said or wrote that we could never know. This points to the difficulty of having students grasp the necessity to keep probing and problematizing what we think we know, and simultaneously accept that after much research, we *can* have a decent, if provisional, understanding of a phenomenon to the best of our current knowledge. Students need to be able to name injustice when they investigate it and reach the reasoned conclusion that it exists.

An additional dilemma that I mention above was the challenge of adequately contextualizing some complex historical issues related to the projects. Issues like institutional racism are not simple to grasp, but the fact that students did not always understand them also points out the difficulty of successfully orchestrating many things at once. Although this occurred in several projects, it was partly due to certain conditions: I taught math, not social studies; I wove issues into the daily fabric of classroom life (like the "everyday racism" story) and returned to them later; and I believed that students would develop their own understanding of the world and sociopolitical consciousness over time and thus did not try to provide too much information, history, or my analyses all at once. This tension is related to Freire's (Freire & Faundez, 1992) point that "they [teachers] must affirm themselves without thereby disaffirming their students" (p. 34), and is an ongoing issue in teaching for social justice. Teachers need to be conscious of the challenge, although we may not easily resolve it.

Another dilemma that surfaced was: Whose questions and whose themes should comprise a social justice curriculum? How should students' issues, concerns, feelings, and experiences interrelate with those of their teachers in determining what curriculum to pursue? I chose the specific topics and designed the projects with little direct input from students. Although some of the projects evolved through classroom conversations,

I made up (or adapted) most without explicitly consulting students. Is this appropriate in a classroom purporting to be about social justice? In social justice teaching, should curriculum be "student centered" and what does that term mean in social justice pedagogy? The dialectic manifests itself in at least two ways: one, developing curriculum based on local, immediate contexts (e.g., neighborhood gentrification) versus ones outside of students' immediate lives (e.g., world wealth distribution); and two, developing curriculum based on student-articulated themes versus teacher conceptions of social justice issues.

For example, projects like the wealth simulations did not start directly from students' experiences or knowledge, although Freire (1970/1998) advocated that curriculum should be based on the "present, existential, concrete situation" facing people (p. 76). I found that every project did not have to be about students' neighborhood, culture, or other characteristics for several reasons. First, it is not entirely clear how to interpret Freire on this point. The inequitable distribution of wealth *is* part of the "present, existential, concrete situation" in the world today, and it did affect my students. It is true that Freirean educational programs develop curriculum based on themes that educators learn from students' communities and that are based in people's immediate lives (1970/1998). However, that does not necessarily mean that social justice curriculum cannot use themes articulated by others that are related to students' own themes (e.g., poverty). Second, many students themselves drew relationships from external situations to their own lives, and these connections often became classroom discussions. These relationships became ways for students to bridge distances across the globe (e.g., to Africa). Third, students needed to understand more about the world beyond their own lives and communities to be able to situate themselves in a broader context. For example, low wages were on my students' minds, but these wages were related to the ways in which globalization, transnational capital flight, and labor migrations affected their communities. Fourth, *all* of the real-world projects related to students in some ways by building on their *sense of justice* (see chapter 4). And finally, many projects did directly connect to students' lives, especially the initial projects, so having some not immediately relate did not seem to be a problem.

Evidence of Students' Growth Over Time

A central question I repeatedly asked myself was: What difference does teaching for social justice make in students' lives and consciousness and in their actions in the world? This is a complicated question because I am *not* suggesting a direct causal relationship between a middle school mathematics class and students' life decisions. I address this question through my analysis of multiple data sources (see Appendix 2 on methodology), but I relied briefly on my students' reflections as they interpreted their own development, and I triangulated them with my observations and with their written and mathematical work. I acknowledge that self-reporting is problematic, but it is important to understand, when and where we can, what contributes to students' growth, and how and why they develop in relation to those factors.

I have continued studying these issues with several students after they left middle school to see if they felt that there was any long-term influence of the classes. In two of my classes, I had students complete an open-ended, anonymous survey at the very end of the year when grades were already turned in—and I essentially had no more "teacher" power over them. As I mention earlier, I had mailed a similar survey to my two-year class in the summer (2001) after their tenth grade. I focus on my two-year class in this discussion because we were together longer, and I have data from them after our class was over.

Marisol disliked math, a lot, a point she made consistently and vocally. However, although she never grew to love math, she nevertheless appreciated its importance as a way to understand the world. One of the questions on the survey I mailed after her tenth grade was: "How did your views about mathematics change from being in my class?" Marisol responded:

> Well, I never liked math and to this day I'm still not very fond of it. But although before I never realized it, I realize now how extremely important it is to have good mathematics skills so we can fully understand what is going on around us. Believe it or not, math can be incorporated into almost any situation. (I learned that in class.)

When Marisol wrote "so we can fully understand what is going on around us," she was speaking specifically about sociopolitical issues. The evidence for this is her response to a different question: "Besides math, what do you feel you learned in my class (academic or otherwise)? Of these things, which are the most important?" She responded:

> By being in your class, I was really exposed to the fact that racism is still very much a part of our world. I mean, I had always known that racism still existed, but I never had so many examples of it staring me right in the face. There were things happening around me that before I had never really paid attention to, but when those same things were brought up in class, it just made me see them in

a whole new light. I (for example) didn't see how building condos in poor neighborhoods was an example of racism until it was talked about in class. It just made me realize.

When I mailed that survey, I included a part of the racial profiling project I had given my class in 2000–2001, which was not Marisol's class.[8] I asked her class, who had never seen that project, to use mathematics to investigate possible inequities, even though it was two years since we were in class. I gave them the data and asked: Is there a problem here? If you think there is a problem, explain exactly what you think it is and what you think is the cause of the problem. If there is not a problem, explain why you think no problem exists. *In either case, use mathematics to justify your findings, and explain **exactly** what mathematics you used and how you used it to help you reach your conclusions.*

I also asked on the survey: "Do you feel now you are better able to understand the world using math? Can you give some very concrete and specific examples?" Marisol's response referred to the racial profiling project.

> I think that I <u>am</u> better able to understand the world now using math. Like everytime I look at any situation dealing w/ numbers, I automatically begin doing some math in my head with those numbers that tie into the situation. For example, right after I started reading that "math problem" you gave us, I had it figured out through the first read. By looking at the numbers, as soon as I finished the reading I already knew there was a problem there—I already knew what the problem was. After the 1st read, I only read it a couple more times to be sure of my conclusions (I was right), and I just wrote down the exact calculations I used. (This time with a calculator for the sake of more accuracy.)

Her calculations were correct. I reproduce them here to demonstrate that she read the world with mathematics two years after our class—and to show her unusual use of mathematics as well. So the data were 500,000 motorists, of which 14,000 were Latinos/as, and 7,375 traffic stops, of which 1,550 were Latinos/as.

> Since there are about 500,000 people taking "personal vehicle trips" and about 14,000 of these people are Latino drivers, it means that one out of every 36 people taking these trips is Latino (500,000 ÷ 14,000 = 35.71). Then, since the police make an average of 7,375 stops per time period, and 1,549 of these stops were Latino drivers, it means that one out of every <u>5</u> people stopped by

officers in those districts are Latino. (7,375/1,549 = 4.76) Is there a problem here??? Damn right! Why is it that the number of Latinos stopped by the police is almost eight times greater than it should be? For the numbers to be even, there should only be about 207 Latino drivers stopped on these "personal vehicle trips"—instead there are 1,549!! (7,375 (# of stops) ÷ 35.71 (# of non-Latino drivers to 1 Latino) = 206.52 ← the # of Latinos who should be stopped. Then, 1,549 (# of Latinos being stopped) ÷ 206.52 = 7.5 which means that the Latinos are stopped 7.5 x more than they should be—when rounded you get 8.)

This is from a student who disliked mathematics but who found that investigating injustice with mathematics "just made me realize," and who voluntarily worked through the racial profiling problem. As she put it when in seventh grade after an early discussion we had about neighborhood issues and the mathematics of gentrification:

> This week I also learned a lot about Morningside and what's happening here. I learned about the people who want to build new condos and the possible racism behind all this. It was very interesting. You might say it was one of the few times I really enjoyed math class.

Most students in her class reported on their eighth-grade survey that their views about mathematics and the world changed after the class. I asked, "Do you feel now you are better able to understand the world using math? Examples?" Of the 23 responders, all but 3 said yes, and 1 of the 3 said "sort of." Elena, who said "sort of" signed her name on the anonymous survey (almost all did). On the same question two years later, she wrote:

> We did some projects in class, math, by means of data analysis, ratios, percentages, absolute/relative comparison, etc., helped me in a way to open my eyes. This let me see how unfair the world really is and all the superiority white people feel above and beyond what they call "minorities."

I infer that she felt that she was better able to understand injustice using mathematics. Omar (also a name signer) also initially answered "no" in eighth grade, then later told me that he came to believe that he could better understand the world with mathematics.

Two students reported on their eighth-grade survey that after the class they disliked mathematics more than before. But one of those also wrote how her or his views changed on using math to understand the world: "I think that now I can understand the world better by using math, but that doesn't mean I like connecting math with what surrounds me. I still think that there are some 'BIG IDEAS' you can understand without using math." So there may be evidence that even students who disliked mathematics or who initially felt they did not use mathematics to understand social realities, may have still begun the process. And some students were quite clear on this point. Paulina wrote:

> Yes, I think I'm able to understand the world with math. All the math problems, projects, discussions about drug testing, Chicano history, etc. have made me understand because knowing about those issues and the discussions that we did made me think of what math might be involved. The math that we did helped me even more.

Guadalupe responded succinctly, "I think that now I am able to understand the world better using math because you taught us how to. Like by doing that U.S. wealth problem you gave us." And Antonio wrote, "Oh, of course! Like learning about the Mercator map and learning about the world using math to see the inaccurateness of the map. I learned more about tomato pickers and tif's[9] concerning the problems people face and the unfairness of it all."

Students in my two-year class overwhelmingly reported that their views of mathematics and the world changed, and that they were better able to use mathematics to understand the world. However, there are some caveats. First, I taught this class almost two years. In the general program class I taught in 2000–2001, fewer students reported change. On the question of being able to understand the world better with mathematics, 15 said yes, 4 said no, 3 said maybe, and 4 did not answer, but only a few gave concrete examples. Second, I had no opportunity to give a survey to the class I taught for half of 2002–2003 because I was removed in the middle of the year with no warning. I have less data on how much students in that class grew in the time we were together, although I suspect quite a bit based on their responses to the four projects we completed, including the mortgage project. Third, even with my two-year class, several students were inconsistent, resistant, or sometimes confused. This is not surprising because they were middle school students trying to make sense with mathematics of complicated social phenomenon for the first time (as they reported), although their seventh-grade homeroom teacher engaged them in somewhat similar ways when she taught language arts. But for the most part, we dealt with difficult conceptual issues, and they worked hard to understand them and learn mathematics at the same time.

Conclusion

I do not want to imply that students easily came to read the world with mathematics. What happened in my classes was a beginning, and it was not always a smooth road. There were factors that facilitated the journey and those that made it difficult, and I stumbled at times and felt my way along at other times. Overall, however, I saw growth in students' capacity to understand complex aspects of society. Sometimes they did so without using mathematics, and sometimes they learned mathematics without reading the world. At other times, though, they used mathematics to make sense of social reality, and they grew over time, with experience, in their capability to do so. Their mathematical analysis may not always have been that complicated, but I argue that one should not assess how well students understand society with mathematics by the complexity of the mathematics. The point is that mathematics became a necessary and powerful analytical tool that students used to study their sociopolitical existence. Mathematics also became an entry point into deeper investigations and more questions. As Paulina said on her eighth-grade survey:

> I liked the way you taught math using real life issues, that is interesting because we had never done anything like that, it got everyone thinking for themselves. It made some people come up with powerful things to say about the math involving those problems. I liked the projects we did because we thought beyond candy, music, soda and it brought out another side of us.... All my views have changed, the world before wasn't very interesting to me because I wasn't aware about all the issues that were happening. Now, math has made everyone interested in the real world because it's something new that catches everyone's attention.

CHAPTER 4

Writing the World with Mathematics
Developing a Sense of Social Agency

Being in your class definitely changed me. Of course, I acquired new math skills, etc., but I also acquired a new perspective on the world. For some reason, after seeing so many acts of injustices happening before our very own eyes, I cared even more about the issues happening in society. For example, the whole TIF [development scheme] situation we went into in class angered me so much because it made me see how the rich white people were sort of getting rid of minority groups by pushing them out of their poor homes so the rich people (whites!) could all live in some expensive condos. It just frustrated me to see how some people can be so selfish and uncaring! Being in your class has <u>definitely</u> made <u>me</u> a more caring person and is the reason why I am currently searching for a profession which will allow me to help others later on in life. *(Marisol, Summer 2001, between 10th and 11th grades)*

In this quote, Marisol referred to the gentrification just beginning in Morningside when she was a seventh-grade student in my class (1997–1998). This was to have major disruptive impact on the community and students' lives, and we discussed it in all my classes. Morningside is close to downtown Chicago and has solid housing stock, and developers have coveted it for years. When I started teaching at Rivera and first discussed gentrification with students, few understood or believed that profound changes were beginning in their neighborhood. In one class, some students said that gentrification was their parents' concern, not theirs. As of this writing (April 2005), however, the changes are dramatic. Realtors rent apartments to students advertising "an intercom system, security gates, security lights; very secure building," all of which had been rare in Morningside. A community resident told me recently that if you want to buy a home in a Mexican neighborhood, "you can't touch Morningside." Rents have gone up drastically, and students, artists, and young singles or couples are moving in. In a local coffee shop frequented by Latino/a and white activists, artists, and others, I recently saw a sign advertising a "dog walking service." In Morningside, this was unheard of, and a mother of one of my students was overcome with laughter that such a thing even existed. The signs of gentrification are all around the community.

My students used mathematics—but not only mathematics—to develop social agency. Sometimes my classes specifically used mathematics to write the world, but other times, our investigations started from, or related to, mathematics—but then moved fluidly away from (and sometimes back to) their mathematical studies. For analytical clarity, I separate the development of students' agency into two components: using mathematics and going beyond mathematics. However, I do not mean that these are two distinct processes, because students learn to write the world in various interconnected ways.

"There Goes the Neighborhood": The Mathematics of Gentrification

In December 1997, my seventh-grade class did the first of two projects on gentrification. Students read an article about a developer who wanted city permission to pave over a tiny park in Morningside so that he could create secured parking for the condominiums he was renovating. My young students rarely went downtown and did not fully appreciate how close they were. Also, because at that time signs of oncoming gentrification were subtle or in bordering communities, students expressed no knowledge of the issue.

The essence of the project was to determine mathematically how close the community was to downtown (see Appendix 1). Students used two city maps, of different scales, to find the distance from the park (at the community's edge) to the Sears Tower, a major downtown landmark that was visible from the school. They then figured out how long it took to drive at 25 mph from the park to the Sears Tower, assuming no red lights. The answer was an astounding time of only about five minutes. When students discovered this, they were amazed, but did not initially connect the close distance to ensuing gentrification. Their responses were not surprising because this was the first real-world project the class completed, and gentrification was a new concept to them.

In May of that school year, students completed a second project about gentrification, "Will Development Bury the *Barrio* [neighborhood]?", the title of an extended newspaper article about Morningside (see Appendix 1). By that time, the end of seventh grade, we had discussed the gentrification for months, and students knew about strong and growing community resistance. Local grass-roots organizations mobilized opposition, the city council held hearings on various development plans (regularly attended by protesting Morningsiders), and residents were keenly aware of the issues. I was involved in the antigentrification struggle and kept students informed of public hearings, development plans, demonstrations, and other opposition. I attended a number of city hearings and rallies and took students along (with parents' permission). My class's homeroom teacher (a lifelong Morningside resident) and I organized an afterschool "field trip" of nine students to attend a hearing, and I took other students to various events as well.

The newspaper article students read thoroughly documented the various development plans including a major housing and retail development (Springfield Heights) just outside Morningside. Springfield Heights was to have 752 housing units with prices far outstripping typical Morningside homes. There were predictions, that proved to be true, that the high prices in Springfield Heights would cause property taxes to soar. These high taxes, in turn, would displace homeowners who could not afford the increased property taxes, and as landlords passed on tax increases to renters, they would have to move as well. All this information was in the article, as were the development plans and the promise that a certain percentages of jobs (construction and other) would go to Morningside residents. In addition, the Tax Increment Financing (TIF) development mechanism would supposedly fund a number of infrastructure improvements, and the city indeed started rebuilding sidewalks and making other long-neglected improvements in Morningside. The Rivera school security guard told me in 2002 that in his 50 years in the neighborhood, the city never before repaired the sidewalks on such a large scale. The local alderperson, a close ally of Mayor Daley, strongly supported both Springfield Heights and other real estate development, as did a sector (not all) of the Morningside business community, but many residents were vehemently opposed.

Students investigated the mathematics of the situation. For the project, they looked at costs and percentage increases of commercial property, examined the average cost of the new properties, found the median income for the metropolitan area and for Morningside, found how much a family would need to earn to afford the different houses in Springfield Heights, computed what house price the average Morningside family could afford and compared that to the cost of Springfield Heights properties, and determined how many jobs were promised for Latinos/as in the city and for Morningside residents. The lowest originally advertised unit in the development was slated to cost $125,000 and the highest was to be $350,000 (but prices soared—the cheapest unit is now almost $300,000 and the most expensive over $1.1 million). Students answered the following questions (among others):

> 5. To buy a $125,000 house, the article says that a family of four would need to make $47,000 a year, which is 80% of the median income in the metropolitan area. So how much is the median income in the metropolitan area for a family of four?

> 6. Using the information of needing an income of $47,000 to buy a house costing $125,000, how much would a family need to make to buy a house costing $350,000?

> 7. According to the article, the median family income for a family of four in Morningside is $22,000 a year. How expensive a house could that family afford?

The answer to question 7 above is about $58,500, far less than the lowest-priced Springfield Heights unit that was advertised as "affordable." In fact, not only was it not affordable for the typical Morningside family, it was out of reach for the vast majority of the community and certainly for the 98% to 99% of Rivera families whose children qualified for free school lunch. By using mathematics, students were clear that almost no Morningside families could afford Springfield Heights, and furthermore, Morningside families would have an increasingly difficult time remaining. In a typical comment, Manuel wrote, "So if they make those houses, people in Morningside are going to have to move because people in Morningside only earn $22,000 a year, and the people are going to have to leave because they can barely afford it [now]." Armando understood the mathematical relationship of property taxes to rents and displacement, as well as the geometry of the city: "The TIF will increase the property value so landowners are forced to raise the rent, and rent payers have no choice but to pay or leave for a cheaper neighborhood away from the downtown area." Antonio put the price into context with respect to who lived in Morningside and who would live in Springfield Heights: "The houses cost

$350,000 at the most ... the price is too high for the people in Morningside. They won't be able to afford it.... In other words, people have to be rich to buy a house at that price."

Thus the notion of affordable took on a particular political meaning. Students realized that affordable was a relative, not absolute, concept. By examining the idea mathematically and placing it into a larger social context involving Morningside's future and economics, students realized that for them and their neighbors, in this situation, "affordable" meant exclusionary.

To finish the project, students wrote essays arguing whether development would indeed bury the barrio. Regardless of their positions, their essays were powerful and from the heart, and many expressed strong resistance to the development. However, the issues were complex. Jobs were promised to Morningside residents, and students had to confront what was more important, jobs and infrastructure improvements or the destruction of an intact Mexican barrio. Many of their essays reflected these quandaries. Jaime wrote, "Although I'm not with the development, there are some good things coming out from it. Houses are being replaced with new ones and sidewalks are being fixed. This is good because there are some very old houses in Morningside." But his last sentence was: "As a resident I do not support it, or else the barrio will be buried." Magdalena's essay also exhibited the complexity.

> I think that the TIF can hurt and help the barrio. But for it to help the barrio it has to be kept a barrio. With the people that live in it still living in it and not just throwing out the people in it because then it is no longer a barrio but a neighborhood.... But it can also help the barrio since Morningside is not such a recognized barrio or neighborhood since it has a lot of gangs and other things. It can make it look better, help the barrio grow economically and culturally and in other ways....

Like Jaime and Magdalena, others believed that good could potentially result from development, yet they simultaneously wanted the neighborhood to "remain a barrio" as Magdalena noted in her nuanced distinction between a collection of people living together versus a coherent community. The desire for improvements to Morningside was widespread because the city had neglected the community for years, and any previous improvements were the result of determined community organizing and struggle.

However, some students believed nothing could save Morningside. Their essays were particularly poignant. Elena wrote:

.... Many people here in Morningside are fighting to do everything possible in order for TIF not to take place, but even with all of the support and fighting these people are doing there is no way, not even the strongest person could stop ... this.... The only thing that these "high quality people" think about is "I, I, I. Me, Me, Me." There is never a single thought about other people, just about how a high price might benefit them. They never stop and think, "Oh these people need good quality things for a reasonable price." People might say that I'm not the person to be saying this because I'm a child. Most grown-ups say that kids don't know about anything that is going on the outside. But some of us do care and understand. I'm not a person of a very high class but I've experienced a lot with people of a higher [class]. Sometimes they come near my block to a corner store and they start saying, "We're in 'ghetto' land." This really ticks me off, but my parents always taught me to ignore anything that bothered me. So I did. All this development will bury the barrio even if we try hiding it and try to get the money to stay, taxes will still go up. They say nothing is fair in life, they are especially right on this one.

Danny echoed this sense of powerlessness.

I believe development will eventually "bury the barrio." It's unavoidable. The odds are against us. The city belongs to white people (mainly men), who do not appreciate the diversity of those they rule over and, therefore, are only interested in expanding their miniature empires. This sounds quite pessimistic, but what most call pessimism, I call reality.... I don't know what I, as a young person, can do to stop this. Attending meetings no longer seems to be an option. You said yourself on Monday that the protests at City Hall were a "last-ditch effort." What else is there to do but wait? I certainly don't know. The saddest thing is that when I one day return to my hometown, it will have gone down in history. Right up there with the lost continent of Atlantis will be the lost Barrio of Morningside.

In contrast to Elena and Danny, many believed resistance was possible and could have an effect. Their essays were often adamantly against the development plans and showed a strong spirit of opposition. If one only analyzed the situation mathematically, one would have to conclude that the barrio would indeed be buried by development, because the data were clear about the increasing financial burden Morningside families faced.

To think otherwise, however, objectively acknowledges the power of human agency to affect the course of history. Those students who attended city hearings or rallies and became more involved tended to more strongly advocate resistance, but one cannot know if they became more involved because they believed they could make a difference, or if they more strongly believed they could have some impact because of their participation. As I note before, the dialectical processes of becoming involved and developing commitment feed each other. Several students who were involved in the resistance wrote strong essays against the development. Paulina wrote:

> They think they will succeed ... but almost nobody supports them (which is good). Yes, I kind of think that the development will bury the barrio because many residents from Morningside can't afford to pay more rent so they will end up in the streets, but it won't bury the barrio if we keep struggling. There is lots of support to what I said. In the meetings we went to there was no support for this development. Everyone was against it except the people who were not really clear on what will happen to them.... Not much can be done as a young person because older people don't seem to take us seriously. Why? Well because they think we don't understand what is going on, BUT WE DO! The most we could do is speak out to the community, especially those who are not informed about this development. In conclusion, the more people that protest, the easier it will be to win.

The meetings to which Paulina refers were city hearings on the Morningside TIF that became rallying points for the community. One time we arrived a little late to attend a hearing with a third of the class. The hearing ended early, and dozens of Morningside residents were coming out. When they saw a large number of neighborhood youth coming to support them, the adults stopped, talked to the students, thanked and hugged them, and remarked how important it was for youth to be involved. They appeared clearly moved. That had a big impact on my students who saw that their actions meant something to their community and that they could move others by taking a stand themselves.

And finally, Freida's voice rang with indignation, pride, and determination.

> .... the city is taking advantage of this development to tell people that if they don't take over, they can't develop. They think people may want development so much that they would give up their houses and neighborhood. But they are wrong.... Justice is in one language, not in many. If we don't strive for our rights,

they will take over us and even the whole world. If people don't get together to fight this, they would all get overthrown. But I know we have a voice, we have a spirit, we have a goal, and even if we suffer consequences, we will fight and get what we want. Will we let development bury our pride, our family and our liberty? NO! NO! NO!

We are humans and have the strength or, even more, power to get what we want. We may not have high places in government, but with unity and hope, anything can be done. So why should we let them bury us? We know the laws more than them. We believe in justice, in freedom of speech and especially that all men are created equal.

Reflections

This project evoked a range of emotions for students, as their writings demonstrate. For some, the harsh reality of ensuing gentrification was demoralizing, but for most, the community struggle contributed to a spirit of resistance and a sense of agency. Of the 20 students who wrote essays, only seven did not mention fighting back in some way. Of these seven, only three expressed despair, while the others were more matter of fact about the future. The students who expressed resistance often did so with passionate determination like Freida. So the project engendered some powerlessness, but overall did not. Given the reality, why did more students not become despondent?

My response is influenced by recalling what happened at one of the hearings. I was sitting next to Lupe, and we were watching and listening to people standing in a line at a microphone giving two minutes of testimony. Lupe nudged me and asked if I was going to speak. I had not planned to and was not prepared, so I told her no. She did not relent, however, and kept prodding. She said that we had not come all the way downtown to do nothing and that I had to get in line and speak out. I finally gathered myself together, made some quick notes, got in line, and spoke. Freire's (1970/1998) words about how people become involved in social movements spoke to the moment. I quote this in chapter 2, but it is worth repeating here:

> Students, as they are increasingly posed with problems related to themselves in the world and with the world, will feel increasingly challenged and obliged to respond to that challenge.... Their response to the challenge evokes new challenges, followed by new understandings; and gradually the students come to regard themselves as committed. (p. 62)

Lupe was only 13 at the time and not yet ready to speak out herself. Yet she felt "obliged to respond to that challenge." Her response, appropriate for her at that point in her life, was to make sure that her teacher took a stand.

In this instance, two interrelated processes contributed to the development of students' sense of agency: studying mathematics and participating in the community struggle. First, students uncovered the details of the situation through mathematical investigations. They calculated the percentage increases of neighborhood property and extrapolated into the future. They saw how much financially poorer Morningside families were, on average, than others in the Chicago area and how Springfield Heights would exclude them economically while simultaneously it would wreak havoc on their community. They computed how many jobs might go to Morningside residents and compared this and the promised infrastructure improvements against the demise of their Mexican barrio. Through their mathematics, they analyzed injustice to their community and developed their own strongly felt positions on the issues. Students' mathematical investigations enabled them to grasp more deeply the mechanics of gentrification, neighborhood displacement, and relations of power. They could appreciate better what and why people were fighting, as they situated their school work in a broader political context.

The connection to the larger social movement created conditions for students to begin to see themselves as actors in the struggle, even if peripherally. They saw concretely how community adults viewed their participation and that resistance was possible even if it did not necessarily mean that they would win all battles. Those that attended hearings and rallies reported back to others, who could participate vicariously, and throughout that year (seventh grade) and all the next, we discussed Morningside's development and engaged in the struggle to save the community. This praxis—the *reflection* embodied in their mathematical analysis, in close relation to the *action* of their involvement in the larger struggle, to whatever extent they participated—contributed to their "com[ing] to regard themselves as committed" and their sense of social agency.

When What You See Is Not What You Get:
The Politics of Map Representations

Some projects were far less connected to students' immediate lives but were meaningful nevertheless. In May 1999, this same class (my two-year class) that completed the two gentrification projects did a project called "Analyzing Map Projections—What Do They Really Show?" in which students explored two different world map projections, the Mercator and the Peters (Appendix 1). By that time, near the end of their eighth grade, we had been together for close to two years. We had spent much time on the projects, in rich discussions, and this was almost the last project they completed. Its purpose was for students to investigate the politics of map representation, raise questions about their previous learning, and develop further their capacity to critique knowledge and determine its truthfulness.

The Mercator projection is a world map created in 1569 by Gerard Mercator, born in Flanders (now Belgium). Its primary purpose was for navigation (Crane, 2002), not to represent the world. In an era of colonial exploration and exploitation of "undiscovered" lands, Mercator's map was an important tool. It marked the first time that one could draw a straight line from one spot to another on a map (e.g., from Portugal's west coast to Brazil's northeast coast), plot a compass bearing (i.e., measure the angle) and follow it to reach the desired destination.[1] As such, it was a tremendous boon to the European powers in ensuing centuries.

However, like all world maps, it suffers from distortions because no two-dimensional map can accurately represent our three-dimensional Earth. The historical role of Mercator's map is evident from its full name: "New and more complete representation of the terrestrial globe properly adapted for use in navigation" (Crane, 2002, p. 114c). The projection accurately represents shapes (but only on a local scale[2]) and compass directions but distorts the relative size of land masses. The distortion increases as one moves further from the equator (the map key of some Mercator maps explains this, in very small print). Although Mexico is slightly larger than Alaska, the Mercator projection shows Alaska to be two to three times larger. Even worse, Greenland appears comparable in size to Africa, although Africa is actually about 14 times larger. Furthermore, on many Mercator maps, the equator is moved down, and the northern hemisphere covers about 65% of the map, diminishing the southern countries. The Mercator projection was the map in all Rivera classrooms and is still widely used despite critiques of its effect on our perceptions of the world because of its size inaccuracies and reduction of the south. It was also the map with which my students reported being most familiar.

In contrast, the other map we examined, the Peters projection, does not distort land mass size. Arno Peters created it in 1974 with the political purpose of fairly representing the countries of the world in a postcolonial era, although it is essentially identical to the Gall Orthographic map James Gall created in 1855. A tradeoff is that it distorts the shape of almost all countries (Kaiser & Wood, 2001), but Peters argued that accurate size was more important politically than true shape.

I began the project by hanging a Peters map next to the classroom Mercator projection and asked students to comment on the differences.

They pointed out the "weird" shapes of the land masses in the Peters projection, the color scheme of each map, and how some places were different sizes in the two maps. As a class, we agreed on certain features that maps should accurately represent, including direction (angles), longitude, latitude, shape, and size. I then divided students into groups of three or four and gave each a Mercator map (borrowed from other classrooms) and the assignment (Appendix 1).

The mathematical essence of this project was to examine how the Mercator and Peters maps represented area. Students used Mexico's area as a unit of measure (760,000 square miles) to compare its size to Alaska on the Mercator map. They also compared Africa to Greenland, and Scandinavia (enlarged because it is fairly far north) to India (relatively close to the equator). I gave no instructions as to how students were to find the other areas, and they invented various methods (see chapter 5). When students completed this part of the project (which took about two periods), they looked up the real areas in world almanacs.

Critiquing Knowledge

Students found that their hard and creative mathematical work to find the various areas on the Mercator map was quite inaccurate. For example, they calculated Alaska to be anywhere from 2 to 3.5 times larger than Mexico, and all found that Greenland was tremendously enlarged on the Mercator projection. They were shocked, especially with the Alaska and Greenland data. In the second part of the assignment, students compared the same land mass sizes on the Peters projection map and answered several questions: Which map was more accurate and why? Which did they prefer and why? What was the effect of moving down the equator? and Who lived mainly in the southern and northern hemispheres in terms of race? In the third part of the assignment, students individually answered more questions including: What did you learn in this project, about using math, about maps, about understanding the world? and What questions does this raise in your mind and what more do you want to know?

A consistent theme in students' responses was that they began to question what they had been taught—and accepted—without critique. All groups did relatively accurate mathematical work, yet their findings about country size based on the Mercator did not match reality. Most students felt that they had been deceived and were upset. They had grown up seeing the Mercator projection, and no one recalled ever hearing that there were alternate representations or that the Mercator had inaccuracies. Several were especially disturbed that Mexico had been diminished. Elena wrote, "With the Mercator, we learned and were taught that Greenland is bigger than Africa and that Alaska, an American state mind you, is bigger, and according to that map 'greater' than Mexico in size and race." Alejandra succinctly expressed the view of many when she wrote, "I feel that we didn't get the right info and that we were tricked [into] thinking some countries were bigger than others when it wasn't even true. And this makes me think what else are they lying to us about." Ricardo echoed this view:

> By knowing we were all raised on the Mercator map, it makes me feel insecure of what other wrong things we have been taught. Since this map was wrong, we probably have been taught more wrong things in Social Studies and in other academics taught in school since childhood.... The questions left in my mind are why would they want to teach us students the wrong information? Why don't they just tell/teach us the truth?

More than a few students expressed incredulousness that their careful mathematical analysis was so far from reality and questioned what that implied for their education. Their responses indicate how students came to question and critique their prior knowledge.

Politicizing Accuracy

By "politicizing accuracy," I mean understanding how accuracy is determined by sociopolitical and historical contexts. A central idea in the project was the political nature of maps, and thus, of knowledge. Because maps, as representations of reality, can influence how we see the world, hanging a projection on the classroom wall that, for example, artificially enlarges North America, Europe, and Russia with respect to Africa, Asia, and South America is objectively a political decision that can shape how students view countries' relative importance. Size matters. Furthermore, the north, as "above" the south is also a social construction that European mapmakers created, because space (i.e., the universe) has no above or below (see the *What's Up South* map that places the south above the north; ODT, 2001).

The question I asked, "Which map do you feel is more accurate and why?", highlights the political nature of maps. On its surface, it asks students to rank accuracy and choose which map features are more important: faithful portrayal of country size but not shape (e.g., the Peters) or accurate compass directions but not size (e.g., the Mercator). But the question actually surfaces the political nature of the choice between a representation designed to demonstrate "fairness to all people" (Peters, 1983) versus a map created for accurate navigation in a colonial era that today privileges imperial powers. The question also raises how sociohistorical context shapes one's view of "accuracy." From a European colonial viewpoint, the Mercator projection *was* accurate, since the criteria for accuracy was being able to navigate to "new" lands, not whether sizes were true.

My students had their own views of what was most important in terms of accuracy. Just as they contextualized the notion of affordable in the neighborhood gentrification projects, they had to understand accuracy in sociopolitical context as well. They agreed with Peters that the most important issue was that maps should accurately represent country size. No student wrote that the Mercator was more accurate, although the group who carefully read the map key realized that the scale shifted away from the equator and wrote:

> ... both maps are accurate depending on how you look at them. In the Mercator map, if you use the scale correctly you'll be able to measure the real size of the countries, something not noticeable when you just look at it.

Danny wrote for his group that the Peters was more accurate because "the land masses correspond more proportionally with the actual areas", and Manuel added for his group that "Peters [is more accurate] because mathematically using the real land areas, we have concluded that Peter's projection has been based on the actual square miles of each continent."

Although students generally stated that the Peters was more accurate, they also realized that no map was perfect, and several raised questions about the Peters. Alejandra asked about it, "Is this true or another lie?" Gloria added, "Another thing I learned, well, not really learned but just remembered, is that <u>nothing</u> is exact in this world.... The question that I have is that are we sure that even the other maps are accurate?" There was much in-class discussion that no map was exact and that although the Peters was "more accurate" in the above sense, several students questioned the knowledge it represented as well. Waking up to the fact that they had believed and never thought to question what the Mercator projected, they were unwilling to accept uncritically the Peters—thus their critique of knowledge extended to both maps.

Several students suggested that having multiple perspectives (maps) was important to resolve partially the quandary about map accuracy —even while maintaining that the Peters was preferable because, as Antonio wrote, "I feel that using a map that doesn't display the world correctly is just wrong. A country with a smaller area can not be bigger than a country with a larger area." That some students wanted a variety of projections suggests that they politicized accuracy and understood the different purpose of the maps. Jasmine wrote, "I learned that using only one map is wrong, we should have a variety. Just because there's one map doesn't mean it's right." Elena added, "I believe that we should have gotten another chance of viewing other maps and seeing how different illustrators showed their maps and expressed themselves." And Rosa wrote for her group, "We would have liked to have both maps to experience. And we would have liked the teachers to explain to us that they are not exact."

The Salience of Race

Another political issue that arose was race, which we also discussed a lot. To surface the issue of race, I asked students to write about the effect on the northern and southern hemispheres of pushing the equator down and who mainly lived in the north and south in terms of race. I wanted students to question how the Mercator map's consistent presence in classrooms may have shaped perceptions about race even though Mercator may not have consciously meant to diminish people of color who mainly populate the global south.

After discovering that the Mercator map misrepresented size and pushed the equator southward, several students wrote that Mercator intended to demean people of color, although I problematized this in class and pointed out that this shrinking in the Mercator map was probably a by-product of the map's design. Elena had a particularly sharp position.

> Well normally people in the north (I'm not stereotyping) are white or European and the other countries are just Other. In the Mercator map, what the illustrator is trying to show is that their country, region or whatever it is, is superior to others in the world. Of course, this only means superior in terms of their race and not everyone in their country.... they wanted to teach ... that all whites (that color and race) are better and superior than us (brown, or lightly toasted hardly white, and Mexican). We were always taught that we were a minority and didn't deserve anything.

Elena's comment about always being "taught that we were a minority" is telling because it relates the effect of the Mercator map to her past experiences of feeling minimized, independent of Mercator's intention (which she inferred was conscious).

Armando focused on the political impact of both maps, without discussing Mercator's intent:

> Yes, it [the Mercator map] shows how the Caucasians oppress others and make others feel smaller as people and as a country or continent. The new map is like the rebellious Chicanos and

African Americans. It is showing the world a reflection of its true perception.

The conversations about race were complicated and contested. Several students suggested that race was not a factor. Rosa argued, "And the fact that [the people who] mainly live in the North are white doesn't mean anything." Antonio wrote:

> Mr. Rico, you have the idea that it is racism that the map is like that, but I cannot accept that reason. It is a probability, no doubt about it, but I don't think that was the reason because it doesn't make them [whites] any better than the other races by drawing an incorrect map.

Although Antonio interpreted that I meant that the Mercator projection was racist, I did not say that, although I may not have been sufficiently clear. But I did raise that question with students, and I asked them to consider if its continual use reinforced a Eurocentric view of the world, minimized people of color, and objectively promoted a view of them as "less." At the project's end, although some students still argued Mercator intended to do so, most came to accept that independent of intentions, one had to consider the actual effect of the map. There was a general consensus that the impact, purposeful or not, was not fair to people of color.

The Politics of Knowledge

Virtually all students came to rethink the issue of representation and how maps influence their perceptions of the world. They were concerned that they had been taught falsities and that their views had been misshaped by schooling, and they came to question that through the project. Sandra expressed this sentiment clearly:

> Doing this project has opened my eyes in different ways. I am learning how small details like maps, etc, have to do a lot with racism and power. Even though these kinds of things are small it can make a big difference on a person's view after learning what's really [going] on. When we found the total area of a country according to the [Mercator] map, the real area we found had a big difference.

Sandra was describing how deconstructing misleading images is both important in understanding the world and is related to significant political issues. She further stated that she became conscious of these connections through the project. This encapsulates the most important goals of the project—that students use mathematical analyses to critique and question knowledge and begin to see it in larger sociopolitical context.

Students, for the most part, came to realize that maps were *political* entities in that they influenced people's views on, as Sandra wrote, racism and power. Maps like the Mercator could privilege certain countries and peoples and diminish others, while the Peters projection could try to represent them fairly—thus maps were political. Students knew that mathematics was the tool with which they learned these ideas. They came to understand the mathematics of political knowledge (Frankenstein, 1998), that is, political artifacts like maps had mathematical features that they could comprehend and use to arrive at deeper awareness of the underlying political knowledge. Javier captured this:

> I learned many things by doing this project. We raised up many thoughts and questions while trying to figure out the amount of area in each region. But one thing I want to mention of what I really learned was how a person's thoughts and putting it into a reference (map) can influence many people thinking it is very accurate, if it is not analyzed. We did analyze the Mercator Map and saw that it wasn't that accurate. All of this information was brought up just by using mathematics to get answers of a social issue. Like I always say, we couldn't have done it without mathematics.

Reflections

In reflecting on this project, several points stand out. First, as on the mortgage project (chapter 3), historical context was important. Mercator's map was historically accurate for the colonial powers, and one cannot evaluate map accuracy without considering this. Second, students grappled with the effect of representations on our perceptions and began to see the political impact of various choices. Third, we again had the problem of objective time limits; I wanted students to learn mathematics while studying the world and simultaneously understand the sociohistorical context of the maps. Fourth, *accurate* in this situation had both political and mathematical meanings, just as *affordable* had in the neighborhood gentrification projects. To first determine whether the Mercator was accurate in representing relative land mass size, students needed mathematics. But to grasp the issues more fully, students had to also develop an understanding of the sociopolitical meaning of accurate. Thus, their mathematical and political thinking were related to each other, each forming an essential component of a larger analysis.

Finally, I made some mistakes on the project. Although I introduced, and we discussed, the issue that Mercator's intentions were secondary and ultimately unknowable, and that one's map choice was essentially political—and what the specific politics were of the choices—I insufficiently emphasized these points. Students' writing and discussions suggest that some believed that Mercator was individually racist rather than understanding that, whatever his personal intentions, he operated in a context that was objectively racist because it dehumanized indigenous peoples in "new lands." That is, some students' overall grasp of the sociopolitical, historical context was limited. But despite weaknesses, the project was powerful in providing students the opportunity to think deeply and raise questions about their prior school learning and to use mathematics to examine the politics of knowledge. The contrast between what they saw on the Mercator projection and what they found mathematically was jarring, and it created the opening for them to explore further, reflect on, and critique and question their own and other knowledge. Mathematics was the enabling medium.

I contend that this project contributed to students' capacity to write the world with mathematics, that is, it furthered the development of their sense of social agency. There is solid evidence that through this project, students questioned their previous teachings. Freire (1970/1998) described how decodification (i.e., decoding the maps) creates opportunities for people to examine prior understandings and create new knowledge: "In the process of decoding, the participants ... reach a 'perception of their previous perception.' By achieving this awareness, they come to perceive reality differently...[and] discover more easily in their 'background awareness' the dialectical relations between the two dimensions of reality" (p. 96). This "discovery" and the juxtaposition of students' "prior understandings" and their creation of "new knowledge" contributed to their sense of agency. In general, they began to understand their own capacity to deconstruct representations, using mathematics, and thus developed further their own conceptions of reality, knowledge, power, and politics. Doing so can create in students the belief that they can effect change. Lupe's words capture the essence of this sense of power:

> This [project] relates to not just accepting what we have but to search for answers to our questions. You have taught us to do that in many ways, and that only makes us grow. Who knows? Maybe we can someday prove things wrong and show the right way!

Students' reflections on Freire's "two dimensions of reality" may have also influenced their orientation toward future learning. It is plausible that their strong reactions influenced how they saw knowledge in the future (I discuss this later in the chapter). This project was unique because it was the only one in which their long-accepted misperceptions clashed so glaringly with reality. Because of that, this project, on top of almost two years of learning mathematics for social justice, may have been a turning point in their development—and may have been a catalyst for them to being to question and critique more sharply what they read, heard, and saw. One student, contrasting his before/after perception of reality, described how the class influenced him and how he started to get socially involved. Adrián Caldéron, a co-author of chapter 7, said, as a high school senior in January 2003:

> … before that class.… I knew about certain historical moments and certain things, but I never really acted on any of them. I didn't really share my ideas with anyone. This classroom really opened it up for me, and this is when I really started to get involved. I started talking to other people, and finding their opinions. And it wasn't just, I'm gonna take what this book tells me and that's the answer. I'm starting to take facts now and making my own decisions. I didn't realize that before seventh and eighth [grades], that you had to make up your own mind, I just figured, oh, people memorize this, people memorize that.

Obstacles to Developing Agency

> The most potent weapon in the hands of the oppressor is the mind of the oppressed. (Stephen Biko, speech in Capetown, South Africa, 1971 [Stubbs, 1978])

My observations were that, for students, learning to write the world with mathematics was as complicated, if not more so, than learning to read the world. One reason is that writing the world entails taking action, or at least seeing oneself as making a difference through one's actions, and that is a step past understanding a situation. It is the more demanding action component of Freire's (1970/1998) reflection-action dialectic (praxis). Indeed, there are multiple challenges involved in helping students see that they can impact the world.

First, U.S. schools socialize students into nonquestioning roles, creating and maintaining passive identities so that students do not believe in their own power to shape the world—what Macedo (1994) called *literacy for stupidification*. Freire (1970/1998), though not speaking of U.S. schools (although he could have been), described *banking* education in which teachers "deposit" dead morsels of knowledge into passive and subservient students ("recipients"). He pointed out that a pedagogy that helps students develop consciousness and a sense of agency is potentially extremely dangerous and an anathema to those with power in an unjust world:

> The more students work at storing the deposits entrusted to them, the less they develop the critical consciousness which would result from their intervention in the world as transformers of that world. The more completely they accept the passive role imposed on them, the more they tend simply to adapt to the world as it is and to the fragmented view of reality deposited in them. The capability of banking education to minimize or annul the students' creative power and to stimulate their credulity serves the interests of the oppressors, who care neither to have the world revealed nor to see it transformed. (p. 54)

Second, Freire (1970/1998) maintained that other impediments to liberation also contributed to the passive identities and disempowerment created by banking education. He believed that the internalized oppression of people from disempowered groups held them back, and he advocated that the oppressed needed to purge themselves of the self-images perpetrated by their oppressors: "How can the oppressed, as divided, unauthentic beings, participate in developing the pedagogy of their liberation? Only as they discover themselves to be 'hosts' of the oppressor can they contribute to the midwifery of their liberating pedagogy" (p. 30). Others have argued similarly that negative self-images and internalized oppression harm the struggles for liberation. Carter G. Woodson (1933/1990) described how the U.S. educational system systematically mis-educated African Americans after emancipation as essentially slavery's extension. He contended that the purpose of education for African Americans was to ensure their subordinate status, and he explicated eloquently the effects of what can only be called the "mind control" of such an education:

> When you determine what a man [sic] shall think you do not have to concern yourself about what he will do. If you make a man feel that he is inferior, you do not have to compel him to accept an inferior status, for he will seek it himself. If you make a man think that he is justly an outcast, you do not have to order him to the back door. He will go without being told; and if there is no back door, his very nature will demand one. (p. 85)

Third, little in conventional education teaches students that they themselves have a role in creating history and changing society (Macedo, 1994). Bill Bigelow (2002), a *Rethinking Schools* editor, explained what students need in contrast to what they normally learn in school:

> It's especially vital that students come to recognize the importance of organization and collective action because so much of young people's education emphasizes the opposite. For example, they learn about Rosa Parks, the tired but heroic lone seamstress who challenged segregation and launched the modern Civil Rights Movement; instead of learning about Rosa Parks, long active in a movement that consciously sought to overthrow segregation and white supremacy. Textbooks and teaching materials often allow Great Individuals their moments in the curricular sun ... but rarely [examine] the social movements that nurtured and ultimately were responsible for whatever accomplishments they are credited with. (p. 332)

What students are taught in school disempowers them in multiple ways. Even Malcolm X has been taught in a way that strips his power, makes him palatable, and commodifies his message (Murrell, 1997; Perry 1996). And high-stakes testing and "accountability" further hinder the efforts to teach for social justice (Lipman, 2004; Lipman & Gutstein, 2001). Finally, some of my students at times exhibited a *sense of powerlessness* (about which I say more below) when they learned about injustice such as on the neighborhood gentrification projects. These are all substantial challenges in encouraging students to see themselves as capable of acting on their environment and making positive social change toward a more just world.

Building on Students' Strengths—Their Sense of Justice

To support students in developing a sense of agency, it is important to build on the strengths that students bring into the classroom. One of my students' most prominent strengths was a strong *sense of justice*. I define a sense of justice as collective and extending beyond the individual, including (at least) members of one's family, community, and ethnicity or nationality, and often other oppressed peoples as well. My data suggest that my students' sense of justice came largely from their life experiences as members of low-income, working-class, immigrant, Latino/a communities subject to immigration raids; police harassment; low-paying, dead-end, exhausting jobs; and various forms of gender, race, ethnicity, social class, and language status discrimination. Students often wrote about their family's and community's experiences when responding to a project about inequity. Many students had little trouble articulating these views, often quite powerfully, given the opportunity. For example, on the world wealth simulation, Marisol wrote:

> Well the world is <u>not, not</u> a pretty fair place. It just gets me mad to see that some people have so much money that they don't even know how to spend it. And others have <u>so</u> little, they don't know which bill to pay off first. It's just so frustrating to see some rich people buy unnecessary things (like a real expensive, legendary <u>spoon</u> for $1000 just cuz someone famous licked it). And other people can't even buy <u>food</u> to eat.

Another example is Omar's reaction when he learned about the application process for a magnet high school. To even take the test, students needed to have a standardized test score on vocabulary of at least the sixth stanine. Omar, fluently bilingual like virtually his whole class, wrote in his journal about a classmate's opportunities:

> I want to talk about what you told me yesterday on admission to Whitney Young. I really would like to go there and it's not fair. I'm a bilingual, and how many people with a stanine six [in vocabulary] can say that. People like Rosa miss a chance to go there when she really deserves to go. That can be one way of discrimination because those tests don't show the hard transition from coming from a Spanish talking home to learning a whole new language, yet we are not rewarded by getting a better education that we have earned and reached very hard for.

The challenge was for students to learn about injustice without paralyzing them into inactivity and hopelessness. Although students' sense of justice was clearly present, about one fourth of the students also at times exhibited a sense of powerlessness. They wrote things like, "but what can I do about it?" Inculcated by the banking system of knowledge (Freire, 1970/1998) and education for domestication/stupidification (Macedo, 1994), a sense of powerlessness could conceivably be made worse by learning just how bad things really were (Bigelow, 2002). I saw this group of students intermittently express a kind of underlying pessimism, a feeling of not being able to change the situation.

What emerges from my analysis of students' writings is that their sense of powerlessness was almost always linked to their sense of justice. Often, the same students who expressed outrage at a particular issue threw up their hands in hopelessness. For example, Marisol, who wrote above so eloquently about the U.S. wealth distribution, ended that excerpt with the sentence, "But then I say, oh well, what can I do about it—I'm not rich." And her comment on the world wealth distribution activity was: "Well of course, as everybody can tell, the wealth distribution of the world is not exactly equal. Some continents have more wealth than others, but what can we do about it? Life is not fair."

The linkage of students' sense of powerlessness to their sense of justice appeared across the projects. In the project, "Racism in Housing Data?", Chuy wrote, "Race has nothing to do with success. [This] is something I feel strong about. There might be some people out there who won't give you a job because of your race, but that shouldn't stop you from succeeding in life." But just three days later, he wrote, "I still think that we shouldn't do a project on Kenilworth. Even if we do discover that there is racism, there is nothing we can really do to stop it."

These data raise several important questions. What can teachers do so that students like those who wrote poignant essays about Morningside's future do not feel hopeless given the seemingly inevitable gentrification of their neighborhood? How do we introduce students to those realities of the world beyond their immediate experiences—which themselves may be harsh—while not paralyzing them into inactivity? What is a pedagogy of hope in this context? How can we build on students' sense of justice, and invigorate, enthuse, and motivate them to work and fight for social justice given the admittedly depressing state of the world? In short, given the nature of both schooling and the current sociopolitical climate in which we live, how do we create conditions for students to write the world?

Developing Agency—Going Beyond Mathematics

To address these questions, I had to find ways to support students' agency that went beyond mathematics. As I describe in this chapter's introduction, there are many ways to develop agency—in my class, these were located on a continuum from having very little to do with mathematics to being deeply embedded in mathematical analysis. But I emphasize again that even the supposedly "nonmathematical" ways of encouraging students to become socially active can have mathematical components—especially in a mathematics class!

First, students need to know their own histories to develop positive cultural and social identities (Ladson-Billings, 1995b; Murrell, 1997). Woodson (1933/1990) advocated strongly that emancipatory education for African Americans include the serious study of their own historical contributions and specific conditions:

The program for the uplift of the Negro in this country must be based upon a scientific study of the Negro from within to develop within him [sic] the power to do for himself what his oppressors will never do to elevate him to the level of others. (p. 144)

This also applies to other marginalized peoples. In one class, we did a project in which students studied the mathematical correlations between SAT/ACT scores and gender, family income, race, and ethnicity (Gutstein, 2002). Armando expressed an idea related to Woodson's in speculating why students of color performed more poorly than whites and wrote:

I have noticed that the people and genders who have been "oppressed" are doing worse than the "whites." I have noticed that many books used at my curriculum (8th grade) have not been related to me in any way because I'm a Mexican American. I don't believe that they relate to anyone [except] "whites." For some reason I believe that's the reason, [but] not the whole reason.

Second, students need to know that positive change can occur and that it is usually the result of mass struggle. I showed my students videos on Chicano/a history (during special days such as school celebrations of *Cinco de Mayo*), and two incidents remained in students' minds long afterwards. One was a scene from the 1950s in which a teacher put a young Chicano in a corner wearing a dunce cap that said "Spanish." The student was to stay there until he could speak English. The other was the story of the "East L.A. Blowouts" in which Chicano/a high school students in Los Angeles organized to protest racist educational practices in 1968, and over 10,000 students walked out (Delgado Bernal, 2000; Ruiz & Racho, 1996). My students did not know that children were punished for speaking their own language in school (Rivera's principal strongly promoted fluent bilingualism), nor that high school students barely older than themselves took strong stands against injustice and actually effected change. This was a profound moment for many, as Marisol commented, 3 1/2 years after eighth grade.

... they [the videos] actually show you people our age do stand up against injustices, it's not something just for the older generations to take care of. It's something for everybody to think about. These problems are social problems, they're not individual problems. Everyone is involved in it one way or another, if it's by contributing to it, supporting it, or fighting against it.

Thus, students do need to know their history, but history can be taught in different ways. When teachers emphasize the struggles of ordinary people for justice (Takaki, 1993; Zinn, 2003) rather than great leaders making history (Bigelow, 2002), students can see that their actions can make a difference.

Third, teachers can provide students with opportunities to take actions themselves. This is, of course, restricted because youth have less autonomy than adults. Because of these limitations, creating room for students to raise their own questions, sometimes just to each other as happened on the mortgage project, can serve as action. Furthermore, even though mathematics classes generally have less do to with social issues than do social studies, history, language arts/English, or even science classes, young people can still take action within mathematics classes (Tate, 1995; Turner & Font Strawhun, 2005).

In the project in which we studied the correlations of ACT and SAT scores to family income, gender, and ethnicity, students wrote letters to the Educational Testing Service (ETS) (the SAT makers) about their analyses and questions. Although they decided not to mail them, they read them to each other and raised significant, provocative questions about the relationships in the data. Juanita wrote:

> I want to know how are people who have a lower income and who study just as hard as those who have a higher income, how are they affected?.... Is there racism or something involved? I also have another question, why are the scores different for each race? How come whites and Asians get high scores, yet everyone else gets lower scores? How does race affect your scores? Now I really want to know, is there racism involved?

Antonio also raised penetrating questions about social class.

> Dear ETS,
> I have a few questions about your SAT scores by income level. It seems to me that people with low incomes have lower scores than people with much more income. Why is that? Your data shows that low income means that kids are not smart, and rich are smart. That data can not be right. Why, all the other people [are] just as smart or even smarter. Because they try to succeed in life and get a job that could bring in some good income. All these people want to become doctors, lawyers, sports players, etc., so why are "rich" smarter?

He then addressed one of his own questions in his letter: "Could it be that normal people go to public schools, while richer people go to private schools and have their own tutors? Is that one reason that might answer one of my first questions?"

The antigentrification struggle was another opportunity for involvement in which students either participated themselves or did so vicariously. My class in the general track in 2000–2001 also did the project in which they found how long it took to drive from Morningside to the Sears Tower, but we did more in that class. I took four students on a "field trip" after school to the Springfield Heights sales office, just outside of Morningside. I pretended to be a quasi-interested buyer, and we went through the motions (I told the salesperson that I brought my students along for them to learn about the home buying process), listened to the sales pitches, looked at the virtual representations and physical models of the development, read the promotional materials, and took pictures of everything. Students then gave an in-class presentation, with the photos, on what they learned as a way to educate others about gentrification. Even if these experiences were limited because of students' age, they concretely gave them opportunities to join in wider social activity, or to envision themselves as active participants via the collective sharing of action and interpretation. These may be small steps, but they provide openings for students to imagine the potential of their actions in the world, especially in the context of social movements.

Fourth, teachers can create opportunities for students to understand commonalities they have with others. One of my students stereotyped Asians one day, which led me to show the film *Ethnic Notions: Black People in White Minds* (Riggs, 1987). This moving film explores the history of how degrading stereotypes of African Americans became a common and harmful part of U.S. culture. In introducing the film, I told students that I was unable to find a film about them as Latinos/as. Instead, I asked them to consider how the film would be if it were about them, seeding the notion of examining common experiences. Although students initially laughed at the buffoon caricatures of African Americans, by the film's end they were deathly silent as the destructiveness of the stereotypes became clear. Ariana, a Mexicana, succinctly wrote in her journal: "… at first we may be laughing, but when we see that they are making fun of *us* [italics added], it ain't that funny anymore." The "us" encompasses both African Americans and Latinos/as (who are not mentioned). Others also saw themselves in the story.

These connections are important because students can see their lives reflected in others' lives and can begin to understand that an injustice to one is an injustice to all. When they begin to recognize common experiences of oppression, they begin also to realize that emancipatory actions by others (like African American freedom movements) can be liberatory for themselves as well. They can see that they have potential allies in their own struggles and can be allies to others, which can create a sense of power, solidarity, possibility—and agency.

My analysis suggests that a critical component for students to begin to see themselves as subjects capable of making history and to overcome a sense of powerlessness was to build on their strengths, especially their sense of justice. The four "beyond mathematics" ways I discuss above for students to begin developing agency—(1) learning their histories, (2) learning that ordinary people, including youth, have changed the world, (3) envisioning and taking actions themselves, and (4) finding commonalities and solidarity with other oppressed peoples—all relate to students' sense of justice. This is in addition to learning to write the world specifically with mathematics as I explain earlier. All the real-world projects I developed built on that sense of justice, one way or another. These projects revolved around issues near to my students' hearts if not also their lives—from immigrant status, distorted representations of the world, and the growth of Latino/a population, to unequal wealth distributions, racial profiling, and racism in housing patterns.

Moreover, these ostensibly nonmathematical practices supporting agency can also involve mathematics. For example, to learn their history, Mexican students can study the mathematics of indigenous Mexico: Aztec pyramids, Mayan numbers, and Olmec sculpture. Or they can contrast Mexican computational algorithms with those of the United States and build conceptual understanding by analyzing common, underlying principles (Ortiz-Franco, 1999). The students who used mathematics on the mortgage project and discovered that both African Americans and Latinos/as were rejected for mortgages at higher rates than whites found commonalities with other oppressed people. And to see themselves as participants in making history, students' involvement in the antigentrification struggle was facilitated by the understanding they gained through mathematically studying the issues.

Thus, more "mathematical" ways of encouraging agency, like the gentrification and map projects, can include nonmathematical practices like studying history and critiquing political knowledge—and developing agency when "going beyond mathematics" can still have mathematical components. We were in mathematics classes, after all, and discussions moved easily back and forth between mathematics and real-world topics, especially because students were studying society with mathematics. That we ventured off into other areas, seemingly less related to mathematics, did not seem to bother students once the pattern was established. And both mathematical *and* nonmathematical ways of supporting agency can be linked to participation in social movements. Experiences like the above, in classrooms in which students and teacher co-create a community that normalizes this form of pedagogy, may be powerful ways for students to begin developing agency.

Assessing the Long-Term Influence

As in chapter 3, I do not assume a causal relationship between these mathematics classes and either the consciousness students developed or the actions they took (or will take) in their lives. Rather, I wish to understand how students saw the influence of the class on themselves. Below, I share some vignettes and student reflections that may suggest this influence, although I do not claim that the students in the following stories necessarily represent all my students, nor that these tales imply definitive changes in their lives. Yet their actions, along with their self definitions, suggest that they were beginning to develop agency and that the class contributed to the process.

When Lupe was in tenth grade, she saw a late-night television report about violent vigilantism against undocumented Mexicans crossing the border into Arizona. My phone rang at midnight, and in a horrified and furious voice, she asked me, "What can we do about this? We have to do something!"

Elena was also in tenth grade when she wrote an essay on the Declaration of Independence in which she made a scathing critique of racism—and used mathematics. She referenced the "We Are Not A Minority" project (see chapter 3). She wrote, "We have been called 'minorities' even though we are not. Statistics say that by the year 2025 the population of Latinos will be greater than any other racial group, so you tell me ARE we a 'minority?'" She made her mother, a Rivera teachers aide, find me and give me a copy of the essay.

It was not unusual that students and I kept in touch. Part of this was my ongoing attempts to study and understand the lessons from our classes. In preparation for a conference presentation in 2003 (Gutstein, Barbosa, Calderón, Murillo, & Nevárez), I had conversations with my four co-authors, then high school seniors, in groups of two. We taped them for the purpose of analysis. Adrián Calderón described how his social studies teacher ended class with five-minute "shoutouts" in which students could raise any issue they wanted by submitting an anonymous note to the teacher. Seeing a Mercator map in his classroom, Adrián took action.

Calderón: I asked, "What's wrong with the map in the back of the room?" And they were all like, "what are you talking about?" And the teacher was kind of like, "what? What is this?" And I just kind of stayed there quiet for a while, because I realized just how big a reaction everyone had, they were like, "huh?".... I said, "well, there are a lot of things wrong with the map," and I explained to them.

Gutstein: Did you go up to the map?

Calderón: Yeah, I went up to the map and I talked about the south and the north, and I compared Alaska and Mexico, Greenland, and Africa and Asia, and how Africa is this really big continent and how it's represented on the map, and a couple of the students were like, "whaa?" They didn't understand it.... But, the teacher was kind of surprised. She was like, "oh wow, I didn't even know that!" And she was really interested. And a couple of other students were kinda "oh, I didn't know that." They got really into it, too. And ever since then, I would put out shout outs about different things, and people would be like "oh, that has to be Adrian's."

Gutstein: And so, how does that relate to this issue of, "oh well what can we do about it?"

Calderón: It proves that not everyone thinks like that. It's just a matter of does one person—is one person gonna make a difference. I made a difference! Like, 7 people, it was 28 people, 7 people out of 28 people, now they realize that, "hey maybe I should take a second look at the map." *And that's just how it starts* [italics added].

I could not keep contact that well with Freida because she returned to her native Dominican Republic after eighth grade. However, she called me in July 2001 (the summer before she entered eleventh grade) when she was visiting Chicago. I had not talked with her since her eighth-grade graduation, and we talked for an hour. I wrote some notes afterward including the following:

I just talked to Freida … this is 2 years since I've seen her. She has been living in the D.R. since then. She told me some very interesting things …

• She took her Peters map into school [I gave every student in her class an 11 "by 17" laminated map for graduation] to show her social studies teacher, but he got mad and told her that this was not a good map. Freida told the teacher that it was, that's why it was made, but the teacher told her to put it away and not show it around. However, she took the map and showed it around to a number of her classmates so that they could see that the areas in the conventional map were not accurate. I asked her if she argued with the teacher, but she said she was in enough trouble with her teacher and that this teacher was on her, so she let it go.

- She had to create a play for drama class in tenth grade, so she created a script from the Chicano history video of the East L.A. Blowouts and used that as the theme. The students in the drama class at first didn't like doing that because they wanted to do a romantic story, but she persisted and they eventually came around to it and liked it. Her drama teacher loved it and started calling her a revolutionary.
- She feels that she thinks a lot about injustice and how Haitians are treated in the D.R., just like the way Mexicans are treated in the U.S. ... and that some of that awareness with issues of injustice came from our class.

One final, and powerful, story about the development of students agency is when they took a stand, but on my behalf. During the 2002–2003 school year, while I was teaching at Rivera, the principal who strongly supported my curriculum moved on. A district-appointed temporary principal did not like the politics of my work and forced me to leave in late January 2003, the end of the first semester (see chapter 8 for the full story).

A special Local School Council (LSC)[3] meeting about my situation was held at Rivera. At the LSC meeting, several of my former students spoke out strongly in support of what they had learned and why it was important. Although one might expect expressions of student loyalty to caring teachers in such a situation, it was significant that students (and their parents) overwhelmingly voiced support of a curriculum in which students learned mathematics and used it to investigate injustice. My former students (then high school seniors) from my two-year class organized themselves and wrote a collective letter signed by 17 of them (all they could reach on a few days notice). Marisol read the letter aloud to start the meeting. In the first paragraph, they wrote, "We are addressing this matter because we believe this act was an injustice to the school and the students in Mr. Rico's math class." The letter also states:

By being his 7th and 8th grade math students at Rivera five years ago, we feel that his way of teaching was essential to our development not only as mathematics students, but also as human beings. His integration of real-life issues into the math projects he assigned to us was an effective way of exercising our ability to think critically about the world we live in and *to the way we respond to it* [italics added].

I had hoped that students would develop a sense of agency, that they would stand up and speak out for that which they believed. I just never expected that it would be on my behalf. Thus, a compelling piece of evidence that these students began to develop a sense of agency may be the events that brought them to take a stand for the very school experiences years earlier that contributed to their development. Coupled with their rich and varied life experiences and knowledge over 18 or so years, and their powerful sense of justice derived from their positions in society and their critical analyses of the world, their middle school mathematics class in which they began to read the world using mathematics may have provided contexts, tools, and space for them to begin the complex process of *writing* the world with mathematics as well. It is important to clarify and name contributing factors in students' growth, when we can. Given the empirical evidence and the admittedly problematic nature of self-reflections/self-reporting, there is enough justification to warrant a provisional claim: teaching mathematics for social justice in urban, public schools—in which developing agency is a central part—can make a difference in students' lives beyond the classroom.

CHAPTER 5

The Relationship of Teaching for Social Justice and Mathematics in Context

Well, I thought of mathematics as another subject in school that I hated. And I didn't bother to think too much about world issues or everyday issues. Now I know it all relates. And I've learned how powerful math can be to help us explain our decisions and help us express our selves, because like I said before, math makes things more clear. *(Lupe, 8th grade, May 1999)*

I have two purposes in this chapter. First, I analyze the interrelationship of using Mathematics in Context (MiC) and teaching mathematics for social justice. I describe MiC's philosophy and how MiC has the *potential* to contribute to social justice teaching. I then analyze what I did to try to actualize that possibility and the complexities involved. I discuss the relationship between teaching mathematics for social justice and teaching it to develop mathematical power. Second, I provide evidence that it is possible to develop sociopolitical consciousness, social agency, *and* to achieve the mathematics goals of my framework—for students to (a) develop mathematical power, (b) succeed academically in the traditional sense, and (c) develop different orientations, from the norm, toward mathematics. I make no claim that this will always occur, and in chapter 6, I describe in detail some of the facilitating conditions and difficulties I experienced.

MiC and Teaching Mathematics for Social Justice

MiC was created to help teachers actualize the National Council of Teachers of Mathematics (NCTM) *Standards* in the early 1990s. Researchers at the Freudenthal Institute (Utrecht University) in the Netherlands originally wrote MiC, then a team at the University of Wisconsin–Madison reworked it for U.S. schools. MiC is a connected, comprehensive, grades 5–8 curriculum that covers the mathematics strands of the *Standards*: algebra, data analysis and probability, geometry (including measurement), and number. Like all 13 curricula funded by the National Science Foundation (NSF), MiC was extensively field tested in schools across the United States (in MiC's case, also in Puerto Rico), and took seven years and roughly $8 million to become fully operational and published, with a team of about 50 researchers, curriculum developers, consultants, and teachers.

MiC Philosophy and Dispositions Toward Knowledge

MiC philosophy is grounded in the *realistic mathematics education* framework elaborated by Hans Freudenthal (de Lange, 1987; de Lange & Romberg, 2004; Freudenthal, 1983, 1991). A central idea is that mathematics is a human activity involved in social interaction, production, and intellectual abstraction. Virtually all the mathematics in MiC is embedded in real-world situations, with no pages of decontextualized "naked" number sentences. The *Teacher Resource and Implementation Guide* (TRIG) (NCRMSE & FI, 1998) stated:

> The real-world contexts support and motivate learning. Mathematics is a tool to help students make sense of their world. Since mathematics originated from real life, so should mathematics learning. Therefore, *Mathematics in Context* uses real-life situations as a starting point for learning; these contexts illustrate the variety of ways in which students can use mathematics. (p. 3)

The TRIG described specific roles for students and teachers. Teachers are "facilitators" and "guides," while students "create mathematics for themselves" and "reinvent significant mathematics" (p. 4). Students are not rushed into procedural efficiency; rather, MiC emphasizes conceptual understanding. The curriculum's philosophy stated that "it is preferable that students use informal strategies that they understand rather than formal procedures that they do not understand" (p. 4). Because MiC spans four years, students have ample time to develop their own ideas and gradually move to abstraction ("progressive schematization," Streefland, 1993). Important ideas resurface across units and grades at increasingly deeper levels of complexity.

The Potential Benefits of MiC for Social Justice Teaching

MiC can support teaching mathematics for social justice for several reasons. First, it engenders dispositions toward knowledge that are generally in sync with teaching mathematics for social justice. MiC consistently positions students as arbitrators of knowledge, correctness, and reasonableness, and it encourages analyses from multiple perspectives. A typical example is from the unit "Dealing with Data." Four middle school students in the unit's story examine a large data set collected in 1904 by geneticists who studied whether children grew taller than their parents. The story characters concur that the children are taller but state different reasons. The real students using MiC analyze the data and have to justify with which of the rationales they agree. Throughout the curriculum, students explain and defend their answers and claims and often have to critique one another's reasoning. Furthermore, MiC encourages multiple ways to solve the same problem and provides problems with more than one correct solution. The criteria for correctness or appropriateness of answers in MiC often lie with logical coherency, real-world reasonableness, and students' own meaning making rather than with outside sources like the teacher or answer sheet.

These features of MiC are similar to some aspects of social justice pedagogy. For example, when students argue whether racism is a factor in racial disparities in receiving mortgages and they decide for themselves whether a community organization spokesperson or bank loan officer is accurately representing the situation, they are arbitrating knowledge. That MiC's contexts derive from the world is also compatible with students analyzing real-life injustices. And MiC's promotion of mathematics as a sensemaking activity is consistent with the goal of using mathematics to understand various forms of discrimination.

Second, all the complex political issues with which my students grappled had mathematical components. Without a strong grasp of mathematical ideas, students have difficulty understanding underlying political issues. The mortgage rejection project required that students grasp the concepts of rate and ratio, and the random drug testing project required them to understand conditional probability. To appreciate more fully how standardized tests results related to student characteristics, students needed to understand correlation and causality (and the difference), and to develop meaning for racial profiling, they had to understand the law of large numbers. And so on. These are not trivial mathematical topics for middle school students, but without them, students can confuse the ideas or be left with surface-level explanations that belie the complexities. For example, on the mortgage project, one group of students consistently misunderstood the meaning of *rate* and argued that African Americans were rejected at a higher rate than whites because more had applied than whites. Many students on that project had difficulty grasping the meaning of the *disparity ratio*, the ratio between the rejection rates. These conceptual complexities hindered their interpretations of the data and claims in the newspaper article they read. Comprehending the mathematical concepts was necessary for students to develop understanding for, and take positions on, the sociopolitical issues.

Third, students (and adults) often view mathematical (and other) phenomena in black and white and can miss nuanced shades of gray. They have been conditioned by learning (mathematics) for correctness and develop binary orientations: either something is or is not racism, for example. MiC helped students see that answers were often inexact, mathematical questions could have multiple correct answers and interpretations, and some questions had no solutions. Countering simplistic right/wrong conceptions was important in helping students develop the mathematical and overall sophistication to probe more deeply for meaning and understanding and to continue questioning. As Tita commented on the mortgage project, "From this project I learned that you should question everything. Like that to have a better project you should question all your answers. That's what I did." These dispositions, fostered in part by MiC, are essential to more deeply grasp the subtleties of racism and other injustices.

Making the Potential a Reality

However, despite the confluence of various aspects of MiC with teaching mathematics for social justice and MiC's importance in helping students clarify the mathematical aspects of political issues, I argue that MiC *by itself* does not prepare students to read or write their worlds with mathematics. MiC does not challenge students to analyze injustice or see themselves as potential social change agents—nor do any reform curricula. Furthermore, there is no a priori reason to suggest otherwise. One can make a similar argument about textual literacy. Certainly there are many high-quality high school English classes in which students learn to interpret and critique literature. But that reading of the *word*, as Freire (Freire & Macedo, 1987) called it, is not the same as a reading of the *world*. Just because students may be able to analyze Shakespeare does not mean that they will necessarily develop political consciousness and a sense of social agency. If that were the case, then we would have large numbers of politically conscious, active youth. That we do not suggests that good "critical thinking" by itself does not translate into social justice awareness and action. And if this is the case for English class, which is generally more connected to the real world than is mathematics class, then there is even less of a reason to assume that learning rich mathematics alone would lead students to read and write the world.

This raises the question of what teachers can do to actualize MiC's support for social justice teaching. In my situation, MiC was essential for several reasons. Although I describe below how MiC interacted with my social justice curriculum and teaching practices, I am not suggesting that these are the only conditions under which MiC, or any other reform mathematics curriculum, can be a partner in encouraging students to read and write the world with mathematics. Rather, I seek to analyze and draw lessons from my experience.

Issues of Context. First, despite MiC's commitment to real-world contexts, its mainly fictitious stories were not that relevant to my students (nor to other Rivera students). In early 1998, I and another Rivera mathematics teacher gave an open-ended, anonymous survey (with 16 questions) about MiC to three seventh-grade classes (including mine) that had been using MiC all year (Gutstein, 1998). Seventy-nine students completed surveys. Question 11 was "Do you like the stories that MiC is about? Can you relate to them?" From the responses that were categorizeable, 40 students said they liked the stories, 12 were ambivalent, and 16 did not like them. However, on the question of relating to the stories, 17 said they could, 6 were ambivalent, and 32 said they could not. A typical response was "Yes I like them but no, I cannot relate to them." When I asked my class about that question, their (verbal) responses included, "they [MiC story characters] do things we don't do" (several students), "it's not us," "they don't deal with things that most people do," "they have a friend who went to England to do a piano recital," "we don't go on canoe trips," "they measure everything they see," and "they put math into every single thing of their lives." One of my students wrote on the survey: "No, we can't relate to them. We don't have family and friends in Africa, we don't go in hot air balloons, we don't go canoeing, we don't go downtown and count cars, they give cheap stories." Of course, not all students responded this way, and one student said bluntly, "I don't think it should matter" (whether the stories were relevant), but the question often on the table was: Mathematics in *whose* context?

I found that I needed go beyond MiC's real-world settings to include ones that were relevant to my students. However, I did not use generic, ostensibly apolitical contexts that might have been personally relevant. This is a significant point. There are *three* types of real-world contexts here: (1) nonrelevant ones (like MiC's); (2) relevant ones (for example, finding the distance between students' homes and Rivera using maps); and (3) *political* ones involving justice, like the real-world projects. In going beyond MiC, I used the last option.

Students generally said and wrote that those contexts were meaningful and relevant to them in contrast to MiC stories. In all my classes, even students who disliked or were disinterested in mathematics generally reported finding the real-world projects engaging. The fact that MiC stories came from everyday activities, even if different from my students' lives, sent the message that mathematics was about the world. But to make mathematics genuinely meaningful, I built on, and extended, the MiC notion that "mathematics originated from real life" (NCRMSE & FI, 1998) bypassing relevant but nonpolitical contexts.

Although MiC encouraged students to create and arbitrate knowledge, it did not ask them to take stands and develop positions on important social issues. But to learn mathematics for social justice, students needed to produce and arbitrate knowledge about meaningful issues of inequality and exclusion. To develop political awareness, it may have been helpful for students to determine which character in an MiC story most reasonably analyzed why children were taller than their parents—but it was necessary to answer questions such as: What impact does viewing a Mercator projection throughout one's life have on how one sees the world and oneself? They had to use mathematics to decide whether racial profiling was a real issue, if more community jobs and new sidewalks were worth displacing neighborhood residents, and how race and class intersected in influencing Kenilworth housing prices. It may seem obvious that context matters, but although MiC's realistic contexts provided a potential scaffold for the investigation of inequality, I had to shift students' mathematical analyses from the less meaningful MiC stories to ones that were personally relevant to my students *because* they were about social justice.

Pedagogical and Curricular Coherence. In a setting like mine in which there were two different (even if integrated) sets of pedagogical goals—for mathematics and for social justice—teachers need curricular and pedagogical coherence between them. Again, this is conceptually obvious, but the complexities lie in the practice. I tried to maintain this cohesiveness and sometimes connected the mathematics content of the real-world projects to the MiC units we were studying. For example, after we completed the MiC unit "Cereal Numbers," in which we studied absolute and relative comparisons and analyzed "consumer price indices" (CPI), we did a project titled "Tomato Pickers Take on the Growers." Students used the CPI and ideas from "Cereal Numbers" to graph wage decreases and cost of living increases to mathematize and better understand the horrific life and work conditions of immigrant agricultural workers.

But I discovered that things were not so simple. After my two-year class did the world wealth simulation (chapter 3), Marisol wrote in her journal,

"This week I learned how to do all that percent stuff we did with the cookies. There were lots of steps to it, they were easy, but I wouldn't be able to do them without someone telling them [the steps] to me." I was quite taken aback because I do not describe my pedagogy as telling students explicitly how to do solve problems. But she was right—I did exactly that. On reflection, I understood why. I planned to use one 80-minute period for the simulation. In that time, I had to present the project, give students the materials, have them divide the class into the different "continents" and calculate the shares for each continent, have them move into different locations in the room, distribute the cookies, get them to equally share the cookies among the continents' members, and have a full-class discussion. When some groups struggled with the mathematics, I told them how to find the answers. In retrospect, the time was unrealistic to do all this and have a thorough culminating discussion about wealth inequality (which continued to another day anyhow). So I hurried, unconsciously transgressing my pedagogical beliefs, and sacrificed opportunities for students to create their own solution methods.

This prompted me to examine more closely my pedagogy and the mathematical content of the real-world projects, as well as how I related the projects to MiC. I realized that although my pedagogy was generally consistent across the different parts of my curriculum, this story notwithstanding, I occasionally weakened the mathematics content and opportunities for mathematical learning. I also realized that I only occasionally connected MiC units explicitly to the projects.

Dialectic of Developing Mathematical Power and Teaching for Social Justice

Given that I sometimes reduced the mathematical challenge, I had to ask: Why had I made those decisions since I wanted the projects to be sites for mathematical learning? I also considered why I insufficiently connected the mathematical content of MiC to the real-world projects. I came to understand that MiC was so strong in developing mathematical power in my students that it actually provided me a certain amount of "pedagogical space." Within that space, I could engage my students in using mathematics to investigate racism, wealth inequality, costs of war preparations, gentrification, and other issues—and be less concerned that they learn as much mathematics as when studying MiC.

I am not suggesting that the real-world projects overall contained nonchallenging mathematics, and in fact, there were projects with quite challenging mathematics (for example, a conditional probability project on random drug testing that I adapted from a tenth-grade Interactive Mathematics Program unit). Nor did I teach the projects without concern for mathematical meaning and conceptual understanding. Furthermore, even when the mathematical content was less challenging, I still had students share and compare strategies, explain their reasoning (verbally and in writing), and connect mathematical ideas—all components of mathematical power. But my data suggest both that MiC was the primary vehicle for the development of mathematical power, and that when we did the projects, I focused more on students learning to read and write the world and less on learning rich mathematics. I realized that one can use mathematics to develop social awareness *with* or *without* also constructing mathematical knowledge, arguably the most important aspect of mathematical power. That is, one can *apply* already known ideas, concepts, and procedures to analyze injustice and meaningfully read and write the world—but not also create solution methods and reinvent significant mathematics at the same time. That occurred when I reduced the mathematical challenges on the real-world projects.

This tension between developing mathematical power and developing sociopolitical consciousness and a sense of social agency was not my preference. But the dilemma was unavoidable because of the difficulties in simultaneously doing both of these things well. It took a vast amount of resources, time, and people to make MiC into a four-year, connected curriculum that intertwines mathematical strands, creates opportunities for students to progressively formalize their mathematical inventions, and develops in students the capacity to reason and communicate mathematically at a sophisticated level. No solitary individual could create a comprehensive social justice mathematics curriculum of the same quality with respect to learning mathematics. Furthermore, even if one wanted to work on this, as I was a classroom teacher (albeit with only one class), a full-time college professor with no release time to teach middle school, a "real-world project developer," and a researcher of my students' learning and my teaching, I did not even have the time to try.

There is a dialectical relationship between developing mathematical power and teaching students to use mathematics to study, and potentially change, structural inequality. The two processes can facilitate each other, under certain conditions, but there is a tension between them. To learn rich mathematics, students at some point have to leave the situation in which the mathematics is embedded and focus on the mathematical ideas themselves. For generic contexts as in MiC, this shift does not matter. MiC's developers did not intend for students to learn nonmathematical content through the stories, such as lock making, canoe paddling, food making, sandwich sharing, trip taking, and myriad other human activities. But when learning mathematics for social justice, context and content *are* important, as important as mathematics, and so teachers need to explicitly reconcile the interrelationships between the different curricular components.

Conversely, to prioritize the sociopolitical context, teachers need to draw students into studying reality and at some point leave mathematics to the side, even though mathematics may be the entry point into the investigation and may be integral to understanding the complexities. There are ways to make the connections between mathematics and social justice more obvious, for example, by having students explain concretely how they used mathematics to understand particular issues. Skovsmose (1994) referred to this as doing "mathematical archeology," the aim of which "is to make explicit the actual use of mathematics hidden in social structures and routines" (p. 95). But it should be clear that when students discuss why immigrants come to the United States leaving behind families and homes, analyze the genesis of bad credit, or discuss neighborhood gentrification, at some point, mathematics may drop out of the conversation. This is inevitable and not necessarily a problem, but it is a tension teachers have to purposefully negotiate. Despite students learning that mathematics can help them understand "what surrounds" them, there are indeed significant ideas on which mathematics can shed only so much light, even if, as I mention earlier, mathematics is important to understanding political issues.

To the extent that snippets of social justice mathematics curricula exist through which students can develop mathematical power *and* simultaneously develop political awareness and a belief in themselves as potential change agents, the contradiction may be resolved. Some of the real-world projects helped students move toward these goals such as the map project in which students both invented and communicated their mathematical solution strategies (see next section) and also began to read and write the world. However, a full resolution to this dilemma—a connected, cohesive, comprehensive social justice mathematics curriculum—does not yet exist, as far as I know. To create one will take a major concentrated effort, perhaps more than what it took to create any of the reform curricula because it will require partnerships between mathematics and social justice educators. This is a future goal.

Mathematical Power, Academic Success, and Changed Orientations

In chapters 3 and 4, I furnish evidence that many of my students began the process of developing sociopolitical consciousness and a sense of social agency through using mathematics. But did they also learn mathematics? Or was this a case of students developing an awareness of injustice in the world and a sense that they could make an impact, but not also learning the mathematics needed to pass the various gatekeeping tests, have opportunities for advanced academic studies, and become effective change agents toward a more just society? In the following sections I discuss this point and also their traditional academic success. I then analyze the shifts in their orientations toward mathematics.

Developing Mathematical Power: MiC and the Real-World Projects

I used MiC with four of the five classes I taught at Rivera. I focus here on my two-year class because I have the best data for them. The three other classes that used MiC were a bilingual general-track class (I taught for one quarter), an English-program, general-track class (one third of a year), and a bilingual honors-track class (half a year). I did not have as much time with any of those classes to thoroughly evaluate their mathematical growth. The other class I taught was in the English-program, general track (one year), but I used the Connected Mathematics Project most of the time because the school had shifted from MiC that year.[1]

Most of my students who studied MiC developed aspects of mathematical power (Gutstein, 2003c). I do not claim that all developed to be excellent mathematical thinkers, and their understanding and competencies varied. However, of the 28 students I taught in my two-year class, 27 provided evidence of mathematical invention, communication, reasoning, and problem solving in their class and homework, tests, quizzes, and projects (both real-world projects and ones based on MiC).[2] In general, these students learned to invent and communicate their own solution strategies, represent mathematical ideas in multiple ways, and justify their arguments. I present work of a range of students from both the real-world projects and MiC as evidence of their varying capabilities and mathematical sophistication.

Students' Work on the Real-World Projects. The project, "Will Development Bury the *Barrio*?" (chapter 4), encompassed several mathematical topics. There were two straightforward percentage-increase problems, one more complicated multistep percentage problem, two weighted-average problems, two ratio problems, and one algebra problem. All were real problems, in words, about neighborhood development, the cost of housing, median incomes, affordability, and allocation of jobs. Of the mathematical topics, we had previously only covered the easier percentage problems. For the other topics, students had no memorized procedures and had to invent solutions. All students solved most problems correctly (except question 4, which was much too hard, see Appendix 1), but all also had some difficulties.

Question 3, a weighted average problem, was:

> The developer is building 752 homes in the area just southwest of Morningside. The houses will cost an average of $198,000; the least expensive will go for $125,000 and the most expensive for $350,000. 20% are supposed to be "affordable," so those are probably the $125,000 homes. Use this information to answer the following question.
>
> 3. Assume for the moment that the article made a mistake and got the average price wrong (but got the other information correct), and also assume that there were only two prices for the houses, $125,000 (20% of the total) and $350,000. What would the average price of a house be then?

Of the papers turned in, 18 students answered this correctly, six were incorrect, and one had no response. Angel's and Omar's invented response was:

> What we did is we took 5 houses. One of those is $125,000 (which is 20%) and the rest is [are] 350,000 so you add all of it up which is $1,525,000 so then you divide it by 5 and get $305,000. So the answer is $305,000.

Although there are 752, not five, houses, they focused on the relationship of 20% to 80% (a 1:4 ratio) rather than on the number of houses and considerably simplified the problem. Although they did not explain that they added four houses at $350,000, the sum of (one house at $125,000) + (fourhouses at $350,000) is $1,525,000, as they stated.

Elena and Paulina solved this differently:

> The average price of a house will be $305,120 (rounded off). What we did was [we] got 20% of 752, which is 150 houses, and subtract[ed] 150 from 752 and got 602. 602 is 80% of 752 houses. Then we multiply 125,000 by 150, then you multiply 350,000 by 602, add both numbers up, and you get your answer.

Although they did not write their final step, "divide by 752," the answer one gets by doing that rounds off to $305,120, their final answer. This solution is more concrete than Omar's and Angel's because one has to compute the cost of all 752 houses. However, it is completely correct, is thoroughly explained except for the final step, makes sense, and was also invented.

Most students solved the problem like Elena and Paulina, although one other pair did it similarly to Angel and Omar. Of the six who were incorrect, three attempted strategies like Elena's and Paulina's, and three had wrong answers with no explanations (I required and graded explanations, so students generally produced them). All the correct solutions had coherent explanations, although some contained minor flaws like the above. And no student suggested using the unrealistic, actual mathematical answers of 150.4 or 601.6 houses, which was gratifying.

Problems 5 and 6 were:

5. To buy a $125,000 house, the article says that a family of four would need to make $47,000 a year, which is 80% of the median income in the metropolitan area. So how much is the median income in the metropolitan area for a family of four?

6. Using the information of needing an income of $47,000 to buy a house costing $125,000, how much would a family need to make to buy a house costing $350,000?

Juanita's solution on problem 6 was unusual and used equivalent ratios:

I divided $125,00 by 5 and got $25,000. I did the same with $47,000 and got $9,400. Then I multiplied $25,000 by 14 to get $350,000, and I did the same for $9,400 and got $131,600, which is what your income must be to get a $350,000 house.

Although she did not explain her reasoning, one can infer possible rationales. She may have reasoned that both 125,000 and 350,000 were divisible by 25,000 and then used an informal ratio strategy. The logic of the solution is that if one scales down both 125,000 and 47,000 by the same factor (5), then one preserves the ratio between house price and income (i.e., 125,000:47,000 is equal to 25,000:9,400). She then apparently scaled *up* the 25,000 by a factor of 14 when she found what she needed to multiply it by to get 350,000. To then preserve the ratio of house price to income, she then needed to scale up 9,400 by a factor of 14 as well—thus her result of $131,600 for the necessary income to buy a $350,000 house.

Other students solved this differently. Danny's solution was:

$133,000 is the required income. 80% of the median income is needed to buy a house of $125,000. This 80% is 38% of the house's cost. I assumed this was true of all houses, so I found 38% of $350,000 ($133,000) by multiplying $350,000 by 38%.

His strategy was to notice that in problem 5, a person needed an income of $47,000 for a $125,000 house, or 38% of the house price, although he does not say how he found this. He then applied the idea of needing 38% of any house's price to the more expensive house and produced his answer. Two other students solved the problem in a similar way (using 37.5%, rather than 38%).

Some students solved problem 6 by setting up a proportion and cross multiplying (one pair used that language), and others invented yet other ways to solve it. Fifteen of the 25 students solved this correctly. Most of the 10 who solved it incorrectly appeared not to know what to do and apparently used clues and numbers from nearby problems. Others used subtractive strategies instead of reasoning multiplicatively. For example, Rosa wrote, "272,000. I saw that the difference from 125,000 and 47,000 was 78,000 so I subtracted 78,000 from 350,000 and got my answer."

From examining the mathematics work on this real-world project, it appears that some problems were difficult for some students (no individual or pair solved all correctly), but all students solved most of the problems. They used very few traditional algorithms (e.g., cross-multiplying), which I did not teach, and most of their solution methods were invented, similar to the ones I show here—I taught none of the nontraditional strategies students used. Furthermore, all students but one coherently explained their mathematical work, even when incorrect, and many also explained why they did things in a particular way.

The above project shows students' invention and communication in the mathematical area of *number*. They demonstrated similar reasoning on the map projection project (chapter 4), but those mathematical topics were *geometry* and *measurement*. The key mathematical task was for students to find the area on a map of a number of land masses given Mexico's area as a unit of measure (760,000 square miles). They then had to find the areas of Alaska, Greenland, Africa, Scandinavia, and India.

There were six groups of students, and all invented ways to find the areas; all but one group clearly communicated their reasoning. Four of the groups superimposed grids over the various land masses, first finding out Mexico's area in square centimeters on the map, and then finding the other areas in various ways. One group wrote:

> To find the area of each country we did the following: We already knew that Mexico was around 760,000 (sq. m [miles]) so we measured Mexico to find its area in sq. cm. (We did this by gridding each country and counting the number of boxes, sq. cm, each country used.) So we knew that 20 cm equal 760,000 m so we divided 760,000 by 20 to get the number of sq. m each sq. cm has which

equaled 38,000 sq. m per 1 sq. cm. Knowing this we gridded all the countries and counted the number of sq. cm. The total number of sq. cm would be multiplied by 38,000 to equal our estimated area.

A different group also gridded Mexico, but then went on to write:

Mexico was measured as a T shaped land mass, side-to-side and top-to-bottom. Alaska was measured only as a square-shaped area. Greenland was measured essentially the same way, as well as India. Africa was measured as a rectangle and we then measured and subtracted the water from the total as seen below. [See Figure 5.1.]

They continued, "Scandinavia was treated similarly. Measuring it as a square and removing the area composed of water demonstrated below" (see Figure 5.2).

Finally, one group attempted to use the map's key, which explains that the scale changes as one moves away from the equator. Their explanation was:

We already knew that Mexico had an estimated total area of 760,000 so we went straight to Alaska. We used the key and saw that it was different at certain latitudes (for ex. at 60°N, 1 in. would represent 100 miles, but at the equator 1 in. would mean 200 miles, etc.).... For Africa, we measured the lower half first, from the equator down (we used the key for that area again). That half was also in the shape of a square so again we measured the height and width. We did the same thing for the top half (it was in the shape of a rectangle, sort of, so when we added the total areas of both the north and south parts of Africa and got 16,146,000 sq miles.

Greenland seemed to cover 3/4 of a square, so we got the height and width. We found those numbers by dividing the total by 4 (to get 1/4) & then multiplied those numbers by 3 (to get 3/4).... For Scandinavia we saw that it sort of resembled a triangle in this shape [see Figure 5.3] so we decided that if we added this [the triangle on top] it'll be a rectangle so we found the height & width & multiplied those numbers. Then [we] divided that number by 2 (because if we added another triangle to make a rectangle, we had to divide it now) so then I got 604,430 for the area.

The group with the above explanation derived their own way to find 3/4 of a number and even re-invented the formula for the area of a triangle.

 ("Africa")

Figure 5.1 Reallocating land to estimate the area of Africa.

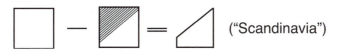 ("Scandinavia")

Figure 5.2 Reallocating land to estimate the area of Scandinavia.

Figure 5.3 Drawing of finding Scandinavia's area.

These examples are typical of the work my students did on the real-world projects. Because I did not teach standard algorithms, students had to create their own for novel problems. If the problems were ones with which they were familiar, they usually used standard algorithms (learned from previous teachers, siblings, or others) but occasionally invented procedures. Because I also generally demanded written explanations, they provided those as well, and after time, became relatively proficient at stating how and why they solved problems in particular ways. The map project was one of the last we did, and their explanations were quite well developed. A couple students consistently resisted writing explanations, although theirs were good when they did them. Overall, students evidenced a range of mathematical power on the real-world projects.

Students' Work on MiC. I believe that most of the credit for developing students' mathematical competencies lies with MiC, the fundamental curriculum that I used 75% to 80% of the time. MiC has the explicit goal that students develop mathematical power, and my data suggest that the curriculum was overall successful, at least in my classes. Students' mathematics may have also developed through the projects, but that was not their primary purpose as I explain elsewhere. I present an example below that demonstrates a range of students' thinking and reasoning on MiC.

My students completed the algebra unit "Comparing Quantities," which, among other concepts, teaches Gaussian elimination[3] in an informal manner called *notebook notation* (see students' solutions next). One of the unit assessments is "A Birthday Party":

TABLE 5.1 Antonio's Chart for a Birthday Party Assessment

Line	M	D	R	Years
1	1	1	0	100
2	0	1	1	64
3	1	0	1	58
4	2	2	2	222
5	1	1	1	111

During Rachel's birthday party, Rachel thinks about the ages of her parents and herself. Rachel says, "Hey, Mom and Dad, together your ages add up to 100 years!" Her Dad is surprised. "You are right," he says, "and your age and mine total 64 years." Rachel replies, "And my age and Mom's total 58." How old are Mom, Dad, and Rachel? Explain how you got your answer.

Of the 25 students who took the assessment, 21 solved it correctly. The four who did not were close; three used notebook notation but either added incorrectly or misread the problem. Fourteen of the students who solved the problem used some variation of notebook notation including combining it with their own innovations. Antonio's solution was:

> I found Rachel's age first by using line 5 and subtracting line 1 to get 11 years for Rachel. Then subtract 11 from 64 (line 2) to get 53 for Dad and for mom was 47 because Dad is bigger by 6 years according to line 2 compared to 3. [See Table 5.1.]

Antonio did not explain how he produced either line 4 or 5 (normal for him as he hated to write explanations). But line 4 is the sum of lines 1, 2, and 3, and line 5 is just line 4 divided by 2. His solution is interesting in that once he found Dad's age (53) by subtracting 11 from line 2, he did not subtract 11 from line 3. Instead he reasoned that Dad must be 6 years older than Mom (by comparing lines 2 and 3) because Dad and Rachel are 6 years more than Mom and Rachel. Algebraically, this is more complicated and requires deeper mathematical reasoning than just subtracting 11 from line 3.

Magdalena's solution did not formally use notebook notation since she made no chart, but it had certain similarities:

> What I did is I added 64 and 58, which is the Dad and Rachel and Mom and Rachel. I got 122 and since the Mom and Dad together is [are] 100 there was 22 years left over. So since Rachel is in both

> combinations I divided the 22 into half so that each parent will get exactly [the] same age for Rachel and I got that she was 11 years old. So then I subtracted 64 − 11 = 53 for the age of her father and for the Mom, I did the same, 58 − 11 = 47. And then I added the parents' ages to make sure it equal[led] 100. So it worked.

Although Magdalena's solution was less compact than Antonio's, she clearly explained what she did and why. She reasoned that the difference between [Dad plus Rachel plus Mom plus Rachel] and [Dad plus Mom] had to be two Rachels (i.e., D + R + M + R − (D + M) = 2R). She merely subtracted 122 − 100 to find that two Rachels was 22 and therefore Rachel was 11. She then substituted Rachel's age into the other "equation" she had for the sum of Dad's and Rachel's ages and solved for Dad's; she did the same for Mom and finally checked her solutions.

Rosa's solution was a fairly sophisticated guess-and-adjust solution (that will always work), but her mathematical reasoning is clear, and her number sense is developed even though her explanation is incomplete.

> I first subtracted 100 − 58 and got 42 for the mom. Then I added 42 + 6 for the Dad's age, 48, but when you add them up [it] is 90 so need 10 more years. So I divided 10 ÷ 2 = 5 and added five to each one. 47 for Mom and 53 for Dad. Then those numbers do equal for [to] 100 so I subtracted 64 − 53 = 11 and 58 − 47 = 11 so that's Rachel's age.

We do not know why she first subtracted 100 − 58, but we can see that, like Antonio, she realized that Dad was 6 years older than Mom (although she also does not tell us how she knew this, unlike him). When she had 90 for the sum of the parents (i.e., 42 + 48), she just split the remaining 10 years between them, preserving the inequality that Dad was 6 years older than Mom, and adjusted their ages accordingly. She then found Rachel's age from the sum of Rachel and the Dad and evidently verified it to make sure.

These three were typical of the solutions, even the incorrect ones. Only Erasmo had no explanation (which was the norm for him), even though he had the correct answer (which was almost always the case). Students reasoned informally, used notebook notation and number sense, made up their own ways to symbolize the problem, used innovative guess-and-adjust methods, and explained (except Erasmo) their thinking relatively coherently.

Overall, my students solved problems with a range of proficiency, often similar to the above. There were, of course, less coherent responses, mis-applications of rote procedures, and responses that made no sense (e.g.,

$400 tax on a $45 restaurant bill). However, when they had time to think and work, and especially when in groups, almost all students demonstrated a relatively solid grasp of the NCTM's (2000) *process standards* (problem solving, connections, communication, representation, and reasoning). They solved novel and challenging problems, "reinvented significant mathematics" (NCRMSE & FI, 1998), developed perseverance, used and compared multiple strategies, and articulated their thinking. They solved ninth- and tenth-grade problems from IMP and knew they were solving high school problems; from this and their overall competence, most also developed confidence in themselves and their mathematical capabilities (see chapter 6). For the most part, they learned mathematics with understanding and developed aspects of mathematical power, albeit to differing degrees.

Succeeding Academically in the Traditional Sense

This class also did well on conventional measures of success. This was not unexpected because they were in an honors-track program (see chapter 6 for a detailed discussion of Rivera's tracking). When they were in eighth grade (1999), 18 students took tests for magnet (selective enrollment, college prep) high schools (there were 26 in the class at the time). Fifteen students were accepted, many by multiple schools, an 83.3% acceptance rate. Because the tests were equal portions of mathematics and language arts, they had to score well in both parts. Although I do not know the system-wide acceptance rate for Latinos/as to selective enrollment high schools in 1999, the 2004 acceptance rate for all students was 6.9%, or about 12 times worse than my students' rate (Chicago Public Schools, 2004). All 26 passed the eighth-grade Iowa Test of Basic Skills (ITBS) exam that determines whether they pass the grade, and all also passed my class in both years. They gained, on average, almost exactly 1.0 year on their ITBS score from seventh to eighth grade. Few had large jumps on their standardized test scores, and few did poorly—only two gained less than half a year and only two gained more than a year and a half (the variance was only 0.18 years). Although I put little stock in these tests to assess what students genuinely know or their mathematical power, they indicate certain competencies and clearly have strong impact on students' lives. As of this writing, most are sophomores in college, ranging from community college to Northwestern University, University of Chicago, and Brown University (one each). That students did well on their ITBS and magnet high school tests, and most went on to attend college, even if in an honors track, suggests that they did not suffer in traditional evaluations while studying MiC and learning mathematics for social justice.

Other data also attest that MiC promotes traditional academic success. In the 2003–2004 school year, the mathematics test scores of Philadelphia eighth graders, all of whom studied MiC, rose by 11.1% (Holt, Rinehart, & Winston, 2004). Furthermore, other preliminary research suggests that students using MiC in a variety of settings succeed academically, though the authors caution against making final judgments (Romberg & Shafer, 2003). At this point, no data suggest that MiC harms students' performance on traditional measures.

Development of Students' Orientations to Mathematics

Given that my students had middle school mathematical experiences that were fairly different from the norm, one might ask how they viewed mathematics and its use and relationship to the world. In fact, I asked them that question, repeatedly, in various ways—on their projects, in class, on journal assignments, in informal conversations, and in open-ended surveys.

Both MiC and the NCTM have the goal that students should use mathematics to connect to and understand real life. The MiC TRIG "is designed to support" the NCTM *Standards* that "emphasize the dynamic, active nature of mathematics and the way it enables students to make sense of the world" (NCRMSE & FI, 1998, p. 3). The notion of mathematical power includes this disposition toward mathematics—that students should see it as a meaning-making tool. However, from a social justice perspective, this definition is incomplete because students should also explicitly use mathematics to understand inequality, critique social structures and arrangements, and become active in movements to restructure society for justice and equity. As I argue throughout this book, the development I seek in students includes what the NCTM and MiC want, but it goes beyond to include viewing mathematics as a way to read and write the world.

This distinction is relevant to the discussion of my students' orientations toward mathematics. An example may help clarify. While studying the MiC unit "Dealing With Data," students collected data from their own families: the heights of mothers and daughters. These data were real and personal. Students then graphed the collective class data and visualized and made sense of the overall pattern, which is that successive generations tend to be taller than previous ones. This is a good example of how MiC actualizes the goal of connecting mathematics to real life and is consistent with the NCTM.

In contrast, I gave my class a journal (homework) assignment to tell me what projects they wanted to do. The majority wanted surveys—of favorite music genre, radio stations, soda, and other real data. At Rivera, students often conducted similar surveys and could be seen asking one another, teachers, aides, etc., these questions. I read their journals and announced that in response to their requests our next project would be a survey. Students cheered. I then said that they could not survey preferred music, shoe types, or anything like that. They booed. I told them that we would instead survey "meaningful" questions, and they were not pleased. But we began discussing what that meant. By the end of the 80-minute period, students had formed their groups, chosen topics, and had produced written justifications for their choices. By the next day, they developed survey questions. These were: "What do you think about abortion and what do you think should be done about it?" "Do you think something should be done about teen pregnancy? If so, what?" "What do you think about abortion?" (a second group) "Do you think there's discrimination against Latinos in Chicago? If so, why?" "Do you believe Charles Darwin's theory that man [sic] descended from the ape?" and "What is your opinion on same sex marriage?" (the last from a group of four seventh-grade boys!).

After the project and class presentations on their findings, I gave another journal assignment (for homework) asking them to complete the phrase, "I think that doing the survey project on real and meaningful questions is a good or bad idea because:" Of the 18 who responded, 15 said "good," two said both good and bad, and one was ambivalent. Several students said good because they could learn about others' ideas, and several said good because the questions were important and real world. Jaime said, "good because we would learn about what people think about real issues of life that are important." Sandra wrote, "It's good because they are questions to really think about and they are very meaningful in real life situations." Danny added, "I think it's a good idea because we learn information that is actually useful in the 'real' world, such as the public's view on politics, racism, etc." This suggests that, despite their initial resistance, students came to believe that it was useful, meaningful, and real to use mathematics to do surveys about their *own* significant social questions.

Thus, I was looking for evidence of orientations that reflected more than students' beliefs that mathematics was important in conducting surveys and collecting and interpreting generically "real" data. When students collect and analyze data about mother/daughter pairs in their own families, as in MiC, or about how far paper airplanes fly with one or two paper clips attached, as the NCTM (2000, p. 250) suggests, they are acculturated into specific mathematical practices (or *Discourses*, in Gee's, 1999, parlance) and develop certain dispositions that do not necessarily include believing in mathematics as a way to understand injustice and change the world. This is the case even if the mathematics is personally connected to their lives as in the mother/daughter data. In fact, I contend that if teachers only use contexts like paper airplane experiments or the mother/daughter heights, students hear and may accept certain messages. They are taught and may learn that politics does not exist in everyday situations and that mathematics has no role in comprehending societal inequities and power imbalances. Furthermore, they do not experience using analytical tools, like mathematics, to understand, and attempt to rectify, unjust situations. These contribute to shaping their views on the roles and purposes of mathematics. Therefore, as I examined the data, I wanted to understand the subtleties of students' views with respect to these distinctions.

Students' Eighth-Grade Survey. One body of evidence about orientations is students' responses to an anonymous survey I gave at the end of eighth grade (and mention in chapter 3).[4] I urged them to be honest and gave them the opportunity to write about my strengths and weaknesses and their opinions about the class. After close to two years of open relationships with students, I am fairly confident that they were generally honest, and, as usual, they did not hesitate to point out my shortcomings or things they did not like.

Other data corroborate much of what my students wrote on their surveys about their dispositions, likes, and dislikes. Their mathematics and written work on the projects provide evidence that they learned how to read the world with mathematics; that work tends to confirm their reports that they saw themselves using mathematics to develop a deeper under-standing of broader social contexts. I also think that, in general, they did not write what they thought I wanted to hear because most had little trouble expressing what they did not like (see chapter 6), and I gave space for that and listened to them.

Overall, the survey data suggest that most students felt that the class influenced their views toward mathematics. The survey had 12 questions; the one that provided the most evidence about their views was question 7: "How have your views about mathematics changed from being in my class over the past two years? Please be specific." On this question, 21 students wrote that their views about mathematics changed (including two who liked it less after my class than before); three wrote that their views did not change; one was unclear; and one did not answer. However, the two who reported disliking mathematics more also wrote on other ques-tions that they were able to better understand the world using mathemat-ics, suggesting that their views may have developed beyond just disliking mathematics. Of the three who said their views had not changed, one of them provided evidence in other questions suggesting that her views about mathematics evolved, and the other two did not. And neither the student with the unclear response nor the one who left the question blank provided any other evidence on their surveys that their orientations toward mathematics were different. Thus, 22 of my 26 students provided evidence that their beliefs about mathematics had changed.

Four of these 22 explained their development in terms of aspects of mathematical power. Paulina wrote about mathematical communication, solution invention, and her feelings for mathematics.

> Like I've said a thousand times, this math was very different because we had to explain more and we had to figure out problems on our own, not by what a math book said. I did like this math a lot because I found that by doing a problem on my own I found easier ways to solve it. That was cool!! Before, math wasn't like this. It was a little boring. And this math has something that just gets to me.

Rosa added the ideas of using multiple strategies and ways to understand: "My views have changed by knowing that there are many different ways to do and to understand math." The other two were similar in flavor and touched on various aspects of the NCTM process standards.

However, 16 students wrote that they believed that mathematics could be used to make sense of real situations. (This does not include the two who disliked mathematics more but who also wrote elsewhere about using mathematics to better understand social contexts.) Their responses were about using mathematics to solve real-life problems and about how mathematics helped them look at and understand injustice. Alejandra's response touched on the map projection project to which she had reacted strongly and questioned repeatedly her former learning. She wrote, "My views have changed on how people change images to make them look different. Like the Mercator map and how countries look bigger than they really are...." Although she did not mention mathematics in her response, the context was the mathematical representation of countries on maps.

I considered whether I misinterpreted students on this question and erroneously concluded that their responses were about understanding injustice when they really meant generic, real-world contexts. So I re-examined the survey to assess that proposition. I discovered that every student who possibly answered question 7 ambiguously also made clear in other parts of the survey that she or he meant justice issues when referring to "real problems" or "real life." For example, Carmen's response to question 7 was, "I think that now I look at mathematics at [in] a different perspective because at first I just thought of math as operations with numbers, but now I realized that it's a lot more and that it has meaning." It is unclear from this quote alone what she means. However, she also responded to other questions.

> I loved that we used problems in the real world to learn about math. I had never been taught math like this before.... I have also learned about things going on in the world that I didn't know about.... Now I know that everything we learned has as much significance as other boring math book things like geometry.

These statements suggest that when she wrote about mathematics having "meaning," it was related to "problems in the real world" that had "significance." In my classroom, the *only* "problems in the real world" we studied were about social justice issues.

Gloria's response to question 7 was similarly ambiguous.

> Well my views now are that anything could be done in math. Some math teachers just give you math problems with only numbers on it. By that I mean that they would just give you math problems like: 375/980. But you did that and more. You taught us with real problems.

But she also makes clear what are "real problems" for her. She wrote elsewhere:

> I did learn about the world, stuff that I didn't know about and didn't think that stuff like that could happen in this world of ours.... You put math into things that happen for real.... I've learned about (like I said before) the world we live in today. How people can be so racist.... I am able to understand the world better using math because you taught us how to. Like by doing that U.S. wealth problem you gave us.

I examined closely the whole survey of every student whose response to question 7 suggested they believed that mathematics was useful in the "real world." For all of them, their other responses imply that they meant social justice issues.

Analyzing the Same Survey—Two Years Later. One cannot easily know how particular experiences will influence individuals in the future, as I note in chapters 3 and 4. Thus, I do not claim that students' orientations toward mathematics remained as they stated on their eighth-grade survey, however much they did or did not grow in the first place. However, as I mention earlier, in the summer before this class started eleventh grade,

I mailed students a survey similar to the eighth-grade one. I again asked the question, "How did your views about mathematics change from being in my class?" Ten of the 26 students responded, and all but two wrote that their views about mathematics had developed, specifically in terms of understanding justice. One of the two, Elena, reported that the class did not influence her views, and she wrote this on both her eighth-grade survey and the later one. However, on the later survey, she also wrote:

> ... we did some projects in class by means of data analysis, ratios, percentages, absolute/relative comparison, etc., [that] helped me in a way to open my eyes. This let me see how unfair the world really is and all the superiority white people feel above and beyond what they call "minorities."

This suggests that the class did shape her orientation toward mathematics, despite her writing that it had not. Her point here that the mathematical analyses we did let her "see how unfair the world really is," suggests that she came to view mathematics as a meaningful tool to understand social reality. And it was she who wrote a tenth-grade essay about the Declaration of Independence with a searing critique of racism, used mathematics in her analysis, and made sure I received a copy (see chapter 4).

Rosa, the other student who reported on the later survey that the class did not shape her views, also wrote, as a high school senior, a letter to the temporary principal who had forced me out (see chapter 8). In it, she wrote:

> ... I have realized that through his teachings I learned of racism and discrimination and its effects on not only our Latino community but other communities through out the United States and the world. I especially remember a project, in which we simulated the distribution of wealth throughout the world. Not only were we applying mathematical skills in the project, but we were also learning of the relations that exist between the powers of the world and the developing nations.

This suggests that she viewed mathematics as useful in understanding unequal relations of power both locally and globally, despite having written on both surveys that there was no influence from our mathematics class on her orientation to mathematics.

These reports suggest that most students saw themselves as having grown in their views about mathematics. The primary way they defined these developments was in relation to important real-life issues of meaning, relevance, and justice and not in terms of conventional notions of mathematical power that do not include investigations of inequality. Although MiC's authors wanted students to see mathematics as coming from, and acting on, our social and physical existence, the curriculum's stories did not engage my students in the same way as the real-world projects in which they investigated and critiqued unequal relations of power—and thus MiC probably did not impact students' beliefs in the same ways. MiC probably played a role in their orientations toward mathematics, but the fact that only four students explained their evolution in terms of mathematical communication, problem solving, or reasoning suggests that the real-world projects were powerful influences on their beliefs about mathematics in ways *beyond* mathematical power.

That students' orientations toward mathematics developed is not surprising because of the dialectical relationship between beliefs and practices. All my students, regardless of their survey responses, used mathematics on the real-world projects to make sense out of actual social phenomena. Our beliefs influence our practice, and the activities in which we engage simultaneously shape our beliefs. Students' mathematics analyses that helped them comprehend their broader sociopolitical contexts no doubt also influenced their understanding of, and their beliefs about, the social practice of using mathematics to interpret the world. In turn, these evolving belief systems may have shaped their future actions with mathematics itself and with using mathematics to read the world. I end this section with Freida's response to the same question on the later survey. Her words capture the essence of my goal about the development of students' orientations toward mathematics.

> I thought math was just a subject they implanted on us just because they felt like it, but now I realize you could use math to defend your rights and realize the injustices around you. ... I mean now I think math is truly necessary and I have to admit, kinda cool. It's sort of like a pass you could use to try to make the world a better place.

Reflections

There is a complex relationship between teaching mathematics for social justice and using one of the NSF reform mathematics curriculum, Mathematics in Context. In my situation, MiC was important because its philosophy and the dispositions toward knowledge it encouraged supported my social justice pedagogy. Furthermore, the political issues we studied all had mathematical components, some of which were difficult and demanded a certain level of mathematical sophistication and maturity; MiC played a major role in helping students develop these, without which the real-world projects would have been less successful.

However, MiC, although necessary, was insufficient by itself for students to develop sociopolitical consciousness and a sense of social agency—nor is that the intent of the curriculum. The primary location for that development was the real-world projects and the related conversations and classroom relationships that facilitated those. The potential for MiC to play a role in students' development as aware and active youth had to be realized in practice. To the extent that I was successful in actualizing this possibility, I had to go beyond MiC's contexts to ones involving issues of justice that were personally meaningful to my students, and I had to try to maintain pedagogical and curricular consistency between MiC and the projects.

That consistency was not always possible to preserve partly because of the objective difficulties in integrating two sets of pedagogical goals and the lack of an "MiC for social justice" curriculum. But because of MiC's strength in developing mathematical power, it allowed me the pedagogical space to provide students opportunities to learn to read and write the world without having to be overly concerned about their mathematical growth. I understand the dialectical relationship between the curricular components to be that each contributed to the other's "strength"—that is, MiC contributed to students learning about their world, and the real-world projects helped students develop mathematical power—and each was a supplementary factor in the other's strong area. Furthermore, there were times when I had to concentrate on one (mathematical power) or the other (reading and writing the world) to the relative exclusion of its partner, even though there was an overall unity and synthesis between the two that contributed to make the endeavor as a whole fairly successful.

My students, for the most part, developed aspects of mathematical power and also achieved traditional academic success, especially the bilingual class in the honors track that I taught for almost two years. Given that MiC's goal is to develop mathematical competencies and that students in an honors-track program are expected to succeed academically, these are not surprising or unusual. What is unusual (at least in the mathematics education literature) and of note is that students' orientations toward mathematics evolved in the ways that they did. I believe one can assert that these transformations are related to the curriculum's explicitly political nature. Since students were consistently involved in the real-world projects whose themes were like threads weaving throughout everything we did, the growth in their orientations was quite reasonable. They began the process of reading and writing the world with mathematics and the experiences were meaningful and relevant to them. The projects tapped into and built on their sense of justice, they learned much about society, and they expressed the value in doing so. Thus, one should expect that they would come to see mathematics as useful in investigating the socio-political realities that shaped their lives, and the evidence is that they did.

Finally, it is significant that students from immigrant, bilingual, working-class Latino/a families developed aspects of mathematical power, achieved some academic success, viewed mathematics as a way to understand unjust social arrangements, *and* began to read and write the world using mathematics. That these students are in a better position to challenge a racist and sexist, class-based system that excludes them and others like them is a contribution to the causes of social justice and liberation.

CHAPTER **6**

Co-Creating a Classroom for Social Justice
Possibilities and Challenges

Mr. Rico,
Was this project ["Mortgage Loans—Is Racism a Factor?"] to confuse us and really make us think? Because that's what it did. After
our last discussion on Friday, everyone was talking about what we
had discussed.

In my first article I said that I thought racism was not a factor,
after our second discussion I thought racism was a factor, but I
think that we don't really know. Even though the rate for Blacks
was 5Xs higher than whites in being rejected, that does not necessarily mean it is racism. It could be because of their debt, income,
or maybe it could be racism. But Mr. Rico, how do we know how
the people at the bank think, and isn't it illegal for many business
to deny service to their customers? And if someone were to be
denied wouldn't the bank give them a reason why?

Does the bank [the people in it] work together? Of course they
do, but I mean, if the boss were a racist, wouldn't he hire people
like him, because if he didn't couldn't they use that against him?
Like if he hired only whites, or only blacks, or only Latinos, who
were racist? Now I am positive that we cannot tell if racism is a
factor using the data and information we have unless we got into

129

the minds of the people at the bank, but we can't, we can only assume. But that's not so great either, because we could assume wrong. So now I think that we can never really know. So in my next journal, can you please answer my questions, thanks! *(Nilda, journal entry, December 13, 2002)*

My response to Nilda:

Nilda,   12/16/02

I mean it, you are really deep. That is really great! You have taken this project and really tried to understand all the very complicated issues (and there are many!!). First of all, the project certainly was to make you all think. I believe that you are very able to think about a lot of complicated, deep things in the world, and the sooner you start, the better. And, of course, it is a very good way to learn mathematics, not only to learn mathematics, but to learn how important mathematics can be in understanding the world. If you remember, in the very beginning of the year, I told you that we would be reading the world with mathematics, that is, trying to understand complicated things using mathematics… and you see, we are doing exactly that. I think you are learning mathematics and also about the world, at the same time. I am very happy about this class, you are a great group of students who are very thoughtful and are learning an amazing amount. Your journals are great, your essays are great, and it's not only you, it's just about everyone in the class.

Yes, you are right, it is illegal to deny service or to discriminate against people because of their race, language, gender (male or female), sexuality (if they are gay or straight), etc. And you make a very excellent point, that we cannot know what is in the minds of individual people to be able to tell whether or not they are racist. That is why I tried to make clear what the difference is between individual racism (e.g., I don't treat you well because you're Mexican) and institutional racism (there is a whole system that exists, that has a history and has been around for years and years that affects whole groups of people—as we see here with the racism in the mortgages). The fact that the disparity ratio exists, and people of color have such a hard time compared to whites in getting a mortgage, to me, is a clear example of institutional racism. To the bank spokesperson who says, "we want to loan money to everyone," I say, "the data shows that you don't!"

And the reason, beyond individual racism (which is there, no doubt, but is not the main thing), is that there is the whole system that has kept African Americans and Latinos from having the wealth to really be able to afford mortgages. Just take a good look at the table I will give you about "Wealth and Race in the U.S." If we understand what that table really tells us, the evidence is pretty clear, and if we were to read the whole book where that table comes from, we would understand much better the whole history of racism in the U.S. Nilda, just think about this. For hundreds of years, millions of African Americans worked as slaves ... all that time, the white slaveowners (not poor whites, just a few rich whites) kept all their wages. When African Americans finally got their freedom, they were still kept down, not allowed into good jobs, kept out of good schools, kept in ghettos and poor communities ... it's no wonder at all that they have so little wealth. Racism is as much a part of this country as the U.S. flag ... this country was built on racism, from the stolen lands of the Native Americans to the stolen wages of African slaves.

These are my views. I am not asking for you to accept them, in fact, I want you to question my views as much as you question any others. Just think about them, and keep thinking about them, as I see you doing.

Mr. Rico

My focus in this chapter is on how I attempted to work with students to co-create a classroom supporting social justice, and the possibilities and challenges. I am clear that there are multiple ways to construct classrooms that support reading and writing the world. Furthermore, my classes had "successes" and "failures," and in analyzing these, my purpose is to theorize by honestly examining my practice. The above dialogue between Nilda, my seventh-grade student, and myself is an example of that practice and provides a glimpse of important issues I address here: the features of a social justice classroom, students' role in its co-construction, my actions, and some of the dilemmas and difficulties in this work.

Features of a Classroom for Social Justice

The culture, environment, ways of being and acting, norms, and interpersonal relationships in a classroom for social justice have a particular character. Certain features, like trust, mutual respect, and open communication are generally accepted as conducive to learning. But there are other characteristics that are not often named "best (pedagogical) practices." They include: *normalizing politically taboo topics*, creating a *pedagogy of questioning*, and developing *political relationships* with students. Although these are not entirely distinct from one another, one can consider them separately for analytical purposes.

Normalizing politically taboo topics means to make topics generally considered as taboo in school part of "normal" classroom life. Discussions of, for example, racism, sexism, brutality against immigrants, gay marriage, and abortion are usually deemed inappropriate for middle school mathematics classes, if not everywhere, in traditional public schools. Furthermore, by normalization, I mean that students not only talk about and investigate topics such as these but also develop their own understandings and positions on them.

A second key feature of social justice classrooms is a *pedagogy of questioning*, which I first discuss in chapter 2. This has several components. First, it is a space in which students have opportunities to pose their own real, meaningful questions about issues of sociopolitical importance, fairness, and equality. Second, it is a setting in which "one question leads to another question, and then you have to answer four more, and those four questions lead to eight more questions," as my student Vanessa wrote on the mortgage project. Answers and "truth" are provisional and relational, and students and teacher keep this in mind as they dig deeply and strive to unravel complex social phenomena, like racism, and understand their interconnections and root causes. Third, these interrelationships and complexities are on the table for all to challenge, question, and analyze. Fourth, students engage and analyze multiple perspectives, not to debate or artificially pretend to take someone else's view, but to build on each others' knowledge and understand that all positions reflect a particular perspective on the world (such as map projections). Fifth, questions are tied to actions and social movements to the extent possible. Finally, questions are integrated and ubiquitous, that is, they are not just posed when a teacher thinks of it, or only at specific times.

A third critical feature of a social justice classroom is the development of what I call *political relationships* between teacher and students. These relationships subsume the personal, supportive relationships with students that some teachers see as essential to their pedagogy. Many teachers build quality relationships with students both in and out of class, and they spend time with students and families when appropriate; share stories from their own lives; and talk, listen, and respond to students about any concerns they have. However, political relationships go further. They include taking active political stands in solidarity with students and their communities about issues that matter. Political relationships also entail teachers sharing political analyses with students as much as possible. Finally, they include talking with students about social movements, involving students themselves in studying injustice, and providing opportunities for them to join in struggles to change the unjust conditions. Linda Christensen (2000) described qualities of her classroom community that are in sync with the notion of political relationships. These included building on students' sense of justice, creating opportunities for students to see themselves as activists, centering the curriculum in students' lives, and developing a "curriculum of empathy" in which students examine shared oppressions and build solidarity with others.

These three attributes—normalizing politically taboo topics, creating a pedagogy of questioning, and developing political relationships with students—are integrated and integral components of what I mean by a classroom for social justice. However, naming them does not explain how they are created in a classroom, to which I now turn.

The Process of Co-Constructing a Classroom for Social Justice

Classrooms are complicated ecosystems, and their culture and climate constantly evolve. My classrooms differed in how much we were able to co-create an environment supporting social justice. The class in which we accomplished the most was my two-year class. That this class was in the bilingual honors program and students did not resist school much was an important facilitating condition which I describe below. Here I discuss five points: (1) pedagogical practices supporting classrooms for social justice, (2) students' vacillations and contradictory views, (3) the dialectic between students developing their own views and understanding sociopolitical context, (4) politicizing high-stakes accountability regimes, and (5) supporting students' identities.

A key idea is the recognition that students actively participate in developing the norms, ways of being and interacting, and overall environment of any classroom. Classroom culture develops through complicated dialectical processes. Students construct their in-class personas within particular institutional structures and interpersonal relationships, reacting to, and in turn shaping, classroom ecology. Although I initiated specific ways of acting and expectations, students' responses were shaped partially by the influences of the larger society, school and district context, and by their own prior socialization and views about "normal" classroom practices. Though one can take the perspective that students are apprenticed into particular ways of being through authentic participation (Lave & Wenger, 1991), they also fashion the classroom environment into which they are acculturated. It is simply not possible to hierarchically impose a given classroom culture on middle school students, especially one that requires them to seriously study social conditions and develop articulated positions about the issues. Young adolescents have their own ideas, energy, and desires, and should they choose to, they can derail the best plans of the best teachers. I could not force students to talk about politically taboo topics nor participate in a pedagogy of questioning if they did not want to participate. Nor could I make them have political relationships with me. The decision whether or not to be co-creators was theirs. This is a significant point.

Pedagogical Practices Supporting Classrooms for Social Justice

There are several pedagogical practices teachers can use to actualize features of social justice classrooms. One approach I used was to provide opportunities with the real-world projects for students to read and write the world with mathematics. Others included taking the field trip with students to the Springfield Heights sales office and having them report back to class (chapter 4), bringing students to the hearings on community development (chapter 4), making space for their questions about September 11, and showing films like *Ethnic Notions* to deal with racial stereotypes (again, chapter 4). I participated in the anti-gentrification struggle in Morningside, kept students regularly informed, shared my own analyses, and involved them as much as possible. I read to students from radical historians Howard Zinn (2003) and Ron Takaki (1993) about U.S. and world affairs that were related, even distantly, to topics we studied; passed out clippings and political cartoons/commentary on current events, such as the Bush administration tax cuts and the Iraq War, pointing out mathematical aspects; and bought books for students (or loaned them) with alternative, anti-imperialist perspectives such as *Killing Hope* (Blum, 2004), a history of U.S. invasions of other countries. When we had time, we watched films about Chicano/a history and civil rights struggles and those made by young Mexican students like my own. Students and I went to political movies and plays outside of school (e.g., *The Last Angry Brown Hat*, about the Brown Berets; Ramos, 1993). And I asked students to think deeply about all these things and write about them, and I tried to engage the class in collaborative dialogue.

In my two-year class, discussion of these "taboo" topics became as regular as conversations about field trips, homework, and weekend activities. Because the real-world projects required students to grapple with, and take positions on, political matters, students generally accepted political discussions at other times as well. The projects set the context for spending class time on, and for serious investigation of, important social topics, and thus political analysis became an ongoing part of classroom life. Although a couple of students felt we sometimes spent too much time in nonmathematical discussions, most students gravitated to them and virtually all participated. Like the example of "everyday racism" with which I begin chapter 3, I initiated discussions about justice that became topics for conversations and/or mathematical investigations on the real-world projects. Since the projects were "official" school work, they validated everyday conversations about subjects rarely discussed in mathematics classes. Over time, students accepted the routinization of taboo topics and brought them up themselves, contributing to the normalization. It was not unusual for them to raise issues in the journal assignments I gave every Friday; these required students to reflect on what they learned during the week and issues we had discussed in class. Several students and I carried on regular, extended journal dialogues, often initiated by them, about the neighborhood, gangs, mathematics, discrimination, families, and the like. In these conversations, it was important to raise questions and/or problematize what students said and wrote, as part of building political relationships.

For example, when Omar wrote that it was unfair for Whitney Young High School (a college-prep, selective-enrollment school) to bar students from testing for admission unless they had sufficiently high standardized test scores (chapter 4), I wrote back:

> I don't quite know what to say—yes, you are absolutely right. It is unfair, and it is racist and anti-immigrant. Rosa is not the only person who deserves to go there, there are a lot of you in this class who deserve to go there—and there are a whole lot of other students at Rivera who deserve to as well. Those tests do NOT show, as you put it, "the hard transition from coming from a Spanish talking home to learning a whole new language." And yes, you are right, you are not rewarded for all the hard work you have done. The people at Whitney Young would say something like, "well there are lots of kids who've worked hard, and not everyone can get to go to WY." And you know what? There needs to be a whole lot more schools like WY so that youth have the opportunity to learn. Every high school needs to be a WY, and there's no real reason in this world why it's not like that. We already know how to build a WY—it's not that we don't know.
>
> So we have to fight. That's what life is, a never-ending fight for freedom and justice, at least in this world where some control lots of "cookies" and others have crumbs.[1] And the purpose of education should be to prepare students to fight for justice, like we saw

the HS students in the Chicano History Video. Without their fight, many other students would not have learned as much as they did, because it's partially because they stood up that bilingual education ever happened at all. Do you know who Frederick Douglass was? He said, "Freedom is a constant struggle." And I'm sure he knew what he was talking about.

Take care and do not give up on this one!

Mr. Rico

I also shared my life experiences for students to see that ordinary people like their teachers and parents (and not just people in films) could be part of political movements. I told the story of the three-day occupation of my high school in 1970. Emulating college students around the country, the school's Black and Latin Students Club, and white supporters, demanded more curriculum materials by and about students of color, and when the school administration consistently refused, we took action. As the Iraq War loomed in late 2002, I shared with students my opposition to the war and explained why, and I passed around pictures I took at a large anti-war demonstration in Washington before the war started. Studying the Holocaust was part of their humanities curriculum, and I spoke about being Jewish, of losing family in the Holocaust, of the dangers of not speaking out against fascism, and about the historical role Jews had played around the world in social justice movements.

Students' Vacillations and Contradictory Views

The process of co-constructing a classroom for social justice was not a smooth one, even for my two-year class. Many students occasionally vacillated or expressed contradictory views about various issues. This was to be expected because they were middle school youth, confronting complex ideas and realities, trying to develop elaborated positions about them, and publicly discussing them, often for the first time. Rarely, they told me, had they done this in school, and virtually never in mathematics class. Furthermore, this ambivalence and even confusion is a natural part of a social justice classroom in which multiple perspectives and the free flow of ideas are desirable. Antonio and Rosa, from my two-year class, often articulated contradictory views on the real-world projects. Antonio was a staunch defender of the Mercator map and argued about its value. He wrote, to explain and perhaps excuse its size distortions, "This map is pretty old, isn't it? Maybe it was never really updated with new area and such." Nevertheless, he also wrote, "I feel that using a map that doesn't display the world correctly is just wrong. A country with a smaller area can not be bigger than a country with a larger area." Rosa, on the gentrification project "Will Development Bury the *Barrio*?" criticized the injustice of destroying the community and advocated that the development could be stopped: "I think that if people get together they would stop the development. I believe that if we give good solid reasons and justice is in our hands, we could prove our point and stop the developers." However, she was also ambivalent:

> I want to point out that in a way I understand the developers' point of view. They are making money for their families and personally I think that if I were an architect and was in charge of building the houses, I would not let the opportunity go by.

And Magdalena, on the world wealth simulation, wrote:

> With the world distribution, I think it's unfair to people. Why is it when people are dying of hunger all these other rich people have more than enough? They throw away [food, things] as if it was nothing. I think this might be the end of many people. But we can all make a difference by helping those in need. The money is very wrongly distributed but sometimes it also depends on how hard a person worked to earn it. But I guess there really isn't anyway to fix the way money is distributed.

Magdalena's reflection is striking in its complex of partially contradictory ideas. She expressed her sense of justice, her own questioning, a sense of pessimism and powerlessness, her sense of agency, and her adherence to the ideology of individual achievement, all in one paragraph. Although most students did not express so many overlapping and competing themes in one short piece, they struggled to develop their own voices on complicated social issues, which was an involved and difficult process.

An additional issue was that students may not have always felt comfortable discussing certain painful experiences in class, especially in my presence because I was a white male professional who could not fully understand their lives, racism, or sexism. This can contribute to students' hesitance in expressing various thoughts and feelings and may manifest itself in their reluctance to name particular aspects of life. More than once, students wrote about how they felt bad when discussing oppression. As Manolo wrote about the mortgage rejection project, "Yes it is, it is a bad feeling to admit it. But racism is a key reason why many Latinos are being denied."

The Dialectic Between Students Developing Their Own Views and Understanding Sociopolitical Context

An important aspect of creating political relationships is to support students' sociopolitical development while at the same time trying to maintain space for them to develop their own voices. This is complicated for several reasons, and the dialogue with Nilda captures some of this complexity. Clearly, when learning (mathematics) for social justice, students must have room to experiment with and create their own ideas. One can see Nilda in her journal working with different conceptions and explanations of whether racism is a factor. However, understanding political issues like racism is an intricate process, and social justice teachers have the responsibility to ensure that students develop deeper awareness. My students had concrete, grounded experiences with, and knowledge about, racism, but their understandings were underelaborated. My knowledge of racism was partial and observational, but analytical and historical—and I could share the latter. Nilda could not easily know about *sedimented inequality*, the layering over generations of inequality that ensured African Americans would have, on average, far less accumulated wealth than whites (Oliver & Shapiro, 1997). This is what I was trying to introduce with the discussion about wealth inequality (and by subsequently providing the information on wealth disparity).

Nilda argued in her journal above that African Americans might have been rejected more often than whites for mortgage applications because of "either [greater] debt or [lower] income." There are at least two ways to respond to Nilda's analysis. One is to provide historical context and a political analysis, which I tried to do in this case. Another is to problematize her analysis and ask her to explain how income or debt were factors and whether they themselves could be related to racism (these responses are not mutually exclusive). Either reply could potentially influence her to rethink on a deeper level. In general, I often problematized students' ideas as part of creating political relationships with them. Here is part of my response to Adalberto's essay on the mortgage project:

> … I have some questions … let's take a look at your possible explanation that education could be another factor … I assume that what you mean is that those people with more education make more money (in fact, there is data to support that, although it's not in this article). But that raises another question, no? Who has more education in this country? How did they get that? Could racism be a factor in that? And what data would you need to know to be able to answer that?

This was typical of my responses to students, and my goal was for them to probe, question, and challenge their own assumptions and beliefs, in effect, to "peel the onion" and go beneath surface-level explanations. However, while challenging students' (and our own) analyses is important, it is not always sufficient. For example, what follows is part of the written interchange between Carmen and myself on the mortgage project. On one of the problems, she wrote, "If I was a staff member for the banks and they asked me why were more Latinos and Blacks being rejected than whites I would say that the reason was because Blacks and Latinos have less collateral…" I wrote back:

> …[you say] that Blacks and Latinos have less collateral. When I asked you why … you said … for Latinos, they have been here less time and had less time to build up their collateral. And you also said that whites could have inherited it from their families…. so a question [for you] … African Americans have been here far longer than many many whites … in fact, the last large wave of African Americans probably came close to 200 years ago…. LOTS of white people's families didn't even come here till after 1900 (like mine). So how do you answer that?…. A second question … suppose it's true that whites have inherited collateral (let's just call it "wealth") from their families more so than African Americans…. So how did these whites get in the position of having more wealth than African Americans to pass onto their children? How did that happen? And does racism have anything to do with that? How?

She responded in her final essay on whether racism was a factor in the rate disparity.

> Racism is totally not a factor in mortgages … the reason why a lot of Black and Latinos are being rejected is because they have less collateral…. Somebody asked me why whites had more collateral and I said because they have been here … longer. Then that one person asked me why didn't Blacks have more collateral if they've been here longer, and to that … I would say that since long time ago whites owned lots of things and Blacks were not able [to] because they were slaves. Even in the 1970's blacks were being discriminated. So I have to say that Blacks had the shortest amount of time to get to own stuff.

Even though I challenged her assumptions (I am the one asking her questions), she was not able to connect her own historically correct reasoning to the racism underlying African Americans' higher rejection rates. This suggests that it can be difficult for students to understand the complexities of institutional racism.

My main point here is to illustrate the dialectical relationship between, on the one hand, providing students space to develop their own ideas, voice, and understanding, and, on the other hand, helping them develop deeper analyses of complex social phenomena. This tension was embedded in the political relationships I had with students, and it was not easy to resolve. I know I did not always create enough room for students to speak openly because they told me so. On the end-of-year survey my two-year class completed, one question was: "What do I need to do to improve as a teacher?" Rosa responded, "You need to understand that not everyone agrees with you. It's like sometimes you say your beliefs out and don't let other people say theirs. You need to balance those things in order for kids to believe more." On another occasion, I was absent one day and another teacher took my class. He divided students into groups, had them race each other for correct answers to math problems at the board, and gave Snickers candy bars to the winners. I was furious when I found out, and we spent the period discussing this. I told the class I wanted them to refuse to participate and show solidarity with each other, rather than be divided into "winners" and "losers." Some students agreed, some argued, and some said nothing. After class, my student Omar said to me in the hall, "Do you know what you just did? You silenced some people in class." Thus, it is evident to me that although I tried to reconcile the dilemma and be conscious, clearly I was not always successful.

The Question of Over-Influencing Students. When teachers share their own views, as I did on what we came to call "Snickers Math," an important question to ask is whether there is undue pressure or influence on students. In *Rethinking Globalization*, Bigelow and Peterson (2002) contrasted what they referred to as "biased teaching" and "partisan teaching:"

> The teacher who takes pride in never revealing his or her "opinions" to students models for them moral apathy.... We would never urge that teachers shelter their students from views that they find repugnant. Indeed, the way to develop critical global literacy is only through direct engagement with diverse ideas. Nor is it ever appropriate for teachers to hand students worked-out opinions without equipping students to develop their own analyses of important issues.... We see a distinct difference between a

biased curriculum and a partisan one. Teaching is biased when it ignores multiple perspectives and does not allow interrogation of its own assumptions and propositions. Partisan teaching, on the other hand, invites diversity of opinion, but does not lose sight of the aim of the curriculum: to alert students to global injustice, to seek explanations, and to encourage activism. (p. 5)

This distinction between biased and partisan teaching is critical because biased teachers cannot successfully teach for social justice. Students who unquestioningly adopt teachers' views for approval, to conform, for grades, or for any other reason do not develop critical literacy. Instead, they parrot views that are not their own and that they do not really believe.

However, one has to be conscious of the difficulty of walking the line between, on the one hand, stating an analysis, providing historical context, and elaborating a position, and, on the other hand, creating opportunities for students (especially younger ones) to develop their own position. As Freire (1994) wrote:

> ... inasmuch as education of its very nature is directive and political, I must, without ever denying my dream or my utopia before the educands, respect them. To defend a thesis, a position, a preference, with earnestness, defend it rigorously, but passionately, as well, and at the same time to stimulate the contrary discourse, and respect the right to utter that discourse, is the best way to teach, first, the right to have our own ideas, even our duty to "quarrel" for them, for our dreams ... and second, mutual respect (p. 78)

There is always the risk of unduly influencing students. But as Freire pointed out and I quote in chapter 2: "Is there a risk of influencing the students? It is impossible to live, let alone exist, without risks. The important thing is to prepare ourselves to be able to run them well" (p. 79). My journal exchange with Nilda at the start of this chapter is typical of how I tried to "run them [risks] well" and reconcile this dilemma of both sharing my views and analyses and urging students to question me as much as anyone.

Did Students Tell Me What They Thought I Wanted to Hear? Given that I wanted my students to develop their own analyses and opinions, I searched my data for evidence that they unquestioningly adopted mine or felt pressure to do so. I found some, such as Rosa's response above about what I needed to do to improve as a teacher, and Omar's critique that I had silenced some students. But I also found much evidence that, in general, most students spoke their minds and took me to task if they felt I deserved it. Sometimes they were polite enough to say, "I don't mean to hurt your feelings, but..." and other times they spoke more plainly. When students were not eligible to test for the selective-enrollment, college-prep magnet schools unless their standardized tests scores were high, I strategized with students, went to one of the schools, and argued with the admissions counselor. A number of my students did apply, and the school subsequently lost one of the applications. The student found out just in time, and we managed to get her records and recommendations to the school. I raised the possibility that the school lost her application on purpose to punish Rivera for standing up and demanding that all students could take the admissions test. I gave them a journal assignment which read:

> ... write about the question I asked about what we should do just in case that high school really did punish Rivera for pushing to let our students take the entrance exam even though their vocabulary stanines weren't what they were supposed to be. Did we do the right thing by pushing? Even if they were punishing us? Should we do the same thing again? Why or why not? What happens if you stand up? What happens if you don't stand up? What would you stand up for and what risks would you take? And what about risks to others?

I got a range of responses, including from some who thought I was totally wrong. Marisol wrote, "I thought the idea was ridiculous.... Why would they punish Rivera by losing one kid's application. That's just stupid." Nor was she alone in her curt dismissal of my proposal. Sandra was even more caustic:

> Mr. Rico, you are exaggerating a lot, and plus you're telling us to defend our rights, what rights? If we don't need to defend nothing [anything], it's her <u>personal</u> business.... you're making a big deal about punishing Whitney Young [the school]. It's truly childish, ridiculous, and stupid, well that's what I believe.

Of course, I did not believe Whitney Young lost the application on purpose, but I did ask students to consider that possibility and write about the issue and potential costs of taking stands. The main point here is that most students generally felt comfortable speaking their minds. Journal responses like these were not atypical, although not all students spoke so forthrightly.

My analysis, overall, suggests that their strong voices on issues of justice were essentially their own and not for my benefit, although I cannot know for sure. I do, however, have evidence that students believed they could disagree with me. The first is from the letter that Rosa (at the time, a senior from my two-year class) wrote to the temporary principal who forced me out of Rivera in 2003.

> While taking Mr. Rico's class, I myself was skeptical of his teaching methods.... Like I said before I myself always questioned him, over and over, but it was that questioning, that ability to even question the teacher that made me grow academically...

I also include an excerpt of the group letter that students from my two-year class wrote at the same time. I share a portion of that letter in chapter 4, but this part speaks to the question of undue influence and whether students wrote or said things for my benefit:

> ... by no means [did] he expect us to believe everything he said. In fact, we were always encouraged to speak up in class whenever we disagreed with him. He never pushed us to believe certain things but instead challenged us to question *everything*. And we did. We not only questioned things going on in our very own neighborhood and in the world as a whole, but we also questioned Mr. Rico and debated ferociously with *him* about his own opinions. That is what he taught us, to question everything around us and not just to take "somebody's word" on an issue, even if it meant not taking his.

Politicizing High-Stakes Accountability Regimes

> To pass the Iowas, we don't have to think things, we have to know things. (*Yesenia, 7th grade, March 2001*)

An important aspect of creating a social justice classroom is providing students the opportunities to politically analyze their lives. An example is to critique the politics of high-stakes accountability regimes, in particular, the standardized tests. In Chicago, the tests are the primary determination of whether students pass to the next grade, what high schools they attend, and whether they attend summer school. The "Iowa" test (Iowa Test of Basic Skills), was the Chicago Public School (CPS) gatekeeper, and it dramatically affected elementary school life, including at Rivera. Because preparing for the Iowa violated everything I believed in, I was loathe to spend any time doing so; because preparing for the Iowa was absolutely essential to students' futures, I had no choice. The question was how to do it in a way that prepared students to pass both the test and at the same time better understand the political nature of the whole stratified educational system of which the test was the most immediate and draconian part for students.

Two key issues were how the Iowa caused students to feel about themselves and how the educational and political systems evaded responsibility for the unequal schooling of low-income students of color—and these two points were related. In my observations, students overwhelmingly blamed themselves when they did poorly on the test. Inculcated by the ideology of individual achievement and meritocracy (MacLeod, 1995), students were susceptible to believing that they were individually responsible for failure. This self-blame was reinforced by the constant, mantra-like proclamations during the late 1990s by CPS officials who proclaimed that success was up to the individual. Thus students were doubly oppressed—first, they were recipients of a racist educational system that had historically devalued their language and culture and failed to educate them, and second, they took the personal responsibility onto themselves for the devastation waged upon them by the educational system. This conveniently obfuscated a group-oppression analysis, shifting blame away from the system and onto themselves, and took CPS off the hook (Lipman & Gutstein, 2001, 2004). In what Conforti (1992) referred to as a "contest society," with limited "winners" and where the majority "lose," the meritocracy ideology was a powerful socializing force shaping students conceptions of themselves, the test, school, and society as a whole. It is one of the ways consciousness is organized by prevailing institutional structures and is extremely difficult to overcome.

I saw the devastating effects the meritocracy ideology had on my students, including those in the honors track, but especially those in general classes. Students not only blamed themselves, but some relatively successful students in the general track blamed those less successful for their school failures, eroding the potential for group solidarity. The fear inspired by possibly failing the test, not graduating eighth grade with one's peers, repeating the grade, having to go to transitional schools (remedial, extended elementary schools for overage students), and/or dropping out permeated almost *all* students' existence, regardless of track. Dating back to at least 1992, Rivera's neighborhood high school had not graduated 50% of an entering class in four years (Allensworth, 2005), and students knew the general situation. They were well aware of their possible life trajectories. A small day-labor center near the school had a big sign advertising that workers were needed starting at 3:30 A.M. When I asked students in my two-year class (in the *honors* track) how many of their parents rose and left home before they did, they laughed as almost all hands went up. Students were aware of their parents' sacrifices, but no student whom I knew wanted to work as hard as they saw their parents toil.

Naturally, I tried to ensure that students passed the tests, but it was also necessary to combat the self-blame. I organized many test-preparation sessions, but I also talked to students about why low-income, bilingual Latino/a students generally performed more poorly than white and wealthy students on standardized tests. In fact, one of my students, Raquel, and her sister, Mónica, both in the general bilingual program, explained it far better than I could have. I was interviewing them about having failed the eighth-grade Iowa and their time in transition schools. At the end of the interview, Raquel asked:

Raquel: Do the white people take it [the Iowa] the same?

Gutstein: Ah, that's a really good question. White people take the test, Black people take the test, Latinos take the test.

Raquel: But I don't think we should take it all together. There should be a different test for each one.

Gutstein: Why?

Raquel: Because white people, they already know. I mean, they're not smarter than us, 'cause they're *not*! But they know already their language and while we're trying to learn our language, we're trying to study and learn the [English] language, and trying not to forget our own language.... And the only problem they have is learning what they need to learn. We have trouble learning the language, but we need to learn mathematics, everything and plus, trying not to forget our language.... I don't think it's fair, I think there should be different tests for Mexicans, different tests for Americans [whites].

Gutstein: Why?

Raquel: 'Cause it's not the same, translating the language.

Mónica: Yeah, because there are words that they know that we don't know and we're reading and we're stuck in one word and they are not. They're like, "oh I know that word."

Raquel: 'Cause that's their language....

Mónica: Because their dads and their moms talk to them ... so they can read it and know what they're talking about in the paper [test].

These two young women, "failures" to the educational system, had the perceptive analysis that they had three simultaneous tasks in school—learn English, learn the particular subject, and maintain their Spanish—while those who "already knew" English only had to learn the academic subject. They realized how the tests were inherently unfair because their own struggles were more difficult, and they had an intuitive understanding of valorized cultural capital and its inherited transmission. Furthermore, they had no illusions that whites were "smarter" than they. But despite being clear on these points, they still tended to blame themselves for their failures, demonstrating the power of the self-blame syndrome.

In my two-year class, to counter this self-denigration and develop a sociopolitical analysis, we did a project in which we analyzed SAT and ACT scores by race, gender, and class (see chapter 4; Gutstein, 2002). One purpose was for students to understand that even though individual low-income students of color excelled on the tests, there were many systemic factors that contributed to the score differentials, including different cultural capital, bias in tests, and unequal education. (Christensen, 2000, did similar work with her high school students who developed their own SAT.) We studied mathematically, and graphed, the correlations of test score to gender, race, and class, but we did more than that. I read to them from Karier's (1972) article, "Testing for Order and Control in the Corporate State," in which he explained the racist history of standardized testing and its relationship to capitalism and labor stratification. Karier explained that on the 1960 version of the Stanford-Binet intelligence test, there was a picture of two women and the question, "Which is prettier?"[2]. One woman is stereotypically northern European and the other is obviously not—possibly southern Europe or African American. The "correct" answer on this "intelligence test" is the northern European woman. I made a transparency of the picture and put it on the overhead for my students as part of the lesson I taught about the racist history of intelligence testing. My students were shocked, but along with Karier's article, it helped them understand the historical tradition from which the Iowa test had emerged and to which they were subject—that is, both intelligence tests and standardized tests have historically been used to rank individuals' supposedly innate qualities and sort them into particular societal slots. I also read to them from Gardner's (1983) theory of multiple intelligences to discredit the one-dimensional Iowa score as a determiner of their worth. This had such an impact on some that when I asked students to answer at the end of the year, "What is the most important thing you feel you learned in my class, math or other?" Freida wrote, "the most important thing I learned in this class was the real definition of intelligence." This was a time when

I explicitly provided an analysis to counter the feelings of inadequacy some expressed and to help them develop a broader understanding of the politics of the tests and the role they played in a stratified society and unequal educational system. Paulina wrote later in her journal, "We might not have the stanines, but we got the brains!"

Supporting Positive Cultural and Social Identities

> ... the White critical educator has much to learn from as well as to teach bicultural students [students of color] in the context of a culturally democratic classroom. From students, teachers can discover what bicultural people feel, think, dream, and live, while the teachers can provide for their students the opportunity to develop their critical thinking skills, examine their histories, reflect on the world, and engage with the dominant educational discourse as free social agents who are able to influence and transform their world. (Darder, 1991, p. 71)

An additional aspect of building political relationships with students is supporting the development of positive cultural and social identities. This was a goal of my teaching as I discuss in chapter 2. I define positive cultural identities to mean that students are strongly rooted in their home languages, cultures, and communities, but at the same time, are able to appropriate what they need to survive and thrive in the dominant culture (Darder, 1991; Delpit, 1988; Ladson-Billings, 1995b; Murrell, 1997). By positive social identities, I mean that students have the self-confidence, perseverance, and courage that are necessary for them act on their sense of social agency.

Supporting Students' Cultural Identities. As a white teacher with students of color, I was limited in what I could do to support their identities. Because I was an outsider with little intimate knowledge of their culture, I obviously could not help them *develop* their cultural identities (Murrell, 1997). However, I could *support* them by validating their language and culture, creating curriculum that was relevant and meaningful to their experiences, and learning about life in their community. This support for who they were as people meant that I needed to view their language and culture as intellectual resources rather than deficits (Ladson-Billings, 1994, 1995b). I also needed to create space for the development of their voices in the classroom (Darder, 1991). And to communicate more openly with and learn from students and their parents, I needed to be "unafraid to raise questions about discrimination and voicelessness with people of color and listen, no, to *hear* what they had to say" (Delpit, 1988, p. 297). I tried to do these things in supporting students to "maintain their cultural integrity while succeeding academically" (Ladson-Billings, 1995b, p. 476).

Darder (1991) discussed the role of white teachers working with "bicultural" students:

> White educators who are working with bicultural students must first come to acknowledge their own limitations, prejudices, and biases, and must be willing to enter into dialogue with their students in a spirit of humility and with respect for the knowledge that students bring into the classroom.... This process truly requires the teacher to share the power more equitably and, in so doing, to empower the student through critically engaging, challenging, affirming, and incorporating into the classroom the knowledge that the bicultural student has about self and the community. (pp. 70–71)

These were things I tried to enact in the classroom, as best as I could. With respect to language, I always told students that they could use Spanish whenever and wherever they wanted, with one another or in written or verbal explanations. If I did not fully understand, I told them that I would ask other students for help. I spoke a little Spanish occasionally in the classroom and made clear that I wanted and expected students to help me learn more. I made the explicit point that people paid good money, in school and to private tutors, to learn what they (my students) already knew, that is, Spanish. I shared with them that my father, like many of them, only learned English at school. I also told them how I did not learn Yiddish, even though I grew up hearing it, and that I regretted not knowing it and appreciated the power of their bilingualism.

I also shared my own culture with students to make culture and history a public part of our conversation and to clarify that whites are not acultural people. At Chanukah, I brought in my family's *menorah* (Jewish candelabra) and a *dreidel* (spinning top with which children play) and showed them to students. My students looked at the dreidel and said, "oh that's a *pirinola*" and others called it a *toma todo* [take all]. I said, "it is not, it's a dreidel!" but they persisted. From this, we came to understand that both cultures had things in common. After asking adult Mexicans in Morningside and researching more, I shared with my students that the connection possibly came from the Spanish Inquisition. In 1492, Spanish Jews were expelled or forced to convert to Catholicism. Some did convert, but secretly maintained their Jewishness. Perhaps, we speculated, those Jews who came to New Spain and Mexico pretending to be Catholic brought their dreidels with them and changed the name, but not the rules, of the game.

And I shared stories of my own family's trek to the United States, strikingly similar to their own tales, as I spoke of my grandfather coming first, fleeing Polish pogroms and the military draft that put Jews on the front lines of World War I; then my grandmother 10 years later walking across Europe with three children, only to set sail and leave two behind who followed a year later. These experiences were important in seeing commonalities across cultures and historic periods. Sometimes my students saw more similarities than I did. They consistently told me I was Jewish, not white, while I argued back and tried to explain that I was both, and benefited from white privilege even while Jewish. However, many continued to disagree, especially since they studied the Holocaust, saw the film *Schindler's List* (Spielberg, 1993) in school, and could not reconcile "whiteness" with Jewish experiences in Europe.

I was much more knowledgeable after 10 years of working and spending time in Morningside, but I remained an outsider to my students' language, culture, and community. Because of that, I never call my teaching culturally relevant in Ladson-Billings' (1994, 1995b) sense. I did build on students' strengths (e.g., their sense of justice) and made the real-world projects relevant, but I do not believe that I used students' culture as a curriculum in its own right nor as a bridge to the standard curriculum. Nevertheless, I took seriously, and tried to make real, what Ladson-Billings (1994) described as liberatory educational practices:

> Parents, teachers, and neighbors need to help arm African American [and other marginalized] children with the knowledge, skills, and attitude needed to struggle successfully against oppression. These, more than test scores, more than high grade-point averages, are the critical features of education for African Americans. If students are to be equipped to struggle against racism they need excellent skills from the basics of reading, writing, and math, to understanding history, thinking critically, solving problems, and making decisions; they must go beyond merely filling in test bubbles with Number 2 pencils. (pp. 139–140)

And, as a white teacher with outsider status, Darder's (1991) analysis about what teachers of any class, race, or ethnic identity need to do to fully support students of color in teaching for social justice is apropos. She argued for

> the need to integrate a critical model of bicultural pedagogy ... that also critically addresses the awakening of the bicultural voice and the development of a social consciousness of struggle and

solidarity that will prepare bicultural students to undertake the democratic responsibility of participation in their world, morally committed to the liberation and empowerment of all people. (p. 71)

Thus, although I was limited in how I could support students' cultural identities, I could still support their development of sociopolitical consciousness and sense of social agency.

Supporting Students' Social Identities. Supporting students' social identities, in the sense I define it, is related to Darder's view above of students' "democratic responsibility of participation in their world." The classroom setting encouraged students to articulate both their sociopolitical and mathematical ideas, and our mathematics curriculum, Mathematics in Context (MiC), was an important factor because it required students to justify their answers and reasoning. Many of the pedagogical practices I describe in this chapter can challenge students' conceptions of social phenomena as well. Darder (2002), using Macedo (1994), explained how students can move to action:

> ... a critical understanding of voice entails "a process that turns experience into critical reflection and political action" (Macedo, 1994, p. 182). This constitutes a political process whereby students come to recognize that their voices and participation are politically powerful resources that can be collectively generated in the interest of social justice, human rights, and economic democracy. (p. 106)

Most of the students in my two-year class developed the capacity to speak about what they thought mathematically and speak up for what they believed, although as I explain earlier, this was an uneven, nonlinear process. In general, these students provided much support to each other, which I believe contributed to their increased confidence. Many had been together in the same class for years. About half of the responses on the survey they completed at the end of eighth grade mentioned feeling more willing to speak out. Chuy wrote about the class as a whole, "The environment in the class is very free where everyone feels confident to speak up and not be ashamed or embarrassed that someone will laugh at them." He also wrote about himself, "Besides the Math and using it and relating it to the 'world' your class gave me a lot of confidence. It taught me to not feel stupid when attempting to answer a question." In response to the question, "What is the most important thing you feel you learned in my class, math or other?" Carmen wrote, "The most important thing that

I have learned is that I am my own person and that I have a right to stand up for what I believe in." And Ariana, who was still relatively quiet, wrote, "The most important thing I feel I learned was that I have to right to speak and if other people don't like it TOO Bad!!"

Of the 15 female students at the time, 10 wrote responses similar to Carmen and Ariana. Nowhere on the survey did I ask about confidence, willingness to speak out, take action, or anything similar. The students were responding to the question of what important things they learned in the class or how the class changed them. It did not surprise me that most of the girls wrote about speaking up because, in my classes, the intellectual and social leaders who emerged were usually girls. Paulina wrote about the class as a whole and captured the general trend.

> Everyone in this classroom has learned to speak out and do what they believe should be done. Many people in the classroom have overcome their shyness and now they participate more in discussions and they don't care what other people say because they know how to defend their position.

The students in my two-year class and I worked together for the most part and created a classroom that generally supported their investigations into real-world phenomena involving justice issues. That their participation was integral to the process and voluntary will become more evident below where I contrast this with a general-track class I taught. We normalized politically taboo topics and created a pedagogy of questioning through the development of political relationships. I initiated these, and students responded, and our dialogues, both individual and group, sustained and deepened the mathematical investigations students conducted through the real-world projects. Conversations about various forms of discrimination permeated classroom life and became threads that we wove throughout almost two years of learning. I articulated my own analyses and views while struggling to ensure students developed their own as well, and I tried to provide the necessary historical and social context at the same time. In the ways I could, I supported their identities as individuals and as members of particular cultures. None of it was smooth or easy, and I felt my way along guided by various theoretical frameworks as well as by intuition and experience. In reflecting on my data and what I learned, the issues of what conditions facilitated and hampered our efforts comes to the foreground. I turn to these conditions now.

Facilitating Conditions and Constraints in Teaching for Social Justice

The conditions that most affected my work included the school and district context, tracking, and the role of administrators. The backdrop for all of these was the larger political context that I discuss in the concluding chapter. These conditions were interrelated and played a major role in my capacity to teach mathematics for social justice.

School and District Context

Chicago is a punitive, top-down, regimented district with a historic record of failing its low-income students and students of color (Lipman, 2004). In 1987, then Secretary of Education William Bennett proclaimed Chicago to be the worst school system in the country. In 1988, the State of Illinois legislature passed a far-reaching law that, among other things, created a certain amount of local community decision-making power. The law created democratically elected Local School Councils (LSC) consisting of six parents, two community representatives, and two teachers, and for high schools, one student. The LSCs had substantial responsibilities and powers, including granting (and rescinding) principal contracts, controlling discretionary budgets, and developing school improvement plans. But in 1995, dissatisfied with the pace of school reforms and pressured by business interests and the mayor (Lipman, 2004), the legislature passed a second law that returned much of the control to the mayor. It reduced LSC powers and allowed the mayor to appoint a school board. Most of all, the law ushered in a host of accountability measures and a chief executive officer for the system who was appointed by, and reported directly to, the mayor. The accountability measures including the use of high-stakes tests to determine whether students passed grades 3, 6, and 8, and increased monitoring and control of schools by central office administrators including the power to close and reconstitute schools.

Discipline was a major concern in the system, but it played out differentially within Rivera's tracks. School personnel generally believed that students had to be closely monitored, supervised, and regulated. The principal was a Mexican American woman who strongly promoted Mexican culture, bilingualism, and close contact with families and community. She also believed in tight discipline and keeping gangs at bay. Gangs and violence were (and are) serious issues at Morningside, but the school administration managed to ensure the school was neutral territory. There were known gang members in school, including sixth graders, and several students had been shot. The security guard kept a close watch on neighborhood streets when students gathered outside before school, and more than once, I saw him hustle particular students inside when rival gang members came near. Thus, there was plenty for school officials, teachers, parents, and students to worry about in the neighborhood with respect to gangs.

The way the school controlled students, however, extended far beyond gangs and violence. Rivera was a *panopticon* (Foucault, 1977), or "all-seeing eye," with over two dozen security cameras, metal detectors, and constant surveillance of students. Students were told, from the moment they walked into the building, when and where to stand, sit, walk, stop, talk, be silent, go to the bathroom, eat, and leave. I saw teachers walk classes back and forth in the hall at 3:00 P.M. until "they get it right" before letting them leave. Once, when teaching my general-track class in another teacher's room, a student of hers told her that one of my students left gum in a desk. The teacher burst into the room, and, to my astonishment and before I had time to react or protest, ordered my class to stand and empty their pockets so she could inspect for gum. The dominant orientation was that "you gotta be tough on them," as one teacher said. The disciplinarian was a tall, severe white male who was also the basketball coach. Although he had good relationships with many students and was known to be fair in his punishments ("you know the streets have rules, you know we have rules"), he inspired fear in many students as well. None of this is unusual in urban schools where teachers and administrators often see themselves as having to "manage" and constantly hold back what they perceive as the "flood of unruly hordes" of Black and Brown youth (Ferguson, 2000). However, the school's differentiated tracks compounded this.

Tracking at Rivera

Rivera's tracking was a powerful and complex force on the school and my teaching, and I have struggled to understand it. The key issue is how to explain the different way students in the honors track participated in school compared to students in the general track. Because students in the different tracks were demographically indistinguishable from one another, and there were not, in my assessment, any differences in students' capacity to conceptualize (mathematical) ideas, my explanation has to do with the extremely distinct school socialization experienced by different track students. But stating that socialization was a major factor does not answer either how this manifested itself nor what to do about it, which I address below. Nor did I study this question rigorously, so much of my analysis is tentative. However, I am most concerned with this question because of the implications for teaching mathematics for social justice for all students. This is especially important because of the potential for some to misinterpret my research as "these students" can learn to read and write the world with mathematics, and "others" cannot. My argument here is that despite constraints, students in the general track can learn mathematics for social justice; the issue is to understand the root of the complexities involved and try to resolve them.

Unlike many tracked schools in the United States where the advanced-placement track is filled with white, upper middle-class students and the remedial track with working-class students of color, Rivera tracks were not differentiated by race and class. In my two-year class in the honors track, only one student did not qualify for free lunch, and her family barely exceeded the limit. In my 10 years at Rivera, low-income students (determined by the free lunch guidelines) averaged 98% to 99% of the student body. There were no white students at Rivera, just a few African American students, and the honors track was a bilingual program with only working-class Latinos/as.

Rivera teachers could not attribute students' placement in the different tracks to race or class. Teachers generally gave two nonmutually exclusive rationales based on individual, not group, differences to explain why students were in different tracks. Like the teachers Oakes, Wells, Jones, and Datnow (1997) studied, many Rivera teachers claimed that students in the honors track were generally "smarter" or "faster." Teachers also suggested that parents of students in the honors track were more involved in, and supportive of, the school and their children's education. When there were students in the general track who fit standard notions of smartness but who "underachieved," teachers generally cited lack of parental support as the cause.

On one level, one could argue that some parents of students in the honors track were more involved in their children's education because some requested that their children be tested for the program, especially when they were younger. However, Rivera overall prided itself on parental support, and the principal had excellent relations with families. Parent attendance at semi-annual report card pickup was extremely high across tracks. In my multiple experiences talking with parents at report card pickup, which were essentially six-hour time blocks for parent–teacher conferences, I saw no difference in the care and concern of parents in the different tracks; virtually all supported their children's education and Rivera, and they strongly emphasized behaving appropriately, listening to the teacher, doing all the work, and learning as much as possible. "Uniform compliance," that is, children wearing the required uniforms, was also extremely high, and parents were the ones who bought the uniforms, made sure they were clean, and sent their children to school in them. Finally, school attendance was very high, and parents had a role in this as well.

The claim of "intelligence differences" between students in honors and general tracks was a myth, in my assessment. However, many teachers accepted the notion in part because of the commonsensical, hard-to-dislodge folklore that "intelligence" was a "measurable" construct in the first place, and that standardized test scores equated with intelligence. In the primary grades, students entered the honors track via a quasi-IQ test, and in the later elementary grades, through a multiple-choice exam. (My students who entered the honors track early remembered little about the tests, except items like forming letters, identifying colors and numbers, and answering at what temperature one bakes a cake.) Thus, it was not surprising that students in the honors track usually scored higher on the Iowa, although some students in the general track outperformed some in the honors track. More to the point, however, and beyond the socially constructed fallacy that standardized tests assess intelligence, was the issue of mathematical power. Because I initially provided professional development to all Rivera teachers who taught mathematics, I worked with students in all grades, in all three programs (general-track monolingual English, general-track bilingual, and bilingual honors). I worked extensively with hundreds of Rivera students over 10 years. I taught and worked with dozens of students in the general track, in both bilingual and monolingual programs, whose mathematical sophistication, conceptual understanding, and grasp of the various competencies comprising mathematical power surpassed most students in the honors track. Few students in the general track with whom I worked would not have succeeded in honors-track classes. In fact, when an ex-student of mine in a general track class was kicked out of his class and sent for the period into the honors class I was teaching, I put him to work with a group. Within 15 minutes, he was thoroughly involved and grasped material that was entirely new to him.

Teachers' differential conceptions of students in the two tracks were reflected in their behavioral and academic expectations. Even some Latino/a educators who taught in multiple tracks or only in the bilingual honors track often expressed and expected that students would act and learn differently according to track placement. One student in the honors track told me that when she was in eighth grade, someone scrawled graffiti in a boys bathroom. Administrators brought all the boys in grades 6–8 into the auditorium for a group interrogation session—*except* those in the honors-track classes. Students in all programs spoke regularly of how students in the honors track could get away with anything because Rivera adults considered them "good kids" who did not misbehave. One student in the honors track told me that when his class passed lines of boys in the general track in the hall, he and a couple friends in his class sometimes bumped the other students and provoked trouble knowing that the "bad boys" would get blamed. A teacher who taught an honors class for the first time in 2002–2003 told me that they were just nicer and were not "mean" like Rivera students in the general track whom she had taught for years. This conception of the "meanness" of general-track students was shared by at least some other Rivera teachers; as an extreme example, I overheard a special education teacher say to another teacher about one of her students, "A bullet in his belly would be too good for him."

Students were extremely conscious of these different expectations. Students in the honors track had a higher grading scale that was posted in classrooms shared by students in the general track (e.g., a 93 rather than a 90 was an "A"). In a series of open-ended interviews we conducted with 22 students in 1996–1997, virtually all were conscious of differentiated treatment and expectations (Gutstein, Lipman, Hernández, & de los Reyes, 1997). One middle school student in the monolingual general program said, "For the honors ... they [teachers] expect them to get straight A's or at least A's and B's. For the lower kids, they expect C's and D's, they don't expect A's." Another said, "The teachers expect more from them [honors-track] because they are higher, but sometimes if they compare you, you feel dumb." The interviewer asked, "Do teachers compare you a lot?" and the student answered, "Yes, they'll say 'This class behaves better than you.' Or, 'They got higher test scores.' Stuff like that." Students in the honors track spoke about disliking the special treatment they received, and students in the general track resented being compared to students in the honors track. I knew students in the general track who either steadfastly refused to take the honors program test or who told me privately that when pushed to take it, purposely answered incorrectly.

Expectations, Tracking, and Teaching for Social Justice. The confluence of differentiated expectations about behavior and learning with the preoccupation about discipline and control had powerful implications for teaching and learning at Rivera. The most obvious effect I saw was how students in different tracks viewed their own intellectual capacities. Students in the honors track tended to view themselves as individuals capable of serious intellectual work and their teachers as partners with whom they were willing to work. Students in the general track did not usually think of themselves or teachers in the same way. Although I collected little specific data on how teacher expectations interacted with students' engagement, behavior, and learning, studies document the power of teacher expectations to shape students' academic identities and futures (e.g., Rist, 1970). Others have argued that students treated as competent tend to learn, while those treated as not intellectually prepared and deficient, or otherwise denigrated, learn to "not-learn" (Kohl, 1991; Ladson-Billings, 1994). Rivera students treated as most (and least) capable (i.e., honors-track versus general-track students) tended to succeed more (and less). In this sense, Rivera was one large self-fulfilling prophecy.

The other disturbing effect of teacher expectations and the almost-obsession with order and "management" was on student behavior. In a climate of almost-constant surveillance, many boys in the general track tried to get away with minor acts of mischief at any opportunity, and there were more serious infractions occasionally as well. Although I observed and experienced these actions, I am still unclear exactly how to understand them. And students' resistance at Rivera was a significant factor in my general-track classroom. When I taught a general-program class in 2000–2001, teachers described the class as a typical, "hard-to-handle" Rivera class with a few male "problem students." When students in the class disrupted, I asked their homeroom teacher for help. She told me, "just give them seat work, Rico. That will settle them down." In fact, that was standard practice for some Rivera teachers with "problem" classrooms because it "worked." However, this was inconsistent with a social justice pedagogy, and I did not take this approach. I examined my class's assignments, homework, and assessments in their language arts, social studies, and science classes. The bulk of their work was recall of discrete facts and definitions, "fill-in-the-blank" questions, problems requiring identification of specific items, "matching" problems, and other nonintellectually demanding work. Nor was there anything about social justice issues. I also observed my students being taught by other teachers. I saw one teacher effectively silence and control one of the disruptive boys in my class by publicly calling him "potty mouth." I did not, and would not, do that.

I struggled throughout the year trying to engage students in this class. Three boys were particularly disruptive and had rarely experienced much school success, despite being conceptually strong in mathematics. Darder's suggestion that "such resistance constitutes the only effective mechanism they [resistant students] have found to protect the self from the alienation they have experienced for years as a consequence of academic oppression" (2002, p. 137), and Ferguson's (2000) analyses of African American male students' disruptive behavior as their attempts to define themselves in the face of, and in response to, an oppressive racialized and gendered society, while maintaining some degree of self-respect and humanity may have applied to these three students.[3] They were able to create enough momentum in the class that made it hard to teach. I talked with them out of class, visited them and their parents in their homes, asked for help, used punishments as a last resort (like detentions, which were particularly ineffective as I knew they would be), and removed them occasionally from class. I was also unable to build a relationship with one of them, who was the angriest. I was frustrated, especially because other teachers had fewer "problems" with them, because, as they said, they gave them seat work and/or publicly put them down. These students were dealing with issues outside of school that I knew about from talking with them and their families. But I was unable to engage them or prevent their influence from creating a classroom climate not conducive to learning.

I also made pedagogical mistakes. Because I firmly believed that there was no fundamental difference in the capacity to learn of students in different tracks, I did not treat them differently. My mistake was in misassessing how general-track students' school experiences failed to prepare them to work independently without constant supervision, and I underestimated their lack of experience with this sort of classroom and how they would interpret a less authoritarian atmosphere. My conception of how my general-track students would respond in my class was based in part on my teaching of honors-track students and also on my work with general-track students in small groups in other teachers' classes, in which these issues did not exist. However, my expectations of my general-track class may have been too different from their other experiences in Chicago public schools. I wanted them to work relatively independently and productively with others and also to approach mathematics problems without directly being taught how to solve them. I wanted students to develop mathematical power, but because of their socialization, they needed more scaffolding than I realized. Like the reform mathematics teachers Martin (2000) described, I did not provide a sufficient transition from students' traditional orientation toward mathematics to doing ill-formed problems on their own. Martin explained students' disruptive acts as responses to their "difficulty adjusting to the demands being placed on them by the new practices being stressed in their classrooms" (p. 181). I believe my actions may have contributed to students' frustration.

In addition, because students in the honors track generally accepted teachers as partners, and because I had good relationships outside of the classroom with students in *all* tracks, I did not accept the view that students and teachers cannot have open relationships in school as well. I believe this was not a problem with students in the honors track because adults took them seriously as learners, and they consequently saw themselves the same way. However, several boys in my class in the general track objectively took advantage of our relationships and did not take me seriously in the classroom. They evidently could not sort out what they may have perceived to be mixed messages from me. Mario, with whom I was close, threw snowballs at me outside, and at first, did not heed me when

I told him to stop. I had to be extremely forceful before he realized that I meant it. One day, Manny saw me in the hall before class, smiled, and said, "what's up Rico dog," as if I were a friend on the street. I grimaced and said, "Manny, you *cannot* call me that, here *or* outside!" Manny looked perplexed for a second, then brightened as he thought he understood what I meant, and said, "Oh, ok! What's up *Mr.* Rico dog." I believe Manny was genuinely confused, which was my responsibility, although he may have been pulling my leg.

Furthermore, I was reluctant, and therefore inconsistent, in using institutional power and punishment which, in my view, only led from more detentions to in- and out-of-school suspensions and dropping out. I knew that my hesitancy was a problem, and students could take advantage of it, but I felt trapped by larger societal structures and the slippery slope of enacting punishments. I knew too many students who dropped out and/or joined gangs, or met worse fates, so I was slow to use coercive power. Christensen (2000) wrote about this dilemma:

> Here we were teaching about justice, tolerance, equality, and respect, and yet when we had a problem with a talented student who didn't want to go along, we turned him over to the deans. Ultimately, what lesson did that teach our students? ... That we might profess to believe in everyone's potential, but in practice could not act on this belief? It's a complex issue. I don't want to keep the class from progressing because of one or two students, but I don't want to "give up" on students either. On bad days, I threw Wesley out. On good days, I tried to look beyond his behavior and figure out what motivated it. (p. 37)

Even without the three students who often disrupted, developing a social justice classroom would have been difficult because of the school's fixation on discipline and control, the powerful way expectations shaped students' sense of what they could do, students' lack of experience in working independently, and my misassessment of the power of students' socialization. My lack of consistency, inflexibility in adapting to students' conditioning, and reluctance to use coercive punishment interacted unproductively with the overall school climate. Furthermore, as an outsider to students' community, I did not know some of the cultural codes (that insiders instinctively know) that might have allowed me to communicate more clearly to students, work through some of their defensiveness, and win their trust. Murrell (1997) points out that " ... it is difficult for those who do not already share the cultural motifs of blackness [Latino -ness] to establish the intersubjectivity needed between learners and teachers in a Freireian literacy [numeracy] learning framework" (p. 37). I concur, and these issues together made it harder to build the mature relationships necessary to co-create a classroom for social justice.

I do not wish to be one sided here. There were many students in the class who wanted to and did learn mathematics and engaged in trying to read and write the world. And students were inconsistent—Alicia, for example, could disrupt one day and lead the class in a discussion about injustice the next. I gave the class the same end-of year survey I gave my two-year class (again, many students signed their names even though it was to be anonymous) with the question: "Do you feel now you are better able to understand the world using math?" Manny responded, "Yes, because you opened my eyes. Before I didn't care and now I do." Yesenia's answer to that question was, "Before I didn't even care. But now I feel like it's important to be aware of the things that are going on such as racial profiling." Of the 25 students who turned in the surveys, approximately three-fourths referred positively to the real-world projects. On the question, "What is the most important thing you feel you learned in my class, math or other?" Alicia answered succinctly, "About our community." When the class did the same "meaningful survey" project as my class in the honors track (see chapter 4), her group's question was, "Why do you think so many Caucasians are moving into our Latino neighborhood?" She wrote on the survey that what she liked about our class was that "we did projects on our community, in our Latino community."

Nevertheless, my data make clear that this class was overall less successful in learning to read and write the world than the class in the honors track I taught for almost two years. Although this class was relatively successful on real-world projects, they did only about half as many as my classes in the honors track. Furthermore, 4 of my 28 students did not pass their Iowa test to get to eighth grade (due to both their mathematics and language arts scores) for which I could not help feeling partly responsible.

Students were more involved when doing real-world projects than when learning regular mathematics. Part of this may have been because I used the Connected Mathematics Project (CMP). It was the only year I taught CMP, and I was less familiar with it than with MiC. My observations were that it interested students less than MiC. When I taught an MiC unit late in the year, students were substantially more engaged in it than in CMP. Students often complained that they found CMP boring, but some of this may have been because of my unfamiliarity with it and my struggles in establishing a climate strongly supporting serious mathematical learning.

Reflections on Rivera's Tracking. Tracking worked in opposite ways for the different tracks. Adults in the building took students in the honors program seriously and expected them to learn. As one student said, "Everyone expects us to be somebody." They, in turn, reciprocated, for the most part, by believing themselves capable of real intellectual work and accepting their teachers as partners in their learning, even though some resisted school for various reasons and virtually all reported disliking the special treatment that isolated them from their peers. In contrast, most adults in the building focused inordinately on controlling and disciplining students in the general programs. Virtually all Rivera students were low-income Latinos/as, but CPS schools were mostly preparing the students in the general track, except for the "few really bright ones," for the military or to be compliant and amiable workers in low-skill service-sector jobs (Lipman, 2004). The "bad kids" were being objectively prepared for dropping out, joining gangs, and/or going to prison. Although many students in the general programs spoke vaguely of attending college, few had appropriate counseling by teachers or the academic confidence exhibited by students in the honors track, and most knew that their chances to get to college were not great. I knew several Rivera students who never even made it to high school, caught by the Iowa test and the transition schools, and who dropped out at the end of eighth grade or after repeating the grade. Trapped by low academic and behavioral expectations held by the wider society and by many teachers and administrators, and taught a curriculum that neither developed critical literacies nor, for the majority, the competencies to reach and succeed in college, only the most persevering Rivera students in the general track made it to that academic level.

The Role of the Principal

The third key factor affecting students' learning mathematics for social justice was the role of the principal. Being forced out of Rivera by an acting principal certainly brought home to me the importance of administrator support. I have a disturbing memory from the special LSC meeting that I requested to appeal her decision. At the end of the night, one of my university preservice students who was born and raised in Morningside and who attended the meeting came up to me and said, "If she does this to you, what will they to do us [new teachers]?" I am often asked how administrators react to teaching mathematics for social justice. In my situation, for eight years, I had the full backing and trust of the principal who wanted students to develop critical literacies. However, when she left and CPS bureaucrats appointed a temporary replacement, the situation changed. In retrospect, I would have done some things differently with the replacement, but I, like many parents, teachers, students, and neighborhood residents, was quite surprised by her views and actions, which ultimately led to the community successfully rallying to oust her. It is clear that because of the power differentials that exist in schools, administrators can support or restrain social justice pedagogy and curriculum, but it is important to recall Carlson's (2002) point that teachers need to find spaces within which to subvert dominant, repressive agendas and teach against the grain. There is always some room to do so, even within oppressive, authoritarian regimes, although one's tactics may vary to preserve one's livelihood or position.

Conclusion

I draw two principal lessons in this chapter. First, it is possible for students and teacher to collaborate in deep and meaningful ways to support social justice teaching and learning. Second, contextual factors play a powerful role in influencing the possibilities of doing so. In my classes in the honors track, especially my two-year class, students and I worked in partnership to create the relationships, classroom norms, and overall climate. They viewed themselves as capable of substantive academic work, engaged the ideas, and delved into the real-world projects using mathematics to investigate injustice in the world. Over time, they, too, began to initiate discussions about racism and other taboo topics and contributed to make these issues a normal part of classroom life. To develop political relationships, I took specific actions and students responded in kind, and my relationships with them took on a different character than just being a trusted adult. Through our collaborative efforts, they began to understand the sociopolitical context of their lives and broader society and started the process of learning how to critique knowledge and question sources of authority such as texts, teachers, and maps.

Despite the "success" with classes in the honors track at Rivera, teaching mathematics for social justice was significantly different in the general-track program. What is absolutely critical here is that this not be read as students in the honors track were somehow "special" and that one cannot teach students in general programs to read and write the world with mathematics. Other evidence refutes this point as well (Brantlinger, 2005; Peterson, 1995, 2003; Steele, 2004; Turner & Font Strawhun, 2005), although none of these authors deals specifically with tracking. Students in the honors track were not special or fundamentally different from those in the general track. My analysis is that the *only* meaningful difference at Rivera between students in the different tracks was their school socialization. I taught students in the honors track with parents who never attended school, with family members in gangs and prison, and with life experiences as diverse and difficult as students in the general track. However, what was different was their school experiences, and the contrast was profoundly stark and dramatic. Furthermore, although it was difficult for the reasons I analyze in this chapter, many students in the general track I taught did begin to understand their community and world on a deeper level through mathematical analysis.

If I were to teach a class in the general track at Rivera again, I would do several things differently. I would suggest that any teacher in a similar situation consider these ideas. First, I now better understand the socialization of students in Rivera's general programs and would therefore more intentionally teach specific competencies, both mathematical and general. I remember writing "spoon feeding" on the board when teaching my class in the general track and almost berating students for the tendency to want and even need such a pedagogy. I would now try to meet students where they were, as opposed to where I wanted them to be, and try to patiently help them develop the dispositions needed to read and write the world. To clarify, this is not "dumbing down" the curriculum, but rather adjusting my expectations to what I believe to be realities, while still challenging students. Second, I would be more careful about how I built relationships with students and would be much clearer in communicating what lines students could not cross (e.g., snowballs). This is not a retreat to the "don't smile until Christmas" line given to new teachers, but rather the recognition of the need to be clear to students about appropriate roles given the history of their socialization and the unequal relations of power enacted in school. Third, I would use more real-world projects because students were more involved in these than in regular math. One of Christensen's (2000) four themes for "building community out of chaos" is to center the curriculum in students' lives. I would do more, not less, of that, even at the risk of leaving the standards-based curriculum aside, to engage students more where they were. Finally, I do not know how to resolve the issue about using punishments. Although I do not disagree with Christensen (2000) when she wrote, "Perhaps it's just letting them [disruptive students] know we [teachers] care enough to take our time outside of school that turns them around" (p. 38), that was insufficient in my situation. This is an open question for me.

This research provides evidence that it is possible to teach mathematics for social justice in urban public schools, but it also describes and analyzes the challenges. My experiences at Rivera suggest that some conditions strongly facilitate reading and writing the world with mathematics, and conversely, others hold it back. School and district contexts that contribute to positioning students as competent/incompetent, good/bad, and smart/not-so-smart play a particularly powerful role. Students who are taken seriously and who consequently view themselves as intellectual learners capable of sincere and thoughtful discussion can generally shed the behavior and immaturity that kept some students in the general track from participating in class. When teachers have difficulty creating conditions for students to overcome the negative effects of low academic and behavioral expectations, students are less likely to work together with teachers to co-construct the classroom norms and political relationships that support learning mathematics for social justice. In a school culture of repressive surveillance and low expectations for specific students, working to surmount students' disruptive actions, whatever their multiple, overlapping causes, is therefore a necessary aspect of a liberatory pedagogy. What is salient, however, is that when positive conditions were present, students' learning was significant and the evidence is substantial that they developed sociopolitical consciousness and a sense of social agency—the real question is how to transform the constraints so that other students can do the same. This is an area in which much more research needs to be done.

CHAPTER 7

"*Lucha* Is What My Life Is About"
Students' Voices on Social Justice Mathematics with Maria Barbosa, Adrián Calderón, Grisel Murillo, and Lizandra Nevárez

The four students who wrote this chapter, Maria Barbosa, Adrián Calderón, Grisel Murillo, and Lizandra Nevárez, were in my two-year class, their seventh and eighth grades, from November 1997 to June 1999. Except for Grisel, they were part of a group of about eight students whom I recruited in their seventh grade to be "co-researchers." I never quite figured out how to maximize their knowledge and insights, but we met fairly regularly for over a year, often at a local *taqueria*, and tried to make sense of the class. Although we may not have learned that much from those sessions, they were at least a time for students and myself to reflect on what was happening in class. During their ninth grade, Adrián, Lizandra, and I presented at a national conference, and as seniors, all five of us presented at two conferences, one state and one national (Gutstein, Barbosa, Calderón, Murillo, & Nevárez, 2003). They have also come to my teacher education classes at my university and shared their perspectives with pre-service teachers. In all those presentations, I gave a short introduction and sat down, and they did the rest. As of this writing (April 2005), Maria, Adrián, and Grisel are

165

college sophomores, and Lizandra is working, helping support her family and saving money to attend college.

I asked them to write this chapter because they have their own perspectives (different from mine) and because they too have been reflecting over the years on what took place in our class. I continue to learn from their insights and various presentations. Their voices add to the story because they are speaking for themselves, rather than through my interpretations. They do not necessarily speak for others in the classes I have had, but their voices and views about teaching and learning mathematics for social justice are real and important and need to be heard.

They wrote this chapter, and I helped only to edit for clarity. I gave them some feedback on their first drafts, but all the decisions about what to write were theirs. We have been discussing these themes for years since I first taught them in November 1997, and I think we all would say that our understandings of, and disagreements about, the class have been partially shaped by these ongoing conversations. Also, our relationships are beyond just "co-researchers"—we are all close friends. With that as an introduction, I turn the chapter over to them.

Maria Barbosa

> We cannot seek achievement for ourselves and forget about progress and prosperity for our community.... Our ambitions must be broad enough to include the aspirations and needs of others, for their sakes and for our own. (Cesar Chavez)

Prior to entering Mr. Rico's class, I was a relatively shy person, but when I walked out of that classroom for the last time I had grown in many ways. I was no longer the shy girl that once entered that classroom. Although the class ended, the lessons learned inside those four walls will always remain important building blocks that helped define who I am today. Currently as a second year student at Northwestern University, I constantly find myself reflecting on the important lessons learned in our seventh and eighth grade mathematics classes. The manner in which the class was conducted allowed the students in the class to obtain a greater sense of agency. It allowed me to see that although often we are taught that we live in a meritocracy, we can be oblivious to the institutional discrimination that is prevalent in our society but that we can make a difference.

I believe that in order to portray fully the impact that the mathematics class had on me, I should explain some of my personal background. My parents, similar to many of my classmates' parents, immigrated to this country in a search for a better life. I am not a native of this country, and I came here when I was three-and-a half years old. Spanish is my first language, English my second, and German my third, which I studied in school. I was raised in a predominantly Mexican-American, low-income neighborhood in Chicago. My parents always instilled in me the importance of an education, as they themselves were not allowed to finish elementary school due to their economic circumstances. My success to this point can greatly be attributed to the parental support that I have received in all of my endeavors.

My experience in Mr. Rico's class at Rivera elementary was very different from any other class in my elementary years. For starters the style of instruction that Mr. Rico employed was unlike any other I had experienced. He taught us math in a very untraditional manner. We learned all the mathematics that is required through our active engagement in projects and through the Mathematics in Context [MiC] curriculum; many of the questions prompted by the book and Mr. Rico required explanations and often were open-ended questions. In many of the projects that we engaged in, we were given limited information and asked to develop our own ways of solving the matter at hand.

There are certain projects that I specifically remember working on and have had a long-lasting impact on me. Among those projects was one entitled "Tomato Pickers Take on the Growers." In this project we were asked to solve for different amounts that the pickers would earn in different scenarios. We were to solve this given data from a newspaper article and through our own mathematical approaches. Many of the math tools that we used in these projects had been developed in the Mathematics in Context books and were further developed and applied in the projects. What made this experience different than other classrooms was a number of factors. First, the issues were applicable to real life, and many were personally relevant to us at more than one level. As low-income, Latino, immigrant children, some of the issues were directly linked to our own neighborhood, while others were issues of social justice on a global level.

In the case of "Tomato Pickers Take on the Growers," this particular project was directly applicable to the class. We first read an article about the situation of Immokalee workers in Florida. This was followed by a sequence of mathematical questions in which we had to use our own prior mathematical knowledge to answer questions about the workers' wages and current job situation. The questions were open ended and required us to develop our own analysis of the data in the article. This was something that was required of us on a daily basis. At times I remember feeling somewhat frustrated with the in-depth analysis that was required of us, especially the constant mathematical derivations that we were asked to develop to answer the questions. Often we were asked to develop our own methods of answering mathematical questions. The frustration that I felt was mainly because I did not possess the confidence to know that I could answer the questions. In many of those cases I remember complaining to Mr. Rico about the level of difficulty, to which he would tell us that we could answer the questions and would follow with questions that would help guide our understanding.

Following the mathematical analysis that we were asked to make were in-depth social questions that were applicable on a global level. For example, on the project "Tomato Pickers Take on the Growers," there were questions such as *what is exploitation?* and *do you believe that the workers are being exploited?* These in-depth social analyses, which we had to construct and justify using the mathematical numbers we computed, helped me to develop a sense for social justice. In particular this project was personally applicable because most of the workers on those farms are of the same ethnic background as me. Further, many of the workers in the article felt helpless since they were not legal workers, which was the situation for many of the people in the community that I lived in. The sense of helplessness is one that I saw in my everyday life. In many ways the questions and the projects not only opened our eyes to the social injustices in the world, but also developed my ability to use the same type of analysis when evaluating other issues that were not dealt within the confines of the class. In particular it allowed us to be able to justify our opinions through the power of numbers, created in our mathematical analysis.

After we developed our answers, we shared our views with the class. Our class was very different than many other classes in that we had been with the same classmates for many years. I, for example, knew most of the students since the first grade. This facilitated our openness in fully expressing how we felt about issues such as wealth distribution, SAT scores, the situation with the Immokalee workers, and so forth. I foresee this as a challenge for teachers to deal with in classes in which the children are only with their fellow classmates for a limited amount of time. Mr. Rico, I believe, also facilitated our comfort level with one another by having us often work together in groups and having us talk among ourselves before we gathered as a class.

During class discussions, I remember the class often challenging some of the analysis we made. When the discussion was coming to an end, some students would ask Mr. Rico his perspective on the same questions he posed, and further questioned his views. Although I have mixed feelings about Mr. Rico expressing his views, I do appreciate his input, though at times I do feel that it created a bias in our own feelings about an issue. Therefore, I perhaps would advise that he not express his own perspective on the issues.

My feelings toward the manner in which we were learning math changed throughout the years. When first presented with this style of teaching, I was very accepting of the manner in which we were learning math. Later in the course, my attitude toward it changed to distrust and, to a small extent, rebellion. What prompted this attitude were different factors. I remember having a large concern and not feeling confident in being able to perform well in the required state testing that would be used by high schools in determining where one would attend. My concerns were personal and were also furthered by other teachers around me who expressed concerned about the manner and subjects that were being taught in Mr. Rico's classroom. Mr. Rico often assured us that we would perform well on the exams. Although to a great extent this was true (the performance of most in the classroom was adequate), to this date I believe his style of teaching could spend more time on developing our mathematical skills, while simultaneously still emphasizing and fostering the sense of social justice.

Reflecting back on the lessons learned in those two years, I must say that the class sparked in me the desire to make change. This feeling only grew through my own personal experiences outside of the classroom and down the line. What the class gave me was the ability to not only recognize social issues, but I also believe it harvested an attitude which does not allow me to feel helpless. In particular I often reflect back on the video we watched about the Brown Berets and the East L.A. student blowouts, a video in which students at predominantly Latino schools walked out in protest of the bad school conditions they were subjected to. Seeing other Latino students creating change in that video helped me develop a sense of power and helped me truly believe that I too can make a difference. In addition, other projects and videos helped me to fully develop a sense of power. Although some projects did particularly pertain to my own ethnic group and socioeconomic status, I believe that there are other projects which we used that could help other students outside of our classroom develop the sense of social justice that I was able to develop. For example the project on wealth distribution is one that I believe would affect anyone in a manner in which it would harvest a sense of creating equality, because it allows one to see the great disparities that exist in the world and the living conditions that people are subjected to. Although some issues may affect some students more than others, this is the case with most issues. Perhaps the questions that students are prompted with could be altered in order to allow the students to see the social issues at hand.

The lesson that I learned in those two years will remain with me forever.

Adrián Calderón

Over the past few years I have come to realize that many people are skeptical whenever there is a new idea, such as really using education in the world. Mathematics is usually taught through tedious repetitiveness and examples. This leads to many students having a faint understanding of mathematical properties and a lack of ability for real world applications from the math that has been drilled into their heads. But mathematics has always shaped our world and how we interact with it. It helps us understand history, literature, sociology, and many more aspects of our civilization. The youth of the nation must realize that they can understand and shape the world around them with the tools of mathematics.

All through school, I was taught a certain way: to complete problems 1 through 100 and then for homework continue through 500. I was forced to follow this mode, and it created a lack of interest in mathematics and real world application. And I was like many when something new is introduced—skeptical. There were many things to be skeptical about when the tall strange man came into my classroom partway through seventh grade: his character and his open-mindedness. The manner in which he communicated and the topics that he brought up were all things that I did not expect.

In my experience there are three types of teachers: those who dictate their lessons, those who attempt to be your best friend, and a balance of the two. My first impression was that Mr. Rico was just another teacher who would try to be my friend. It wasn't until later that I realized the influence that the class had on my life and how I see the world. Whether it was through the irregular textbook or conversations that we had outside of class, he was always challenging and teaching me, not by example, but by raising questions that forced me to create my own questions. The skills I learned during class, of mathematical reasoning and real world application, raised an awareness of the world around me and shaped my political consciousness.

With realization and consciousness came anger, frustration, and the feeling of being deceived. The transformation to a conscious person came slowly at first. I began to question all of the construction that was taking place in my neighborhood, the increasing property value of the surrounding area, and finally the property tax increase that increased rent in the area. Why was this happening?

This class instilled a sense of agency, a belief in myself that as an individual I can make a difference in my neighborhood and the world. We did a simulation in class of world wealth and distributed cookies to each group according to the estimated wealth of each continent. We found the population and wealth ratios using mathematics and eventually ate the cookies. I left class that day very frustrated because I didn't get as many cookies as I would have liked, but I was really frustrated by the inequity of wealth in the world. At the same time I became more conscious of the financial situation of my friends and their families.

My transition to high school was difficult: It was back to the old textbook method and tedious drills. There wasn't enough time for any critical thinking or application. My interest in mathematics decreased and my frustration grew. There was no longer room for discussion in math class, only in classes like history or literature. I needed another outlet, and it came through community service as I began to become more concerned with and involved in my community. The sense of agency instilled in me by my middle school math classes was still there. I wanted to spread pride and the concept that mathematics lets you read the world. Using the lessons from the math projects we did, I showed others how to question and how math plays an intrinsic role in the process of changing your neighborhood.

Throughout high school, I presented at math education conferences. The more I participated, the more I realized the effects of my seventh and eighth grade math class. The picture was becoming clearer, especially when I tried to develop political consciousness, a sense of agency, and a positive cultural identity for the younger children in my neighborhood.

Now with college experience, I can truly appreciate the value of that math class. Everything in college is about applying it to the real world so the transition wasn't as harsh like moving to high school. In retrospect, the period when I learned to read and write the world with mathematics was the only time I had an interest in mathematics. It was also the time when I chose to serve my community and overall was a great experience. I learned that I am a part of the solution to justice, and I will always be. This is an important concept that all children should know and understand. I gained political consciousness at an early age and a belief that I can make a difference, and grew proud of my cultural identity. With all that, I also gained a friendship that continues outside of classrooms and conferences.

Grisel Murillo

> Student: Mr. Rico! What's the answer to number four? What would a tomato picker's salary be?
>
> Mr. Rico: (to the whole classroom) Given the answers to the last three problems, how can you figure out number four? What ways do you think this problem can be solved? Just throw some ideas around and I'll start writing them on the board....

This type of dialogue is one that is extremely familiar to those of us who were students in Mr. Rico's seventh and eighth grade mathematics class. Although this exact exchange didn't really happen, it's close enough to embody the way Mr. Rico taught and interacted with us. I use it to show the way he listened to us and was perceptive to our needs, the way he made us connect to math by not giving us straight answers and letting us figure things out for ourselves, the way he allowed us to teach each other, the way he helped us look at problems differently, and most importantly, the way he used topics that were of relevance to our lives. All of this rolled into one classroom proved to make it a very dynamic and different one than any other class I had witnessed before or since in the Chicago Public School system. This huge change of pace is probably what also helped me become one of Mr. Rico's most rebellious (and probably most annoying) students.

In middle school I was a very vocal and opinionated 12- and 13-year-old, and if I felt something wasn't being done right, I made sure I let it be known. And that's exactly what I did in Mr. Rico's class. At the time I greatly disliked the way we were being taught because I didn't feel it prepared us for the Iowa tests (standardized tests) that we needed to do well on in order to pass to the next grade level. The way we were learning math was through real life issues, and although I didn't mind that aspect of the teaching so much, I did mind the fact that we weren't doing the same type of math the other classes were doing in our grade level. I felt we were behind, and what's more, I already hated math. I don't think I grew to really appreciate that math class until I didn't have it anymore and until it sunk in that I did exceptionally well in the math portion of my seventh and eighth grade Iowa tests. As a current sophomore in college reflecting on the class, I'm able to see how the skills I learned at such a young age have had a hand in molding the person I am today.

What I feel I took the most out of my seventh and eighth grade math class was surprisingly not the math (although as I mentioned earlier I did very well in the subject). I learned and took the most out of the relevant real-life issues Mr. Rico used to teach us about numbers. Or was it that he used *numbers* to open us up to real problems going on around us?

Regardless of which he used to teach with, we were able to learn about both effectively. The way we studied issues facing the poor and people of color in our math made me think deeply about issues I had only superficially thought of before. I mean, I had those issues staring me right in the face everywhere I looked in my community, but until that point I had only seen them as realities that everyone had to deal with and didn't question *why* those realities existed to begin with. These deep reflections really allowed me to form opinions on issues having to do with injustices, stereotypes, racism, and prejudice at an early age, an age when I believe it is crucial for young people to develop a sense of awareness of our world and the role we play in it.

One of the most important things I learned in the class was how to open my eyes and really take note of everything going on around me and question it, everything from small injustices occurring in Morningside (the neighborhood most of us lived in) to the magnified ones occurring in our world as a whole. To teach us about those things, Mr. Rico, of course, usually had to incorporate some of his own views about the topics discussed in class. I personally believe that this was a good idea, or it worked in our classroom at least. It was a good idea to tell us what side he was taking on the issues at hand because that challenged us to try and prove the teacher wrong, which we often did, which in turn brought up many thought-provoking discussions in the classroom. Although he gave us his views, I wasn't forced to look at things in a certain *one-sided* way—instead I was challenged to question the world and everything going on around me, which let *me find out for myself* if injustices really were present or not.

Through his math projects on real world topics, I built up a stronger critical eye for socially unjust and discriminatory issues that presented, and *still* present, themselves to me. Not only that, but I also gained confidence and faith in myself by realizing that there is always something you can do to try and change a situation if you deem it unjust. I won't deny how many times the topics we discussed in class made me feel helpless as a young Latina who had to face the truths of our society every time I stepped out of the classroom. But the fact that we watched films in class of people like the Brown Berets (*young Latinos*) standing up for their beliefs and making long-lasting changes during the 1960s, made young Latinos such as ourselves see that change, and change by us, was possible. That change was possible, and we could make it happen, even if we were young, even if we were Latino, even if we didn't have all the financial power. Mr. Rico encouraged us to attend protests too. I remember being a middle school kid and going to downtown Chicago to protest against development schemes that threatened to gentrify the neighborhood I lived in. Just attending and showing my support made me feel as if my voice was heard and showed us that despite our age, we could still make an impact in our world. This in itself allowed me to see first-hand that I wasn't as helpless as I felt I was.

It is because of this and the surroundings I grew up in that I am now striving for a profession that will allow me to give others the justice and resources they need to live a better life. Right now I'm working toward obtaining an A.B. in History and Hispanic Studies at Brown University, and a Master's in Teaching after that. Yes, I want to be a teacher! I feel that there is a dire need for more well-qualified, truly caring and progressive teachers in the public school system. I want to teach either in the neighborhood I grew up in or another urban setting where I can influence students coming from disenfranchised, low socioeconomic backgrounds. To me, teaching is one of the most important professions out there because I know from experience how much impact a teacher can make on the lives of his or her students and how much a teacher can support his or her students to gain the power and the strength to see that *anyone* —regardless of race, gender, and economic background—can make a positive long-lasting change in our society.

It might sound sensationalistic to say that I owe the person I have become to my seventh and eighth grade math class, so that is not the case. But I *can* say that many of the critical thinking skills and reasoning tools I acquired through this class developed over my high school years and have helped make me who I am today. I can definitely say that the class helped me *begin* thinking deeper about the issues present in my community and the world as a whole, and this in turn has influenced me to get a great education so that I can one day change—or begin to change—those unjust situations occurring in my community and in the world.

[The rest of Grisel's contribution is her advice for teachers and teacher education.]

For teachers to allow their students to experience *some* of the things I experienced in this class, I would suggest they set up a trust system in the classroom. By this I mean that the teacher should try and make the students feel as comfortable as possible during class time. The teacher can do this by telling the students some personal stories about some issues they will be discussing in class. For example, I remember Mr. Rico telling us about the different ways he stood up against injustices when he was a teenager like us. He talked about the different issues that faced him and the ways he dealt with them. This way of opening up to us helped facilitate discussions on topics of injustice, racism, and prejudice in the classroom because it showed us that it was okay to discuss these usually taboo topics in his class. I don't remember *ever* holding anything back from Mr. Rico; I always spoke my mind no matter how crude and offensive my comments might have been deemed by people outside the classroom. I knew he wasn't there to judge me as a person, he was only trying to learn from us and trying to get us (the students) to learn from each other. For this type of teaching to have an impact on students, the teacher must be able to show them that they will not be judged and that the class must be taken seriously because the topics discussed are serious and important.

I honestly believe that this curriculum and way of teaching mathematics can work for anyone. True, each class is different, and each teacher teaches differently. Some might point out that the reason our class took so much out of this method of teaching was because we were all students of color and whether or not we wanted to, the issues of prejudice, injustice, and racism presented to us were already much a part of our lives. Although I can see some truth in this reasoning, just because you have dealt with an important issue firsthand does not mean that you are the only one who cares and should find out more about it. It is equally important for the financially upper-class students as for the financially lower-class students to learn about the unfairness of the world wealth distribution and possible reasons as to why it is distributed the way it is (one of the projects we did covered this topic). It makes no sense to only have the people on the bad end of the deal understand the injustices present in issues of wealth distribution.

It will probably take a little longer to get students who are not usually exposed to injustices to open up about them in the classroom because they might not feel as strongly about those issues as someone who has been exposed to them. But I can almost guarantee that after doing some of the projects our class did that they would undoubtedly have to think about them profusely. I feel that just informing them about these issues would be enough, whether or not they decided to ignore or do something about them in the future. I personally believe that in the long run, this type of class can work in any type of setting.

Lizandra Nevárez

When you watch the news to catch up on current events and are slapped in the face with the reality that immigrants at the border are being hunted, that children are not given the opportunity for higher education, that people are being persecuted for their religious beliefs, or that an entire country suffers in the dilemma of poverty, infection, and malnutrition, you cannot help but wonder when it will change. Many will take it upon themselves to ask, "what can I do?" That humanity in us allows us to look beyond our well-being on to others—the passion to make change, the desire to fight for others and ourselves, for social change. How do we rid ourselves of prejudice, racism … intolerance? In a larger perspective, how do we rid the world of injustice?

One finds this need to resist and challenge inequity from within; it is not something you can feign. In many cases, family embraces social justice in one's upbringing, but as we grow so do the questions about the world around us and we look elsewhere for answers. Learning institutions have been the perfect place to persuade young minds into thinking a certain way or another. By telling incomplete stories, teaching geography with disproportionate maps of the world, using strictly computational mathematics, and teaching conservative literature, minds are not allowed to think beyond standard boundaries. Social justice is not part of the curriculum; therefore, injustice is rarely a topic discussed.

I feel very fortunate to have been part of a class where I was not lectured to; instead I was given the freedom to look at the bigger picture and question what was told to me. I was able to express my opinions freely. I asked questions about the work and often answered them myself through projects that allowed me to see the answers in the numbers. The numbers spoke for themselves, and this sometimes provoked questions. I often thought about ways to change the results that I saw, because I did not want to believe such injustices occurred, but in the end there was nothing I could do immediately to change the reality that the numbers gave me, although we could always maybe do something in the future.

We worked on projects that pushed us to think about real world issues, and although the realization of just how "real" these issues were hit me hard, I learned to think about cause and effect. For example, once I knew that there was an issue of injustice of any type, I thought about what caused it and who it affected. One of the most difficult things was thinking about the issues in my community and realizing that I was part of these issues. I considered the possibility of my being part of the statistics of Latina high school dropouts, or teenage pregnancy, or as in many cases, both! I felt like I could look beyond the walls of my neighborhood. For the first time I was actually looking at the big picture.

This is very particular to my case. Maybe the political fire was already in me, but the class allowed me to feel like it was okay to question the status quo and find ways to support my arguments. I am part of a family who has lived in the United States as immigrants, lived in Mexico in poverty, and was molded by single women. Being in a class where my voice counted gave me confidence—it gave me strength.

Although everyone in our class had different opinions, no one was ever wrong, and their opinions were respected. That is what made this class so different and empowering in a very different way. Everyone was free to speak for what they believed in, as long as they supported their opinion.

The things that I learned in this class will be with me for the rest of life. Although others may not have been affected in the same way that I was with this form of teaching, they were given the opportunity to explore their sense of justice. I know that this class itself did not make me a strong person, or one who fights for justice. That was already deep within me, but it made me stronger and helped me develop ways to fight for what I believe in. This "fight," or as my mom says in Spanish "*lucha*," is what my life is about, it is what makes me who I am.

CHAPTER 8

"The Real World As We Have Seen It"
Parents' Voices on Social Justice Mathematics

> And for me, life is political. To say you have nothing to eat, to say you have no money to pay for this, it's all political, so then why not learn it this way? *(Vanessa Arroyo, November 2003, mother of Tita, a student in my 7th-grade 2002–2003 mathematics class)*

While I taught at Rivera, I knew little about what parents really thought of my mathematics class. I was aware that they were generally supportive, and I never received any complaints about my teaching, but I certainly did not know specifics. However, all that changed when the acting principal forcibly removed me at the end of the first semester in January 2003. That precipitated a struggle, including many of my students' parents, to reinstate my position. And that led me to ask about the parents who backed my curriculum: Why do these Latino/a parents support teaching and learning mathematics for social justice? In this chapter, I explore what some of my students' parents thought about a curriculum and pedagogy oriented toward social justice.

Researchers know little about how parents in general, let alone Latino/a parents in particular, think about social justice mathematics curriculum. Although much has been written about "parent involvement" in education, this is an entirely different matter. Graue and Smith (1996) point out,

"In particular, we do not know much about how parents perceive their children's mathematics instruction, in either traditional or reformed contexts" (p. 396). We know even less in social justice contexts. The larger point is that we know very little about parents' perceptions of their children's mathematics education in any context. We do know, however, contrary to some deficit mythologies, that parents of color generally value education highly and support their children's mathematics education (Civil, Andrade, & González, 2002; Civil, Bernier, & Quintos, 2003; Guberman, 2004; Martin, 2000, 2004; Ortiz-Franco & Flores, 2001). These studies point out that parents of color are invested and involved in their children's mathematics education. However, little research documents what parents of color (indeed, any parents) think specifically about social justice pedagogy. Martin's (2000, 2004) work documented that the African American parents he interviewed understood their experiences in a sociopolitical (specifically racialized) context and saw the relationship of their own mathematics education to their lives, but it did not explain how they would feel if their own children were in classrooms where they learned mathematics to analyze social inequality and understand issues of justice.

In this chapter, I extend the ideas of reading and writing the world as a theoretical perspective to frame parents' views on social justice curriculum. I wanted to understand how their interpretations of their own lives influenced their views about education and their children's mathematics class. I asked their children to read their own world with mathematics, and I wanted to know their parents' views of that. I also wanted to know how those views about their children's mathematics education related to their own understandings of life and education as parents, adults, Latinos/as, and members of a marginalized community. Finally, I wanted to know how their reading of the world influenced them to take action and become involved in supporting social justice mathematics curriculum—that is, writing the world.

The data in this chapter are primarily from 10 open-ended, audiotaped, and transcribed interviews with parents in their homes (8) or my university office (2). I conducted the interviews either in English or Spanish with translation help (see Appendix 2). I also regularly communicated via e-mail, phone, and in person with several of the parents after I was dismissed, so I had multiple opportunities to probe further particular issues and get to know people better. Additional data are the actions that parents took with respect to my teaching, the school, and my removal, as well as what they said about their children's response to my class. I collected these latter data from observations and from what the parents said about their children's actions. I selected the parents because they supported my teaching in some way (e.g., speaking out at the special Local School Councils [LSC] meeting about my situation). Thus, this research was not to see who did or did not support social justice curricula, but rather to understand the reasons of those who did.

I realize that parents may not have wanted to be totally open in the interviews for several reasons. First, they may have censored their responses because they did not want to offend me. Second, the explicitly political character of my curriculum had the potential to make some people uncomfortable. A third reason was my status as a white, male professional, and a fourth reason was that I was an "authority figure" in a position of relative power with respect to parents, although at the time of the interviews, I was not teaching. However, these particular parents were not reluctant to voice opposition to school policies with which they disagreed (e.g., my termination), nor were they hesitant to criticize forcefully an administrator in public (as I explain below). This willingness to critique openly "authority" figures at least suggests the possibility that they would express any disagreements or discomfort with my teaching. I also had relationships with most of them that I believe were fairly open, but I have no way of knowing how forthright with me the parents really were.

Parents Read the World

When the acting principal was appointed at Rivera in September 2002, I met her and explained my curriculum, pedagogy, and the real-world projects, but it became apparent later that she had not really understood. In January 2003, as the Iraq War was approaching, the Chicago Teachers Union passed a resolution essentially endorsing a major anti-war rally in Washington, DC. I wrote a letter the next day to the parents in my class inviting them and their families to attend a local anti-war rally. The letter emphasized (twice) that it was personal, not school, business. I put the letter on the back of a flyer advertising the rally, told students briefly about it in class, and put the letters on a table for students to take if they wanted. Parents were generally familiar with my political views by this time as we had done the B-2 Bomber project (chapter 1), another project about diminishing public opinion for the war, the world wealth simulation, and the racism in mortgages project. I had also given students materials about Bush's proposed tax cuts, the impact of sanctions against Iraq, and other issues, and I always urged students to discuss what we were studying with their families.

The acting principal saw one of the letters, called me in, and told me I violated a policy by sending something home without permission. I apologized for breaking the rule, but it was clear from then on that she would remove me from the school, which she did three weeks later at the end of the semester.

When her intention became clear, I asked a couple former students and parents to write letters to convince her to change her mind. They wrote letters, but she refused to change her mind, so I requested an LSC meeting. The LSC planned a special meeting about my situation and informed the school's parents that there would be a meeting about a "seventh-grade mathematics classroom."

Over 150 people showed up, including 25 of my then-current and former students and dozens of their parents. A former student from my two-year class started the meeting by reading a collective letter written by her class. For the next three hours, students, parents, and community members collectively railed against the acting principal to reverse her decision and reinstate me, and the LSC voted unanimously for her to do so, but she refused. Twenty-three parents and a former student then went to Chicago Public School (CPS) headquarters the next day to push a high-ranking official to take action. He listened but told them he could not reinstate me nor remove her. The struggle to reinstate me turned into a successful five-month battle to remove the acting principal, which was appropriate in my view, as she had done much to alienate and antagonize others at Rivera. While my situation may have been a catalyst to galvanize people into action, it was more important that the school community choose a principal who met their needs. After they selected a new principal, I returned to Rivera the next spring to provide professional development to the primary-grade teachers in a new mathematics program.[1]

As I listened at the LSC meeting, I realized that I really did not know what motivated the parents who appeared so supportive of a social justice curriculum. No one at the meeting took the acting principal's side that I should be terminated. The explicitly political nature of my teaching—for example, sending home the anti-war flyer and having students use mathematics to investigate racism and neighborhood gentrification—surfaced and was openly discussed. There were also other issues, such as my qualifications, my history with the school, and student achievement. As I tried to make sense of the evening and later analyzed the interview and other data, certain themes emerged, which I now examine.

Parents' Voices on Social Justice Mathematics

Five connected and overlapping themes arose in my analysis, but I separate them for conceptual clarity: (1) oppression and resistance are dialectically related, and both are part of life; (2) mathematics is a central part of life—utilitarian and critical views; (3) education—including mathematics—should prepare students for life; (4) education should be specifically about politics; and (5) parents wanted their children to know more—not less—about the real world. I also acknowledge, as an outsider to the parents' community attempting to make sense of their world views through my own, that these are only my interpretations.

The synthesis of the themes is more significant than the individual themes themselves. My analysis suggests that the parents who supported teaching and learning mathematics for social justice did so because the curriculum (in the broad sense) aligned with their world view. My interpretation is that the parents saw mathematics, oppression and resistance, and politics as interconnected, integral parts of the real world. Furthermore, they all stated that education should prepare students for that unified reality. They essentially reframed the meaning and connection of *real world* and *mathematics*, starting from their understanding of the "real world as we have seen it," as one parent, Ms. Serrano, named it. Their perspectives on life, mathematics, and education were integrated and shaped by their own experiences as marginalized people. Thus, a (mathematics) education that helped prepare their children for the harsh realities they would have to face was of value to them.

Oppression and Resistance Are Dialectically Related, and Both Are Part of Life. "One of the things that I don't like is injustice. Never." This statement by Ms. Serrano succinctly captures what all of the parents expressed about justice and discrimination. All ten parents immigrated to the United States (eight from Mexico, one from Colombia, and one from Chile), and all struggled in various ways. All were working class when I interviewed them, although Ms. Candula, who cleaned houses in Chicago, described herself as middle class growing up in Mexico. Mr. Cárdenas attended divinity school in Mexico to be a priest, and at one time worked as a paralegal in Oaxaca, but in Chicago worked third shift in a hospital delivering supplies. Their lives varied, but all who worked were in manual, industrial, clerical, or service occupations. Mr. Montoya was a construction worker from a working-class family of 14 children, while neither Ms. Burgos nor Mr. Jibarra ever attended school in Mexico because their families were too poor to pay the transportation costs in the countryside to send them to school. Each parent narrated stories of discrimination she/he, or her/his children, faced, from minor slights to major injustices, but often put them into a larger social context. Mr. Montoya, who coached his son's baseball team, explained how their small neighborhood park had to support many teams of Mexican youth, while in better-off, white neighborhoods, there were larger parks and fewer children. Ms. Candula talked about how her husband faced job discrimination and related it to larger sociopolitical structures:

As my husband's been working there for a while, he learns these things. He's trying to become like a chef, but instead they'd rather hire white people to come in and take the higher end positions, and him who's already been working hundreds of hours. And they pay different wages. To them they pay $24 an hour, and to him they raise him a quarter an hour. My husband says that a lot of times they give him the responsibility of a chef. Everybody leaves, and he's in charge of everything, but when it comes to the money, they don't recognize that. I think it's the system in general—whether it be politically, socially, economically, or nationally—or worldwide.

Many of the parents discussed the necessity of standing up to, and defending themselves against, various injustices. Ms. Vargas was a factory worker who described her life to me:

My life has been all the same since I remember and always trying to defend ourselves. We were five, our sisters, and we always had to try to defend ourselves. And I live for that, I live defending myself.... This is why I say we need to learn to defend ourselves.

Ms. Burgos spoke about the discrimination she felt her children might undergo, and how and when they should be prepared for it:

When we go into the store, they think we are going to rob them. They wait on whites before us even though we've been there first ... these actions are pretty much the everyday things I see. It's important to talk to your children about this so that they do not grow up to be a victim, but they grow up able to defend themselves. For me, five years old is about the right time when you should start talking to your children about these things because they are themselves going to be dealing with these things, and they need to know.

She also talked about her brother who was in prison partially because he could not afford a lawyer and had to settle for a court-appointed, uninterested, and over-burdened public defender. Ms. Gómez told a poignant story about how her younger daughter was traumatized in a downtown bookstore by a white couple who accused her of "mistreating the books and throwing them all over." Her daughter broke down and sobbed and was affected for quite a while, "in a way that she will feel [as] if she's less than others."

For the parents, their reading of the world gave them an awareness of societal injustice that they knew their children would also confront. The parents' collective experiences reflected those of other Rivera parents. Having to deal with racism, language discrimination, discrimination against immigrants, and economic hardships was common to not only the 10 parents I interviewed, but to the whole Rivera community—as was the necessity to stand up to the various forms of oppression in life. Factory raids by *la migra* (the Immigration and Naturalization Service) looking for undocumented workers who traveled long distances in the early mornings in overcrowded, seatbelt-less vans to work at low wages in sweatshop-like conditions; racial profiling, discrimination, harassment, and prejudice in public spaces; unequal allocation of resources such as better parks, schools, and public transportation for whiter and wealthier communities; and a public education system that had consistently failed to graduate more than half of the Latino/a youth in Chicago who started school and that overall devalued students' language, culture, experiences, and communities—*all* were part of the common life experiences and consciousness of Rivera parents. In such a process in which oppressive conditions become a normal part of a community's existence, the necessity to maintain one's dignity and humanity and to resist becomes part of one's world view. This dialectical relationship between the various forms of injustice that people faced and the need to stand up to them was clearly expressed by the parents—and my interpretation was that this was integral to how they understood their lives.

Mathematics Is a Central Part of Life—Utilitarian and Critical Views. Parents also saw mathematics as very much part of life, in various ways, including for utilitarian purposes. Mr. Montoya spoke about the necessity for students to know about fractions in case they had to lay floor tile and do measurements. Ms. Candula explained that we needed to know mathematics for interest rates in case people wanted to buy a car and get a loan. Ms. Serrano said that "everything moves around mathematics in certain ways." Ms. Arroyo declared math was everywhere but added that we needed to know how to use it in life beyond just in school: "All of life is basically mathematics. It's best that they learn it in the best possible manner—not only do they need to know how to divide or add, but rather, how to incorporate it in their life."

Mr. Cárdenas, like these others, believed that mathematics was central in people's lives:

> I believe that mathematics is important because math is part of our life, perhaps the most important part of our life. There are

numbers when we wake up, there are numbers when we eat, there are numbers when we work, there are numbers wherever we go, there are numbers when we go to sleep, everywhere in life there are numbers.

However, he went further in his analysis beyond just a utilitarian view of mathematics. He continued:

The problem is that many times numbers are used and these numbers are misused. Then there are statistics, for example, they tell us what is the per capita income but no one ever sees this money. They tell us that there is justice in society because there are X numbers of Hispanic representatives in key positions, but in truth, we never see these people who represent us.

Several parents echoed his alternate view of the relationship of mathematics to life. In fact, the same parents who said that mathematics was an integral part of life in a utilitarian sense also did so in a critical sense. They read the world with mathematics to clarify the injustices that existed in society—exactly what I tried to do in mathematics class with their children. Ms. Candula remarked:

When you get to being forty years old, you don't really do four times four, but you sit down and you look at the statistics and look at the 75% you do have and the 25% you don't have, and that really helps you.... The other day in the news, they showed percentages of buying a car. I don't know if you saw it. To whites they gave a low interest rate, and to Latinos they tripled it. And that's what they say in the news, imagine what they don't say.

Mr. Montoya also used mathematics as an analytical tool to explain discriminatory lending practices. I was describing the "Mortgage Loans—Is Racism a Factor?" project that his son's class had completed. Before I could finish, he interjected by saying how different rates were charged to different races, and, by implication, how mathematics played a role in understanding the injustice of it. Ms. Candula also commented on that project and explained why it was beneficial for students to use mathematics to investigate whether racism was involved.

Ms. Candula: ... they know how to use the percentages, they look at the percentages and they know how to use it. I imagine that Anglos get 75% of the mortgages they applied for and the Blacks get 30%. They're numbers. They're

Gutstein: | important. It's information. In everything they give you percentages, and from percentages come numbers so when you look at the numbers that's where everything comes from. That's what you did with them. It could've been anything.

Gutstein: So why not just study about mortgages. There's lots of percentages there. Why study racism as well?

Ms. Candula: ... That's something you see. You can't hide it. The percentages [pause].

Gutstein: What is something you see?

Ms. Candula: Racism you can see, but they don't want to recognize it.

Gutstein: Who are they? Whites? The system? The students? Teachers?

Ms. Candula: From top to bottom and bottom to top.... You can see racism. It's there. But some people don't want to make it conscious, and they want to keep it [hidden]. But everyone can see it is there.

The implication here is that mathematics is a tool that makes hidden phenomena (e.g., racism) visible, even when those in power want them to remain concealed.

Finally, Ms. Gómez's family actually *did* some of the real-world projects along with their daughter, who was in my two-year class, something I did not know until I interviewed her years later. She explained:

I remember when I was first told by somebody else that they would have a new way of teaching math, I was a little bit, not reluctant, but, not even confused, but I was not ready to accept a change from the way that students were taught. But, as the time passed, and I saw Elena bringing all that kind of homework, I remember there were a couple of math problems that had a lot to do with real situations in life, that she had to figure out and that involved how there's—I don't know how to explain it—how justice is not everywhere. I got interested in what she was doing. And most of the times, when she brought those kinds of problems home and she was trying to figure out an answer, all the family got involved. We ended up all working on it.

That parents saw mathematics as central and important in life (and education) is neither surprising nor revealing. What may be somewhat surprising, at least from the mathematics education literature, is that they spontaneously, and in various ways, used mathematics to describe inequality and discrimination—or that they participated as a family in mathematically investigating injustice along with their child. Furthermore, the different ways these families viewed mathematics, like oppression and resistance, were part of a connected whole. They saw mathematics as a way to make sense of the world, whether it was in a utilitarian sense (e.g., making change, measuring tiles, computing interest rates) or in a critical sense, that is, reading the world with mathematics. Because their lives included dealing with and resisting oppression, mathematics, as a part of life, could be a useful tool in understanding their social realities. This is consistent with a philosophy of teaching and learning mathematics for social justice that suggests that mathematics should be learned meaningfully and related to real-life struggles against injustice.

Education—Including Mathematics—Should Prepare Students for Life. The experiences spoken of by the parents influenced their views on the purpose of education, both at home and in school. The idea that oppression and resistance were linked and part of life was connected to what parents articulated was the reason for education, including mathematics education. Their main position was that education should prepare students for life. However, no parent said they expected schools to provide this preparation. Rather, it was something they believed was important. They wanted specific things from school, including that their children do well (e.g., good grades), attend college, succeed economically, and be happy in their lives, though some parents differentiated between success in school and in life. But their views of education also showed that they wanted school to prepare students for life in various ways and that they were skeptical about school's capacity to do so. Mr. Cárdenas articulated this concern:

> I have had, for a long time, the worry with them about their grades, 10's in Mexico, A's here. And afterwards, they went to the store and didn't know how to count their change. Or they were afraid of buying something or lacked confidence in how to manage what they should know how to do. So I believe that it's true that in one sense, [school] subjects have to be only theoretical, but in another sense, they have to be involved in life.

The idea that education needed to prepare students for life was repeatedly and clearly expressed by most of the parents, but for different purposes. There were practical views, like Mr. Cárdenas' above quote, about using mathematics to go to the store and count change. But there were other aspects as well, including about developing one's identity and learning to view the world in multiple ways. Ms. Gómez expressed this and related it to mathematics education:

> But they also need to know about life, about what's going around. And if there's a way that the math could be applied to it, I don't see anything wrong with it. That, in certain ways, gives them self confidence, to express what they feel, something that might be hidden there, and they don't know it.... Because as I told [you], we are a different culture, we have different way of thinking. If there's a way that you could be helped to open up your mind and see that there are different ways of thinking, that could help you to find yourself.

All the parents wanted their children to succeed with the standard curriculum, learn what was required and what would help them get to high school or college. But they also wanted their children to have a deeper understanding of "their real world," as Ms. Serrano put it:

> Sometimes, you know, I ask my son Adalberto about your class, and I have talked to other parents about your class.... For me it's not only important that he learns to say what is 2+2 or 3+3, it's not really important. What is important in life is how they are going outside to their real world and how are they going to face the world, and struggle toward goals in the world. For us, this is important in our society, and our economic situation, and what is the real-world outside.

This concept of the "real-world outside" reverberated through a number of the parents' comments, though some focused more on this than others. Ms. Vargas was a single parent with three children at home, and she also helped raise two grandchildren. Besides her full-time work in a factory, she occasionally worked extra hours as a janitor. Their family continually struggled financially, but her children were successful in school, and the family was close. She was most concerned that her children grew up strong and independent, based on her analysis of her own life, and she wanted their education to support that goal. I taught both her son and daughter in different years.

Gutstein: When I taught your son and daughter, what did they say to you about the class?

Ms. Vargas: They didn't just learn math, but they learned other things in general, what she told me. And I did like it, I do like it, for them to learn different things, and that is very important in life.... I know that you taught them a lot of other stuff, and you even got yourself in trouble for passing out flyers. She talked to me about stuff that she goes to, as an activist, that even I think I would go do, and defend the rights of others.

Gutstein: And Julio [her son]?

Ms. Vargas: Julio also. He likes it. He talked to me about that problem that happened [my dismissal]. And I liked it. I do support them. I want them to learn, because for me that is important, for them to learn to defend themselves. Because here it is very important for you to learn to defend yourself in life. Here, with the people, because I've been through so many things with people and I would have liked to have been taught this in school.

Gutstein: Why do you think I was teaching them to defend themselves?

Ms. Vargas: It's not just about telling them what they have to think or what they have to do.... It is about, you told them about what was happening, what was going on. "This is what we can do, and this is what I do," that's what they [her children] would say you told them. I don't think that you directly told them to do this. I feel that you were teaching them about these things because they would come and tell me about protests [e.g., against community gentrification] and about things they were gonna go to and they were gonna be involved in. And specifically, I would see that she [her daughter] would raise her head up high and that she liked these things. And I personally liked it a lot, too.

These parents valued education for multiple reasons: Education should contribute to practical life, identity development, and political awareness. Because their own lives required them to have certain stances and perspectives toward the world, they wanted, though did not expect, an education that would prepare their children for similar outlooks. All wanted education to prepare their children for the "real world." However, they had different views about which aspects of real life were most important. In particular, some put more emphasis on education for political consciousness (e.g., Ms. Vargas wanting her children to learn in school about demonstrations). I turn to that theme next.

Education Should Be Specifically About Politics. This theme was expressed by only six of the ten parents, manifesting some of the differences in how parents saw the relationship between education and politics. However, although the other four did not specifically express the importance of this interconnection, they in no way suggested that political life should be (or was) disconnected from education. The six who stated that education should directly relate to politics said the relationship was broader than just having to do with mathematics. Some explained their political views as connected to religious convictions, and some to other life experiences. Ms. Arroyo was one of the most overtly political in the connections she described between life and education. I explained my purpose for teaching mathematics for social justice and asked her opinion. She replied:

> I am in total agreement because I believe that you have to open their eyes that each one of them has a history. They need to know what their race is, to know what is their history, not only of the country in which they live, but rather of the world in general. And how this country has wanted to show that it is the world. I believe that one needs to make children socially conscious from when they are little so that when they are big, they are not racists nor ignoramuses.

Mr. Cárdenas' response to this question was similar:

> I believe that it's fundamental not only in mathematics, but also in any subject. One should do the same for two reasons: in speaking of the world, because this [the lack of critical education] has permitted this country to exploit and to benefit from the exploitation it exercises on the rest of the world. But at the same time, inside the country, it has served to create the illusion and the deception that the problems are over there, and that those problems do not exist here. The poverty is in Africa, but if we go to Appalachia, we see that the poverty is here, then the poverty is not [only] in Africa, the poverty is not [only] in Latin America. Not only there, there is poverty as a consequence of exploitation, on the one hand, that this country and the global powers have created with the collaboration of the corruption and incompetence of the local governments over there, but the same thing is here. There's poverty, there's violence, there's false reality, there are illusions.

Ms. Serrano echoed these sentiments as well. My question was why should her children learn about racism and discrimination while they were at school. Her response was:

> All of us should learn, and all of us should fight against these injustices—against racism. We should teach and prepare the students what is it we want, and who are we, and why should we fight in life. I think that yes, it is important that our children learn about this above everything else.

Ms. Candula, Ms. Vargas, and Ms. Burgos said similar things about how education should provide children with an understanding of discrimination so that "they grow up able to defend themselves."

Although all the parents felt that education should prepare students for life, these six were explicit that life was about politics, from the individual to the global level. They said that they wanted (but did not expect) school to get children ready for specific battles against racism, exploitation, and other forms of discrimination. In addition, they wanted (but again did not expect) schools to create the opportunities for children to know who they were as people, and even more, that they understand the reasons behind the specific injustices that they faced. Ms. Arroyo advocated that children needed to be made "socially conscious from when they are little" and Ms. Serrano argued that children should know "why should we fight in life;" I believe that these statements were calls to teachers to contribute and play a role as agents of social change (hooks, 1994).

Parents Wanted Their Children to Know More—Not Less—About the Real World. The parents clearly had reasons to support social justice mathematics curriculum, but I also wanted to know if they had concerns. I asked parents if they believed there were negative aspects to this form of teaching. Also, a few Rivera teachers questioned whether I "propagandized" students, and I specifically wanted to investigate parents' views about that. Near the end of our interview, I asked Ms. Vargas about negative aspects, including the possibility of propaganda or "brainwashing." She said there were no negative aspects, and that if she were to allow herself to be manipulated, that was her problem. I persisted, though.

Gutstein: Okay, but these are boys and girls, right? I have the power in class because I'm the teacher. Isn't it possible to brainwash them?

Ms. Vargas: No, because I think they're mature enough, and I have a lot of faith in them and a lot of trust that they're not going to let themselves be brainwashed or influenced in this way.

Gutstein: Okay. Other possible negative aspects of this kind of teaching?

Ms. Vargas: I personally don't think anything negative in this. I see that—they tell me that they were comfortable in your class, that they learned.

Gutstein: Suppose another parent said this kind of teaching is too political. What would you say?

Ms. Vargas: … I don't think this way.… I think that everything that they can learn that is to their favor is good. It could be that I'm possibly thinking this way because I wish that with my life I could do many things.

Other parents responded in similar ways. Ms. Serrano's response about overly influencing students was, "No, I don't think so. I think that a person who is thinking this, it is because they don't have quite the intelligence or imagination for what we really want for our children." Of all the parents, I knew Ms. Gómez the best because her daughter was in my two-year class, her English was quite strong, and she was a parent aide at Rivera. Through the years, we talked a lot because we ate lunch at the same time. I had been to her house and knew her other family members. She was extremely thoughtful and open, and her interview was by far the longest. She responded:

> I didn't ever focus it like that. Even though I've heard this about you [from a couple of teachers]. But, as I am telling you, I never thought about this like that. I keep saying the same, I always thought that knowing about what the problems are here, and I mean here in the country, with our community, or with our race, that's the only way they could open up their hearts, they could open up their minds, they could think about what needs to be done. Because we are here. We are going to remain here, we as Hispanics. And I don't mean we as individuals, but as a community. So something needs to be done.

Mr. Cárdenas' response to the question was: "It is absurd to think that the result of a method whose objective is to teach students to question reality would have precisely the contrary result, to not question." And Ms. Arroyo said:

> No, if we [the parents], who spend so much time with them, can't do it [influence them], how could you do it? They are going to let themselves be influenced by those who they want to. If it were not

like this, how can one explain that they follow trends that make themselves ugly or put themselves in danger?

It is also relevant that Morningside children often had adult responsibilities, such as childcare, house cleaning, laundry, work outside the home, and other tasks. It was not unusual for the adults in the community to have worked as children in Mexico, especially among those who were not wealthy and for whom economic survival was a collective, family responsibility (Valdés, 1996). This was the case for Ms. Burgos and Mr. Jibarra who never attended school and who started working at age five but was also true for others even if they went to school.

Thus, there were a number of reasons why parents seem to think "brainwashing" was a nonissue with respect to their children. They believed that their children had a certain amount of agency and would only allow themselves to be influenced if they chose to be. This was somewhat contradictory because some of the parents also spoke of children not always making wise choices, but for the most part, parents expressed confidence in their children. Parents also believed that they had enough information about the class and my curriculum to be satisfied that their children were not being led astray. Furthermore, contrary to what some may suggest about shielding children from the harsh realities of life, these parents felt it appropriate that their children be aware of, and more deeply understand, the real world. The parents knew that their children had to deal with oppression and discrimination, and it did not seem to disturb them that their children confronted those concepts within the classroom. In fact, it may be for precisely this reason that they wanted their children to know *more*, not *less* about real-world injustices. Several stated that they wanted their children to learn to defend themselves against oppression—and most said that they themselves prepared their children this way. It is reasonable to infer that these parents would then see as allies those teachers who shared that value with them. As Ladson-Billings (1994) said about African American students, but it applies to Latinos/as as well, "Parents, teachers, and neighbors need to help arm African American children with the knowledge, skills, and attitude needed to struggle successfully against oppression" (p. 139). Brainwashing had been raised, not by parents, but by a few middle-class teachers and the acting administrator whose experiences did not reflect those of the community. For the parents, it was important that their children received the opportunity to study real-world issues of racism and other forms of discrimination and perhaps grow stronger.

Conclusion

My analysis of parents' views on social justice mathematics curriculum and pedagogy reveals five interlocking themes: (1) oppression and resistance are dialectically related, and both are part of life; (2) mathematics is a central part of life—utilitarian and critical views; (3) education—including mathematics—should prepare students for life; (4) education should be specifically about politics; and (5) parents wanted their children to know more—not less—about the real world. The first theme suggests that the parents themselves experienced injustices, knew their communities lived with it, and were aware their children would have to deal with it, or were already dealing with it, in their lives. Standing up and defending themselves and their rights was important to these families, although none of the parents was overtly active politically and some even defined themselves as passive. Mr. Montoya referred to Mexicans as "timid" in his interview and acknowledged that he neither spoke out often nor planned to speak out when he came to the LSC meeting about my removal. Yet he was so angered by the acting principal's intransigence in the face of what he and many others felt was an injustice that he did speak out, and forcefully.

Theme two implies that parents saw mathematics as an integral part of life and that they saw the connections of mathematics to life in both utilitarian and critical ways. "Everywhere in life there are numbers," as Mr. Cárdenas said, but they also read the world with mathematics. The third theme reveals that the parents felt education should prepare their children for the real world. Because the real world included for them a consciousness of oppression and the necessity to resist it, as well the connection of mathematics to that world, it made sense that a mathematics curriculum that brought these things together would serve their children well. In other words, the sense of connectedness between mathematics and life, on the one hand, and between life and standing up to injustice, on the other, meant that a curriculum in which mathematics, life, politics, and social justice all came together—and that could possibly help prepare their children for the real travails of life—was not inconsistent with their orientation to the world. It *was* different from their expectations and experiences with school, both for themselves and their children—but it did not violate their beliefs about what school potentially could or even should do. Ms. Serrano's words capture the essence:

> You combine it all. Because we are accustomed to see that a math teacher focus only on math, and social studies only on social studies, and reading only reading, maybe, for her [the acting principal] and for many people, combining it all in only one class is

difficult. Maybe. But for me, no. Because the students were learning everything in general. The real world as we have seen it. The one the students are going to have to face. The day they leave high school or the university, this is what they are going to face. They're not going to face only specifically mathematics. They're not going to have to face only racism. They're going to face everything in general. And this is how they should live, how they should learn.

In a sense, the parents were placing themselves, their experiences, and their world views in the center of the educational process. They were expressing that, for them, life was connected—it included mathematics, injustice, and the need to learn how to stand up to it as well—the interrelated, inseparable "real world as we have seen it." They lived in an interconnected way and felt that their children would also.

Furthermore, what the parents did themselves and what they saw in their children support these themes. Ms. Serrano talked to other parents about my class and became an active organizer in the campaign to oust the temporary principal. Ms. Vargas talked about and supported her daughter who she saw get involved in the anti-gentrification struggles, go to protests, and "raise her head up high." When I was forced out by the temporary principal, Mr. Cárdenas sent me a personal letter stating his support and asking how he could help, and he also sent her a letter asking her to reinstate me. Ms. Gómez's family involved themselves in doing the real-world projects. Ms. Candula, Ms. Serrano, Ms. Burgos, Mr. Cárdenas, and Ms. Arroyo all went downtown to argue with a senior CPS official and protested my dismissal. In several ways, the parents' actions and how they analyzed their children's reactions showed concretely their support of teaching mathematics for social justice.

It is indeed ironic that several parents did not view themselves as activists, like Mr. Montoya or Ms. Burgos, whose own daughter predicted that she would never speak out at the LSC meeting. Yet when faced with what felt to them as a marked wrong, they not only spoke out, but some became much more active themselves. Ms. Burgos, whom I had known fairly well for six years as a quiet, calm woman, was livid at the LSC meeting and yelled forcefully at the acting principal—and continued to be active in the struggle to oust her from Rivera, to her daughter's surprise. Nor was she the only parent who became more involved in the school through this struggle. For these parents, speaking out *for* a social justice curriculum was a way of speaking out *against* injustice at the same time.

This raises the question of what exactly was it that parents were supporting. I wondered whether the support at the LSC meeting was for the curriculum (again, in the broad sense), against the perceived injustice of my dismissal, or simply for a teacher who cared about students. But distinguishing between these may be irrelevant because just as the parents perceived life as interconnected, perhaps they viewed people the same way. That is, when they looked at social justice curriculum coming from an involved teacher, they may not have compartmentalized a person, but rather saw a connected human being. Ms. Vargas captured this when she said, "For me personally that [the political aspect] interests me a lot. I think the humanity in you has a lot to do with it and is very important. But I think this other part [again, the political part] is also very important for me."

I always ended interviews by asking, "Do you have any questions for me?" About half of the interviewees did and all asked essentially the same question: What motivated me, a white outsider to the community, to do the things that I did? That is, they essentially turned around and asked me the exact question I had asked them: What is it in people's lives that brings them to make particular decisions? They allowed me to probe them about their lives, dig into their pasts, rationales, and motivations—but then they wanted to know the same about me. In that way, they renegotiated the power relationship between researcher and respondent to know better who I was, on a deeper level, just as I wanted to know who they were. They extended their reading of the world to include reading their child's mathematics teacher as well.

My goal was to understand why this particular set of parents supported a social justice curriculum. I believe that the reasons may be summarized by saying that they chose to stand up to the oppression and injustice they faced and they intended to ensure that their children could also. They viewed mathematics as an integral and important part of life, as was the struggle for justice, to which they all felt committed, albeit in different ways. Since (mathematics) education should prepare one for life, it followed that an education was meaningful if it helped prepare their children to be aware of, and respond to, the injustices that they would face as members of marginalized communities. Such schooling may be unusual, but it was in sync with their core values and worth standing up for.

This has important implications for proponents of social justice curriculum. While I make no claim to generalize from this small set of parents to how all Latino/a parents feel about social justice mathematics curriculum, there is a rich historical record of Mexicans and Chicanos/as within the United States fighting for educational justice (e.g., Acuña, 1996; Delgado Bernal, 1999, 2000; Donato, 1997; Getz, 1997; González, 1999; Gutiérrez, 2004; Ruiz & Racho, 1996; San Miguel, 1997). The views of the Rivera parents can be contextualized within the larger record of Latino/a history in the United States and the struggles against various forms of marginalization and discrimination faced by their communities. The reasons why the parents of my students supported this curriculum could well be similar to those of parents in other marginalized communities of color and/or working-class or low-income communities. At a minimum, more research is needed about the views of parents in schools in which teachers are using social justice curriculum. This is needed beyond Latino/a parents in an immigrant working-class Chicago community and beyond middle-school mathematics.

The other implication of this work is the untapped collaboration between teachers and parents, as well as students, in developing social justice curriculum. Scholars have long made the point that appropriate education for communities of color can only be devised with the genuine participation of adults from those communities (Delpit, 1988). But little has been written on the possibilities of specifically developing social justice curriculum in partnership with parents who have long experience dealing with oppression. Given the support of the Rivera families (both parents and students) for such a curriculum, it is plausible that teachers could work collaboratively with parents to design social justice curriculum for their children based on *generative themes* (Freire, 1970/1998), that is, key social contradictions defined by the community. How this is to be done, given the standardization of education and high-stakes accountability regimes (e.g., No Child Left Behind Act, 2001) is complicated. I return to this in the final chapter.

CHAPTER 9

Conclusion
Revisiting Mathematics Education for a Global Context

> ... all of us should learn and all of us should fight against these
> injustices—against racism. We should teach and prepare the
> students what is it we want, and who are we and why should we
> fight in life. *(Sonia Serrano, December 2003, mother of Adalberto, a
> student in my 7th-grade 2002–2003 mathematics class)*

In this concluding chapter, I discuss the implications of my work in three
areas: developing curriculum, educating teachers, and teaching mathematics. I then revisit mathematical literacy; situate my research in a larger, global context; and argue why teaching mathematics for social justice is
needed now, more than ever, given the current world situation.

Implications for Developing Curriculum

In chapter 5, I discuss the interrelationship of teaching mathematics for
social justice and Mathematics in Context (MiC). I argue that MiC can
potentially support social justice teaching because it encourages dispositions that are in sync with reading and writing the world. Furthermore,
students using MiC develop mathematical power, and they need that
mathematical sophistication and maturity to access advanced education
and understand mathematical issues embedded in complex phenomena
like racism and other injustices. However, MiC by itself will not advance

the causes of equity and justice. The curriculum, like others, could be taught in uncritical ways, benefiting those already in power in society and making them more efficient and effective in maintaining the unequal status quo. That is, MiC has no intrinsic value system for the common good—nor do any other mathematics curricula of which I am aware, reform or traditional.

I say this not to criticize MiC, but to think about what kind of partnerships need to be developed to maximize the social justice potential of a strong curriculum. I find MiC to be exemplary, both in its own right—it reaches the goals its creators set for it—but more importantly, as an aide in teaching students to develop sociopolitical consciousness and a sense of social agency. Social justice and mathematics educators could together develop an MiC-like curriculum for social justice. I am certainly not suggesting that one curriculum could be relevant for everyone, as Rivera students made clear (see chapter 5). But a curriculum that combined the best parts of MiC with a social justice focus (that could be adapted to the local level) would be a real contribution. However, more is needed. I propose an exploratory orientation toward building curriculum with three integrated components: what I call community knowledge, critical knowledge, and classical knowledge. These are not novel ideas, and I borrow heavily from other frameworks, but I believe how they interconnect in developing mathematics curricula has been undertheorized. The three components overlap but are distinct enough to consider separately first and then examine their interrelationship.

Community Knowledge

> We must keep the perspective that people are experts on their own lives ... they can be the only authentic chroniclers of their own experience. (Delpit, 1988, p. 297)

The basic orientation toward *community knowledge* is that "ordinary" people have and produce knowledge about their lives, experiences, and contexts. This perspective is an epistemological rupture with the idea that only individuals in universities and other professional institutions create knowledge to be used or learned by others. It privileges neither community knowledge nor that produced in academia or various professions. Freire (Freire & Macedo, 1987) pointed out that those with power always label as "nonintellectual" the thinking of those without power, but a Freirean pedagogy proclaims that those without power create viable, valuable knowledge. Freire (1994, pp. 46–49) recounted a story of a gathering with Chilean farmers who, in the middle of a lively discussion with him, suddenly silenced themselves and self-effacingly yielded to his "professional" knowledge. Freire challenged them to a game, he against them, in which each side took turns and scored a point when they stumped the other with an unanswerable question. Freire asked about arcane, academic philosophy, and the farmers asked about "contour curves, green fertilizer, and soil liming." After a good deal of mutual enjoyment and humor, the score was 10 to 10. The point was obvious—each had substantive knowledge lacked by the other.

Community knowledge is knowledge of farming practices, social relations, production, community life in all its complexity, and of perspectives and interpretations of the world. One's language(s) and culture(s) are also part of community knowledge. It is knowledge that resides in individuals who live in a particular community context and that teachers may not understand, unless they share the culture and experiences of the students. Freire's approach toward community knowledge is exemplified by the way he and a team of coworkers based in Geneva planned to collaborate with educators in newly independent Guinea-Bissau in the 1970s:

> As a team, we had talked in Geneva about the best way to see and hear, inquire and discuss so that the plan for our contribution might result [in] a plan for a program that would be born there, in dialogue with the people, about their own reality, their needs, and the possibility of our assistance. We could not design such a plan for them in Geneva. (Freire, 1978, pp. 12–13)

This view that communities have and produce knowledge is shared by researchers who have studied *funds of knowledge* (FoK), "the knowledge base that underlies the productive and exchange activities of households" (Moll & González, 2004, p. 700). In the FoK approach, teachers investigate community knowledge through semi-ethnographic methods for several reasons including that teachers reconceptualize their orientation toward working-class households as creators of knowledge rather than as deficient.

Community knowledge also has a mathematical component, that is, both adults and children use mathematics outside of school and have and produce mathematical knowledge (Lave, 1988; Nunes, Schliemann, & Carraher, 1993). This is often referred to as "informal mathematical knowledge" and is a resource upon which teachers can build (Mack, 1990).

From a Freirean (1970/1998) perspective, educators can develop curriculum by studying community knowledge and uncovering *generative themes* (or *thematic complexes*), which are key social contradictions confronting the people. For Freire, liberatory educational practices always began with generative themes: "The starting point for organizing the program content of education or political action must be the present, existential, concrete situation, reflecting the aspirations of the people" (1970/1998, p. 76). Teachers and other researchers conduct community investigations to learn about generative themes and then use them to develop curriculum; all this is a complicated and long process. These ideas have been practiced in São Paulo (O'Cadiz, Wong, & Torres, 1998), Porto Alegre, Brazil (Gandin, 2002; Gandin & Apple, 2003), and elsewhere to create curriculum. Gandin (2002) described the process in Porto Alegre:

> The starting point for the construction of curricular knowledge is the culture(s) of the communities themselves, not only in terms of content, but in terms of perspective as well. The whole educational process is aimed at inverting previous priorities and instead serving the historically oppressed and excluded groups. The starting point for this new process of knowledge construction is the idea of Thematic Complexes. This organization of the curriculum is a way of having the whole school working on a central generative theme, from which the disciplines and areas of knowledge, in an interdisciplinary effort, will structure the focus of their content. (p. 140)

There are various ways to develop curriculum based on community knowledge. They are not all the same but share with Freirean approaches the idea that teachers and other researchers first need to learn about community knowledge and then use that knowledge as a bridge to school curricula. Teachers and others often create curriculum in the process. These approaches include the FoK work, in which the purpose was to "learn from the community and to build our mathematics instruction on these adults' knowledge and experiences as well as on their forms of knowledge" (Civil, in press). Others have studied teachers who taught mathematics by building on students' knowledge, including their culture and language. The research on culturally relevant mathematics teaching is a further example (e.g., Gutstein, Lipman, Hernández, & de los Reyes, 1997; Ladson-Billings, 1995a; Tate, 1995).

Critical Knowledge

Critical knowledge in this context has two aspects: *critical mathematical knowledge* and *critical knowledge in general*. By critical mathematical knowledge, I mean the knowledge of how to read the world with mathematics. A principal focus of this book is the development of critical mathematical knowledge, so I will not rehash that here. But I also consider critical knowledge in general to mean knowledge beyond mathematics that students need to understand their sociopolitical context. My data suggest that students needed both knowledges to comprehend complex phenomena. For example, on the "Mortgage Loans—Is Racism a Factor?" project (chapter 3), to understand why African Americans and Latinos/as had worse mortgage rejection rates than whites, students needed critical mathematical knowledge but also a grasp of the history of wealth inequality and its genesis in institutional racism—critical knowledge in general.

Classical Knowledge

I define *classical knowledge* of mathematics to include mathematical power as well as the specific competencies students need to pass gatekeeping tests and to pursue advanced mathematics and mathematically related careers. I have spent less time discussing classical knowledge than critical knowledge in this book, but MiC falls under the category of classical knowledge. Morrell (2005) discussed classical and critical knowledge in a way that captures their essence. He referred to a *pedagogy of access*—learning classical knowledge to get access to advanced studies, and to a *pedagogy of dissent*—learning critical knowledge to disrupt the status quo. Morrell argued that students need both, simultaneously.

There is an important caveat here about classical mathematical knowledge. In our society, it is a particular form of high-status, valorized knowledge that has both macro-economic (Apple, 2004) as well as cultural value (or capital) (Joseph, 1997). Resources in industrialized countries (e.g., funds for commercial research or educational curriculum development) have flowed to mathematics and other scientific and technological fields, as opposed to, for example, the arts, precisely because of their payoffs in terms of "return on investment" (Apple, 2004). The Eurocentric nature of the school mathematics taught in the United States (not to mention most of the world) has effectively diminished not only the contributions of others and of indigenous peoples to mathematics but has also skewed how "primitive" mathematics is seen and understood in the so-called West (Anderson, 1990; D'Ambrosio, 1985). Furthermore, the epistemological and philosophical basis of this mathematics in positivism has been and should be critiqued in how it limits other forms of knowing (Frankenstein & Powell, 1994). So this particular form of classical knowledge needs to be set into context and its historical and sociopolitical roles problematized when it is taught and learned in school. In essence, one has to examine, with a *critical* eye, this classical knowledge.

The Interrelationship of Community, Critical, and Classical Knowledge

Conceptually, the three knowledges have equal importance in social justice pedagogy. Students need to develop both critical and classical knowledge, and teachers need to learn about and then build on the community knowledge that students (and community adults) already have. It should be a given that teachers have classical knowledge, but the distribution of mathematically knowledgeable teachers is still inequitable—white, wealthier schools still have more knowledgeable and qualified mathematics teachers than schools of low-income students of color (Oakes, Joseph, & Muir, 2004). And although students have informal (i.e., community) mathematical knowledge, it is not classical knowledge and, by itself, will not allow students to access higher mathematics and pass gatekeeping exams.

Students have to create critical mathematical knowledge, but there is yet another caveat here. Although students do not usually have critical mathematical knowledge, they may have some critical knowledge in general. Depending on their age and experience, students may already read the world, although not necessarily with mathematics. My student, Raquel, and her sister, Mónica, demonstrated their critical knowledge in their interview when they deconstructed and analyzed the unfairness of the Iowa exam (chapter 6).

Also, adults who have community knowledge often also have critical knowledge, including using mathematics, as shown in the parent interviews (chapter 8). In fact, at times their knowledge is far more critical than that of the individuals who teach their children. The particular parents I interviewed arguably understood the political interconnections of oppression, resistance, mathematics, and education far better than Rivera teachers. This is not to suggest that all parents in a community like Morningside already have critical knowledge but rather to caution against paternalism or the presumption that it is the role of the outsider (e.g., teacher) to bring light to the "uncritical" community residents. Freire (1970/1998) was clear that those who experienced oppression would play meaningful, leading roles in their own liberation: "Who are better than the oppressed to understand the terrible significance of an oppressive society? … Who can better understand the necessity for liberation?" (p. 27). Furthermore, while teachers (or revolutionary leaders) have a role to play, " … we cannot say that in the process of revolution someone liberates someone else, nor yet that someone liberates himself [sic], but rather that human beings in communion liberate each other" (p. 114). Here he is speaking about the partnerships of those within communities (i.e., the oppressed) and those from without (e.g., teachers) who are committed to working with them toward their full mutual humanization. But fundamentally, Freire spoke of a pedagogy of the *oppressed*, "a pedagogy which must be forged *with*, not *for*, the oppressed (whether individuals or peoples) in the incessant struggle to regain their humanity" (p. 30). One only has to listen to the voices in chapter 7 of Maria, Adrián, Lizandra, and Grisel, now young adults themselves, to realize that although they may have been in a mathematics class that helped created conditions for the development of their sociopolitical consciousness and sense of agency, their own life experiences, community knowledge, and sense of justice was the basis. Lizandra captured this well when she wrote, "I know that this class itself did not make me a strong person or one who fights for justice. That was already deep within me."

For Freire, community knowledge and critical knowledge were inextricably linked, and his goal was for community knowledge to become critical. As I explain briefly above, Freire advocated that teams of researchers and teachers first investigate the community's generative themes and use those as the point of departure for the "educational program" (see Freire, 1970/1998, pp. 78–105, for details). But the purpose of starting from community knowledge was always to move forward to write the world. He wrote, "… we must pose this existential, concrete, present situation to the people as a problem which challenges them and requires a response—not just at the intellectual level, but at the level of action" (1970/1998, pp. 76– 77). When anyone—a teacher, community member, or student— poses a situation back to people as a problem, community knowledge can become critical knowledge as people begin to read (the "intellectual level") and write ("the level of action") the world. In chapter 6, I explain how teachers might problematize students' ideas and analyses (i.e., to develop critical knowledge), and I give the example of how I tried to do this with Carmen's analysis (community knowledge) of why African Americans and Latinos/as had higher mortgage rejection rates than whites. This is how a problem-posing pedagogy supports the construction of critical knowledge while starting from community knowledge.

From a Freirean perspective, community and critical knowledge are closely interconnected, but currently in U.S. schools, classical knowledge is generally divorced from both. Students do need to develop mathematical power to understand the complexities of society, but some aspects of classical knowledge are unnecessary and imposed. For example, students need to pass various high-stakes assessments and do well on the ACT or SAT to go to college and access scholarships. Some of the mathematics they have to know, and how they have to know it (e.g., rotely memorize formulas to quickly produce correct answers on narrow, multiple-choice questions), may have little to do with either understanding mathematics or with making sense of and changing the world. Furthermore, NCTM *Standards*-based (i.e., reform) curricula, like MiC (classical knowledge), are themselves uncritical and do not connect directly to students' communities.

Connecting and synthesizing the three knowledges is not simple. For the most part, I did not draw on community knowledge in my teaching as much as I could have, and instead focused on critical and classical knowledge. In contrast, the FoK approach draws on community knowledge to develop classical knowledge, but it does not focus on developing critical mathematical knowledge (Civil, 2002; personal communication, April 2004). The same can be said of the *Algebra Project*, although both it and the FoK work clearly emanate from a broader social justice perspective. It is possible for teachers to conduct community investigations, uncover generative themes, and codevelop, along with members of school communities, interdisciplinary curriculum projects, but given the intensification of their work and the pressure for test scores, it will be difficult. In both Porto Alegre and São Paulo, significant, long-term work that also involved restructuring the entire school system was required, and these efforts were in the context of radically different (and progressive) relations of power in the respective cities (Freire, 1993; Gandin, 2002; O'Cadiz, Wong, & Torres, 1998). In the United States, given the political climate, teachers may have to use small-scale ways of uncovering and developing curriculum from the themes community members express as important. Teachers can also investigate students' themes and, for example, create real-world projects that build directly on those themes, or they can work across subject areas and create interdisciplinary curricula, but this, too, is a challenging, time-consuming process.

There are other complications. First, there may be tension between student-generated ideas and adult-generated ones. In Porto Alegre, teachers have for years investigated thematic complexes by talking with adults in the *favelas* (poor, informal settlements). Slowly, teachers also began to investigate students' themes and discovered that they were not necessarily the same as the adults' themes (I. Martins de Martins, personal communication, March 22, 2005). One could certainly see that as being an issue in U.S. schools as well.

Second, it is challenging to create curriculum based on generative themes, whether from students or parents, that actually develops both critical and classical knowledge. The experiences in Porto Alegre and São Paulo attest to this. At Rivera, it was complicated enough to integrate MiC with the real-world projects. To build curriculum based on student- and family-articulated themes (i.e., draw on community knowledge) and ensure students have the opportunities to read and write the world with mathematics (i.e., develop critical knowledge)—while *also* simultaneously developing the required classical knowledge—would be even more complex. The key question is: How does one connect and synthesize all three knowledge bases, while fully honoring and respecting each, to develop liberatory mathematics education in urban schools given the current high-stakes accountability regimes and larger political climate? This is a significant, open question for researchers, curriculum developers, and social justice educators to jointly pursue.

Implications for Teacher Education

As a teacher educator whose responsibilities include preparing mathematics teachers, I am confronted with the question: How does one learn to teach mathematics for social justice? Much has been written on learning to teach for social justice (e.g., Darling-Hammond, French, & Garcia-López, 2002), and certainly some of those ideas apply, but there are fewer documented efforts of learning to teach mathematics for social justice than, for example, social studies, history, or literature. Tate (1994) wrote that "the disciplines that undergird mathematics education—mathematics and psychology—place great stress on objectivity and neutrality. As a result, school mathematics has been tacitly accepted as a colorblind discipline" (p. 477). One can extend this to say that it has also been accepted as apolitical, and this makes it difficult for researchers, teacher educators, teachers, and pre-service teachers to conceptualize teaching and learning mathematics for social justice.

In mathematics education, we know some of the knowledge bases needed to be effective mathematics teachers: content knowledge (both specific and common, Hill & Ball, 2004), pedagogical content knowledge, and curricular knowledge (Shulman, 1986). We also know, in education generally, that knowledge of the community where one teaches is important (Ladson-Billings, 2001). In considering the knowledge one draws on to teach (mathematics) for social justice, we can add knowledge of the sociopolitical, economic, and cultural-historical workings of society— precisely what we want *students* to know when learning (mathematics) for social justice. Teachers themselves need to understand how U.S. society structures inequality and the history and dynamics of social movements and change (Bigelow & Peterson, 2002). They need an analysis of the political development of our country so that they can support and involve students in the study of their own social realities. For example, to really comprehend why Morningside's housing prices and rents are increasing, one needs to understand the alignment of various political forces, the mechanisms of gentrification, the history of the displacement of people of color, and the city's development plans and tax incentives. And much of this knowledge is not learned in school or books, but in the actual practice of teaching and participating in social movements.

Clearly, there is a circular problem here. If students learned to read and write the world in K–16 education, teachers themselves would have learned how and would be more able to teach others to do the same. However, Macedo (1994) pointed out that, instead, schools in the United States engender "education for domestification, which borders on stupidi-fication, [and] provides no space for critical students … who question the received knowledge and want to know the reasons behind the facts" (p. 18). This applies to teacher education. The typical teacher education program has one, or at most two, courses in social foundations, and whether those courses are taught from a critical perspective depends on the faculty. This is in contrast to the seven to ten history, sociology, and philosophy of education courses that students in Brazil usually take in their education programs (L. Gandin, personal communication, March 2005).

In short, teacher education programs in the United States need to be more like those in Brazil. The downplaying of social foundations in colleges of education and overemphasis on "methods" (Bartolomé, 1994), along with the standardization and "accountability measures" enforced by No Child Left Behind (NCLB) (2001) structure teacher education to "produce" teachers to raise test scores, "deliver" packaged and mandated curriculum designed to improve narrowly assessed "achievement," and teach for functional literacies. This is related to the push by the National Science Foundation for more content area "specialists" as opposed to edu-cators in its funding of projects and research centers. This can also be seen in alternative certification, fast-track programs that privilege content knowledge and de-emphasize social foundations. The underlying presumption is that content and practice are separate from, and more important than, pedagogy and theory, and that foundations courses are the lowest priority because they do not teach anything "useful."

But teacher education programs need to prepare critically literate indi-viduals who can teach for social justice. Mathematics teacher education could and should teach preservice students how to read and write the world with (and without) mathematics, deconstruct media images and representations, and ask the type of questions that their own future stu-dents should ask. I am not suggesting that we sacrifice the crucial mathe-matical content preparation. But it is not enough, and definitely does not prepare students to teach for social justice. I do realize that teacher educa-tion programs are packed, especially for elementary-certified teachers who have to be multifaceted and teach all subjects. I do not know how to resolve the time crunch, but I know that, as currently configured, most teacher education programs barely scratch the surface in teaching critical literacies.

One more implication is that pre- and in-service teachers need to learn how to study their own teaching of mathematics for social justice without being overwhelmed. This again speaks to the current intensification of teachers' work that constrains reflective praxis. But there are no blueprints for social justice pedagogy, and we need reports from teachers who theorize their practice as they try to create conditions for students to read and write the world with mathematics. These would be valuable contributions, and journals like *Rethinking Schools* exist that will publish reports by teachers about social justice pedagogy in their own classrooms.

Implications for Teaching Mathematics

The primary implication of my research for teaching mathematics is that it is possible to teach mathematics for social justice in an urban Latino/a school. Middle school students from bilingual, working-class, immigrant families can begin the process of reading and writing their world with mathematics and can change their orientation toward mathematics. It is not an easy process, and there are facilitating and constraining conditions, but it is doable. A key enabling condition was that adults believed that certain students were capable of genuine intellectual work, and these students held similar perceptions about themselves and willingly participated in the journey as more-or-less equal partners. Conversely, a principal constraint was that most students who were *not* considered capable of independent, challenging work did not take themselves seriously as learners nor fully participate in coconstructing classrooms oriented toward social justice.

I spend a good deal of time arguing why tracking was so detrimental at Rivera (chapter 6), so one implication is that tracking should be eliminated and the same challenging expectations accorded to all. (I realize that tracking is more of a school organization issue than one of teaching.) Untracking is problematic for many reasons, including social class, race, power, and the social constructions of ability and intelligence (Lipman, 1998; Oakes, Wells, Jones, & Datnow, 1997; Wheelock, 1992), but tracking does powerful, long-lasting damage. One way I might have mitigated its impact with my class in the general track program (2000–2001) would have been to focus and build more on students' lived experiences, that is, their community knowledge. When they did the "Meaningful Questions" project, in which they chose their own questions to research, they were quite engaged. Thus, another implication for teaching is to build more on all students' community knowledge but especially those who are disengaged in school partially because they have accepted negative, low expectations placed upon them.

At the risk of being repetitive, to teach mathematics for social justice one needs to normalize politically taboo topics and create a pedagogy of questioning. Further, one needs to build meaningful relationships with students, both political ones as well as those that establish the "intersubjectivity" between students and teachers that Murrell (1997) spoke of as necessary for liberatory education (chapter 6). Murrell's point was that this was particularly hard when teachers did not share students' culture(s), and I found that intersubjectivity even more necessary when students were less engaged in school. Those of us teaching "other people's children" (Delpit, 1988) have to work all that much harder to build the relationships.

Rethinking Mathematical Literacy

In chapter 1, following Apple (1992) and Macedo (1994), I argue that mathematical literacy (in the United States at least) is generally understood as a set of competencies comprising mathematical power (see Jablonka, 2003). It acts as a form of functional literacy. The pedagogical practices and curricular materials that try to develop mathematical literacy in the United States serve the needs of capital accumulation because they contribute to labor force stratification and do not try to teach students to question unequal structural arrangements of society. Mathematical literacy, as generally defined, can be used for a variety of purposes, including destructive ones (Apple, 1992). Mathematics and technology can further imperial conquest; for example, Pentagon engineers and Enron ex-financial officers are clearly mathematically literate in the conventional sense. To counter this, we need to reconceptualize mathematical literacy as *critical* literacy for the purpose of fundamentally transforming society, in its entirety from the bottom up toward equity and justice, and for all students whether from dominant or oppressed groups. This is in accord with what Skovsmose (1994) described as *mathemacy,* a form of mathematical literacy that he framed as parallel to Freire's (1970/1998) conception of *emancipatory literacy,* and also with Frankenstein's (1998) concept of *critical mathematical* literacy.

To reframe mathematical literacy as critical, for the express purpose of restructuring society, is a goal of this work. As I write in chapter 1, my principal argument is that *students need to be prepared through their mathematics education to investigate and critique injustice, and to challenge, in words and actions, oppressive structures and acts—that is, to "read and write the world" with mathematics.* The default in mathematics education is *not* to use mathematics to critique institutional structures with the goal of transforming them and reinventing society for justice and equality. I do not mean to oversimplify, but if mathematics educators and teachers do not consciously resist the status quo and teach mathematics as one of many tools with which to change the world, they may unwittingly support mathematical literacy as functional literacy, and at best, generate a few more individual successes. Instead, we need to conceive of mathematical literacy as knowledge for liberation from oppression. Freire (Freire & Macedo, 1987) wrote:

> To acquire the selected knowledge contained in the dominant cur-
> riculum should be a goal attained by subordinate students in the
> process of self and group empowerment. They can use the domi-
> nant knowledge effectively in their struggle to change the material
> and historical conditions that have enslaved them. (p. 128)

Mathematics, and mathematical literacy, are important components of that essential "dominant knowledge" that educators can help students develop.

Why Is It so Important to Teach Mathematics for Social Justice Right Now?

The preceding discussion on mathematical literacy highlights a potential role for mathematics teachers and educators—to teach mathematics for social justice and to support the development of mathematical literacy as critical, not functional, literacy. But why is it so important to teach mathematics for social justice right now, and is this particular time period sub-stantively different from others? To address this, I examine the broader sociopolitical context enveloping this work and speak to that question, starting with Rivera and moving outward to the larger society.

Chicago and U.S. Schools: Labor Force Preparation

Rivera's tracking and containment of youth disciplined and controlled their bodies, minds, and spirits. Except for the small percentage of students in the honors track, and the even smaller percentage of students in the general track who really went against the tide and "made it," the majority were (and are) educated (in Rivera and other Chicago public schools) for low-skilled service-sector jobs or the military. Some who refused to submit to the routinization, "education for stupidification" (Macedo, 1994), and preparation for servitude were driven out to the margins, the streets, prison, gangs, or early deaths. Louis Farrakhan, in Murrell (1997), provided an alternate way to think about these youth as he addressed a group of African American leaders:

> I was not the smartest in my class. I was mediocre. And I am willing to bet that most of you that are leading today, you were not the best in your class. You were mediocre. But what happened to the top of the class? It's gone, it's dead, it's on drugs, it's destroyed! We just got through. We were more submissive. We submitted to our teachers. And we let them bend us and mold us...(p. 52)

I knew students who dropped out of Rivera or high school—they were among the most perceptive and socially conscious youth I knew. They resisted and reacted to school's attempts to "bend and mold" them, but absent a strong social movement today, they had few alternatives. Some joined gangs or the military, some were sent to prison, some had children early, some just drifted, and some eventually returned to school or went to work, perhaps trying to get a GED along the way. They clearly needed a different education—and that missing social movement—that might have supported their rebellious spirits and equipped them to challenge the injustices that oppressed them.

Understanding schooling at Rivera requires examining the larger social forces that influenced its policies. Rivera is one of 600 Chicago public schools, one of tens of thousands in the United States, and must be seen in that light. Stratified education in the United States has historical roots in the racism of the eugenics movement (Selden, 1999) and a long relationship to labor force preparation (Spring, 1976). Chicago's schools are entirely tracked; there is a hierarchy of a few college-preparatory, selective-enrollment high schools and many neighborhood high schools with a smattering of specialized programs (Lipman, 2002). Its elementary programs are also tracked, with some magnet and specialty schools and also a vast array of racially segregated neighborhood schools of low-income Brown and Black youth. Although Chicago had over 106,000 high school students in 2004–2005, the selective-enrollment high schools had around 10,000, less than 10% of the total (CPS, 2005). Almost all high schools are tracked internally, with up to six tracks. Like urban high schools throughout the United States, Chicago schools overwhelmingly prepare low-income students of color for low-status jobs in a segmented economy (Lipman, 2004). In that sense, they do their job well.

Schools and Military Preparation

But urban schools do not just prepare workers, they also sort out a sector of working-class youth of color for the military.[1] This is particularly relevant to Rivera because many of its students go into the military, and its neighborhood high school has a thriving Junior Reserve Officers Training Corps (JROTC) program. Furthermore, military recruiters especially covet Latinos/as for the Iraq War. According to a media report,

> Senior Pentagon officials have identified Latinos as by far the most promising ethnic group for recruitment, because their numbers are growing rapidly in the U.S. and they include a plentiful supply of low-income men of military age with few other job or educational prospects. (Gumbel, 2003)

Latinos/as are overrepresented in the armed forces (considering that recruits need to be citizens or permanent residents and have a high school diploma or equivalent) and are concentrated in more dangerous positions (Pew Hispanic Center, 2003).

In this time of permanent "War on Terror" and the prospect of open-ended occupations of Iraq, Afghanistan, and who knows where else in the future, schooling serves a particular function. Those working-class students with the grades, immigration status, and test scores can attend college and get financial aid. However, students in Chicago's neighborhood high schools had a mean ACT score around 15.3 in 2004 (CPS, 2005); few of them will receive college scholarships if they are even lucky enough to be accepted. But as Pentagon officials cynically said, Latinos/as (and other low-income youth) have few options, making them ripe cannon fodder for the military's offers to pay for college in exchange for joining. Several analysts have commented on the "poverty draft." That was why my student Lucia's brother was in the Navy and why we did the B-2 bomber project in her class (chapter 1).

Furthermore, the U.S. military is short on soldiers right now and is recruiting heavily. The Army recently lowered its educational standards and increased its age limit. In January 2005, for the first time in 10 years, the Marines failed to meet active-duty recruitment goals, and for the first time in five years, active-duty Army recruits fell below quota in February and March 2005 (Cave, 2005; Kilian & Horan, 2005). The Army now offers signing bonuses: $2,000 for recruits who start training within 45 days of signing; $20,000 for new, active-duty, regular personnel; and $150,000 re-enlistment bonuses for highly trained, special forces veterans (Kilian & Horan, 2005). In April 2003, an Army recruiter crossed into Tijuana,

Mexico, looking for two students who allegedly expressed interest at a San Diego recruiting office (Stevenson, 2003), setting off vigorous protest from the Mexican government. The Tijuana daily, *El Mexicano*, subsequently reported "an intense campaign to recruit young [Mexican] high school students" (Gumbel, 2003).

Chicago public schools and the U.S. military have close relationships. The first public military high school was in Chicago, and in 2005 CPS had three whole-school military academies and nine smaller military academies within schools. The military has given millions of dollars to CPS (Moody, 2004). Also, students in Chicago's military schools are disproportionately of color. In 2004, in the three military schools, 1.3% of the students were white, although 8.8% of all CPS students were white (CPS, 2005), and all three schools were in African American communities. Ten percent of the 2003 graduating seniors from Rivera's neighborhood high school reported planning to join the military, a higher percentage than students in all but three Chicago high schools (CPS, 2005). Teaching students to deconstruct the military's role and its relationship to U.S. foreign and domestic policy, as well as ensuring they have the mathematical and other competencies to carefully read various enlistment documents, is genuinely relevant and important to the whole Rivera community.

Chicago School Policy and Gentrification

Chicago school policy is not only implicated in producing inequality in the future employment of Rivera (and other) students but also in their very places of residence. As I write this in spring 2005, gentrification is rampant in Chicago and deeply linked to CPS policy and Chicago's drive to be a global city (Lipman, 2002, 2004).[2] My students and their families are being priced out of Morningside, a community that they have made their own and that is strongly identified with Mexican culture. Teachers in Morningside schools near where new upscale housing development is encroaching report declining enrollments as families leave who can no longer afford higher property taxes or rents. Across Morningside, rents and housing prices are soaring. My students used mathematics to study these realities, and they have only worsened with time—and the story is the same in many neighborhoods across the city.

In a move seemingly unrelated to this gentrification, in June 2004, Mayor Daley unveiled Renaissance 2010, a bold plan to close 60 to 70 schools and open 100 new ones. Ostensibly a plan to turn around "troubled schools," Renaissance 2010 is actually much more (Lipman, 2005). This became clear when the *Chicago Tribune* leaked a July 2004 report that 20 of the 22 initial school closings were planned for the "Mid-South" area

(Dell'Angelo, 2004). Mid-South is a historic African American community in the heart of Chicago's south side. It is also one of Chicago's fastest gentrifying communities. Mid-South was home to the Robert Taylor housing projects—28 towering buildings, two miles long, with over 27,000 people in 4,321 apartments. It was the largest U.S. public housing project ever built, erected between 1959 and 1963 as part of Chicago's racist containment of its African American population. Isolated partly by an expressway to its west, the land has become increasingly valuable, partly because, ironically, that very highway provides rapid transportation downtown as does the elevated train that runs through the center of the road. Robert Taylor was just a few miles from downtown, but all except two buildings have been demolished as of this writing, and those will follow shortly.

In its place will be *Legends South* with 2,388 new units (MDC, 2005). But only 794 will be public housing units, 434 will be market rate, and 1,160 will be "affordable." My students learned on the "Will Development Bury the *Barrio*?" project that "affordable" was relative and politically contextualized (chapter 4). These 794 public housing units represent 18.4% of the original units, so from Robert Taylor alone, over 22,000 public housing residents were displaced.

Although resistance from community organizations and residents managed to derail the full-scale closing of the 20 schools, CPS has moved ahead and closed a number of Mid-South schools (and others around the city) and "re-birthed" some as charters that will be populated by the middle-income families, both Black and white, who are moving into the neighborhood. Nor are the schools likely to have local school councils, as two thirds of the 100 new schools will be publicly funded but privately managed with no community accountability. Furthermore, as neighborhoods gentrify and public housing closes or communities like Morningside get priced out, school populations drop giving CPS administrators a rationale for closing under enrolled schools and re-opening them as renaissance schools for the "newcomers" who will "stabilize" the "new" neighborhoods. The Kenwood Oakland Local School Council Alliance, a leader in the Mid-South struggle, perhaps captured it best in their Mid-South Education Plan/Renaissance 2010 fact sheet:

> ... The resources pouring into these schools now, have always been there but because the children were low-income, it was never a priority. CPS has a tradition of under-serving our children! ...

> Over 90% of the students who attend Mid-South schools are from low-income, African American families. The Mid-South plan says

that the schools will serve 1/3 middle-income, 1/3 moderate-income and 1/3 low-income students. What happens to the other 2/3 low-income students? DISPLACEMENT!

Where is CPS Accountability for decades of second-class education? Has Chicago Public Schools done such an outstanding job of delivering quality education to low-income and working families that they have earned the community's trust? Absolutely not! Where is the accountability for a probation system that has not worked, student retention (another failed initiative), direct instruction (a disaster), and social promotion? How many thousands of students have dropped out as a result of being mis-educated? …

As a 34-year veteran south side teacher said at a forum I attended to save her community's high school, "African Americans are being pushed out from the city under the guise of school reform." She could have said, "poor people of color" in general and been right.

A Globalized Context

Most people accept that our world is increasingly shrinking. Morningside families live with the realities of a fluid, transnational community and world in which the U.S. president opportunistically bounces back and forth on plans for guest status and temporary residency for Mexican workers. It is the height of irony that Mexican farmers cannot afford to grow corn because imported, subsidized U.S. corn costs less—so displaced peasants come to the United States for work and are then laid off from nonunionized manufacturing jobs because their company relocates to Mexico in its race to the bottom for cheaper labor!

This competition does not manifest itself solely in the economic sphere. In the post–9/11 world, the United States, in contention with European and Asian countries and capital, uses its dominant military to further its drive for strategic, long-term control of oil supplies and pricing. With permanent military bases planned for Afghanistan and Iraq, a large U.S. military presence will be able to control uprisings in the area and intimidate others. The current U.S. administration is heavily influenced by the Project for a New American Century (PNAC) with their well-articulated design for U.S. global supremacy. Key members include Vice-President Dick Cheney, Secretary of Defense Donald Rumsfeld, ex-Deputy Secretary of Defense Paul Wolfowitz, and the president's brother, Florida Governor Jeb Bush. The PNAC (2000) wrote in their highly influential document, *Rebuilding America's Defenses: Strategy, Forces, and Resources for a New Century,* "At present the United States faces no global rival. America's grand strategy should aim to preserve and extend this advantageous position as far into the future as possible." By all indications, the current administration appears to be trying to implement this strategy and reverse the progress of national liberation and anti-colonial struggles in the twentieth century.

Domestically, we see similar attempts to turn back the clock. The Right has stepped up its attacks on legal abortion and contraception, affirmative action, separation of church and state, gay rights, civil liberties and privacy rights, evolution in the curriculum, stem cell research, academic freedom, an "unembedded" press, and even the right to die (Apple, 2001). Before the Terri Schiavo case, the U.S. Congress had never even considered a federal law intervening in the personal medical decision of one family. We now see attempts to legislate, formally and informally, the values and morality of a nation.

The Implications for Education

To a greater or lesser degree, most CPS students face educational preparation for functional literacy and servitude, active military recruitment in a time of war, and gentrification and displacement from their communities. Chicago may be an advanced example, but the story is fundamentally similar in other urban areas (e.g., Valenzuela, 2005). All of this is occurring in the context of the U.S. drive for global supremacy (Harvey, 2003) that has potential to wreak havoc internationally and cause more disasters like September 11 internally. I start this book by telling how I wanted my students to raise their questions about September 11, but I then asked them to interpret the question posed to the United States by others: "Americans, think! Why You Are Hated All Over the World?" If we do not address this question, we may acquiesce to governmental policies causing irreparable harm to the planet's environment, civilizations, cultures, and peoples. But if we teach our students to think deeply about questions like this, both the local, immediate questions that directly affect their lives, communities, and futures as well as the broader, global ones; critique sources of knowledge; and seek to understand underlying contradictions and who benefits—and to take action—we can contribute to a more just and sane world. The urgency is what can happen if we do nothing in the present except to continue with business as usual. This is the immediate and strategic importance of teaching (mathematics) for social justice—*now.*

Conclusion

But this book is not just about oppressive conditions, because they are only one side of the dialectic. It is also about resistance, both real and potential, by parents in Morningside and similar communities, students at Rivera and other schools, and teachers who want to, and do, teach against the grain and for social justice. Social movements always exist, though they ebb and flow. And although those of the 1960s and 1970s have dimmed, people continue the struggles to change their lives. From Morningside streets where people fight for their neighborhood, to the *latifundos* of Brazil where the *Movimento Sem Terra* (landless peasant movement) occupies vacant farms, to South African townships where residents protest utility shutoffs, people keep working to improve life, even when or if popular governments are elected.

There is resistance in educational arenas as well. Social justice schools are starting around the country, in greater numbers, in Oakland, Los Angeles, New York, Chicago, and elsewhere. The story of Chicago's first public school for social justice is a powerful tale. In 1998, CPS allocated funds to build three new high schools. Two were to be selective-enrollment schools (one in a moderate-income community, the other bordering the "gold coast"), and one was to be a neighborhood school in the low-income Mexican immigrant community of Little Village. CPS built the two selective-enrollment schools, then ran out of money. Little Village residents repeatedly protested and pleaded but to no avail. Finally, in May 2001, 14 residents, mainly mothers and a grandmother, staged a 19-day hunger strike (Russo, 2003). They called it off for health reasons, and shortly afterwards, CPS discovered the money to build their school. The new school building, the most expensive ever built in Chicago, will house four small high schools to open in fall 2005. All four will be infused with the hunger strike values: *autodeterminación* (self-determination), democracy, community accountability, and empowerment. Organizers held meetings and surveyed residents to determine the school's themes, and based on responses, one of the four will be a school for social justice. This school may be one of many future models of teaching for social justice.

Final Thoughts—"Another World Is Possible"

Although this is a dangerous period in Chicago, the United States, and the world, it is also a time of opportunity. In Chicago, the mayor's plans ironically have laid a basis for city-wide resistance. Because gentrification affects many parts of Chicago, Renaissance 2010 does too. When south side African American community leaders wend their way, street map in hand, to the multi-racial north side to fight Renaissance 2010; when white teachers and Latino/a service workers go to Mid-South or the African American west side to support activists there; and when the advisory council of the new schools in Little Village call a press conference to renounce Renaissance 2010, putting their new schools in jeopardy, and activists from around the city join them, the mayor and his plans may be in trouble. For the past 50 years, outside of two brief periods,[3] the Daley family (father and son were both mayor) has ruled Chicago except when the grassroots groundswell from the African American community that had been growing for years came together with Latino/a and white progressives in 1982–1983 to register massive numbers of new voters in two months and elected Harold Washington as the city's first African American mayor. The current Mayor Daley may have created a similar situation by attempting to privatize schools and gentrify communities across the city. This is the opportunity for real change in Chicago in this present period.

Simultaneously, peoples' movements around the globe have arisen to challenge global neoliberal policies enacted by the World Bank and International Monetary Fund, and to confront the U.S. empire, in ways that have not occurred before in their interconnectedness. Some call it "globalization from below," and the World Social Forum (WSF) is an important example. In 2005, at the fifth WSF, there were 155,000 registered participants from 151 countries (WSF, 2005b). These numbers suggest this is not a "passing fad." Popular movements around the world are coalescing and uniting in new ways. A document from the 2005 WSF reported (WSF, 2005a):

> Four years ago the collective and global call for ANOTHER WORLD IS POSSIBLE broke the lie that neoliberal domination is unavoidable as well as the acceptance of the "normality" of way, of social inequalities, racism, casts, patriarchy, imperialism, and the destruction of the environment. As people take this truth as their own, their strength becomes unstoppable and it starts materialising in concrete actions of resistance, for demands and proposals. Therefore what is new about our proposal is the outbreak and the scale of the social movements in all continents and their ability to build, within diversity, new convergences and common actions at global level.

Such a common action was the unprecedented, coordinated, worldwide opposition preceding the Iraq War on the weekend of February 14–16, 2003, when 11 to 12 million people demonstrated in over 60 countries to oppose the war. The *New York Times* reported, "The fracturing of the Western alliance over Iraq and the huge antiwar demonstrations around the world this weekend are reminders that there may still be two superpowers on the planet: the United States and world public opinion" (Tyler, 2005). These local, national, and global organizational forms and actions represent the opportunities and possibilities that coexist with danger today.

The perspective that dangers and opportunities are always interconnected yields hope—and this book is also about hope. Freire (1994) wrote, "hope is an ontological need" (p. 8), which I understand to mean that hope is necessary to be human. But Freire always related hope to the fight for a better life: "... hope needs practice in order to become historical concreteness ... without the struggle, hope ... dissipates, loses its bearings, and turns into hopelessness" (p. 7). Furthermore, hope comes not from faith but from an understanding of social agency and history that human beings make the social world:

> Just as ... social reality exists not by chance, but as the product of human action, so it is not transformed by chance. If humankind produce social reality ... then transforming that reality is an historical task, a task for humanity. (Freire, 1970/1998, p. 33)

If humans can create a social system that always puts profit above human needs—capitalism—then human beings can develop alternatives that put people first. We may not know what precisely those new social relations will look like, but surely we know that a system is fundamentally inhumane and flawed if it produces and promulgates what Dr. King called "the giant triplets of racism, materialism, and militarism" (King, 1986). And although the experiments with one alternative—socialism—in the twentieth century had serious flaws, we can consider them like early people's efforts with fire and look at their strengths and weaknesses dialectically and learn from their attempts:

> As humans discovered and learned how to use fire, there must have been thousands of people, entire families and villages, burned to death. But we cannot condemn human experiments with fire—they were attempts to control nature for our own benefit, thus freeing ourselves from nature and developing society to a higher level. Socialism is change of the same order. It opens up a new era, and controlling social organization is as hard for us as controlling fire was for early... humans. (Tung, 1981, p. 7)

Hope springs from the youth in Rivera, like Maria, Adrián, Grisel, Lizandra, and others, whose sense of justice and social agency and whose capacity to begin the complex process of reading and writing the world with mathematics makes clear that they *are* the future. Like teachers in African American schools who look at their students and see their own lives and futures (hooks, 1994; Ladson-Billings, 1994), we too can look at our students and cocreate with them conditions that support their participation in emancipatory struggles benefiting all of us.

It is important to declare that we, as educators, are not powerless, even within repressive educational systems. While we cannot always directly or immediately affect macro political and economic structures, although ultimately that is essential to creating a more just society, we do have social agency ourselves. And our agency includes seeing ourselves as active participants. Freire (1998) wrote a letter to "those who dare teach," in which he said:

> We are political militants because we are teachers. Our job is not exhausted in the teaching of math, geography, syntax, history. Our job implies that we teach these subjects with sobriety and competence, but it also requires our involvement in and dedication to overcoming social injustice. (p. 58)

My perspective here certainly includes the efforts of teachers, as well as administrators, families, and community members in rectifying inequities. But most of all, it sees students themselves as key participants in the social movements of the day. They need tools with which to join the local, and ultimately the global, struggles for justice, peace, and true equality. Among those tools is the capacity to read the mathematical word and to read and write the world with mathematics. As Lupe said in a focus group interview the year after she had finished almost two years in our social justice mathematics class:

> This class taught us math. It taught us how to put things together. And more than that, it helped us fight for what we believe in. Fight for what we know is right, not only for ourselves. Not only for our benefit, but for other people. Just the simple fact that we fight for what we believe in and what we believe is right, and fight against what we believe is wrong. It made us grow up a lot as people. It helped us develop a better way of expressing ourselves. Not just taking the things, feeling it, and not talking about it. But most important of all, it just made us strong. We're all stronger in a lot of different ways. *(Lupe, 9th grade, April 2000)*

Notes

Chapter 1

1. Throughout this book, I use students' words extensively. I gathered students' voices in many forms: journals, mathematics assignments, surveys, interviews, letters, emails, and informal conversations.
2. I have had the nickname "Rico" for 35 years. My mother taught Spanish at my neighborhood junior high school and sometimes called me Erico; Rico came from that. When I first started working at Rivera, a Colombian teacher called me Mr. Rico, explaining that it was customary in Colombia to address teachers by "Mr." or "Ms." and their first name.
3. When the Soviet Union intervened in Afghanistan, the United States funded the *mujahedeen* in the hopes of weakening the U.S.S.R. (Blum, 2004).
4. *Knowledge worker* refers to highly skilled and educated, professional-sector employees who often use advanced technologies.
5. The NCTM, with approximately 100,000 members, is the largest and arguably most influential professional association of mathematics teachers and educators in the United States and Canada.
6. According to NAEP (2004) data, between 1990 and 2003, when comparing "Hispanic" students to Whites, and Blacks to Whites, in fourth and eighth grades in mathematics, the only gap narrowing was between Black and White fourth graders, while for other categories—Black to White eighth graders; Hispanic to White fourth and eighth graders—the gaps have *increased*, although not statistically significantly.
7. Hilliard (1991) estimated 200 African American mathematicians at that time.
8. In the early 1990s, the National Science Foundation (NSF) funded the development of 13 ("reform") mathematics curricula to help bring the *Standards* into the classroom.
9. *Transitional schools* were separate, remedial schools for students who did not score high enough on the ITBS to attend high school but were too old to repeat eighth grade.

Chapter 2

1. I draw on African American traditions because they are very well known and extensively documented. However, I am not suggesting that others lack such a history. For example, Mexicans and Chicanos/as within the United States fought long for education as part of a larger emancipatory project (e.g., Acuña, 1996; Delgado Bernal, 1999, 2000; Donato, 1997; Getz, 1997; González, 1999; Guajardo & Guajardo, 2004; Gutiérrez, 2004; Ruiz & Racho, 1996).

2. In the postliteracy phase, Freirean teams worked differently in that they uncovered *generative themes* that emerged from the collaborative community investigations. These themes were codified and culture circles decoded them in similar ways as in the pre-literacy phase, but the goal was just to develop sociopolitical consciousness rather than also learning to read. (See Freire, 1970/1998, pp. 91–105.)

3. Again, this only refers to the preliteracy phase. In the postliteracy phase, codifications were not only pictorial, and people read texts as well.

4. I used the Federal Reserve Bank's (http://www.minneapolisfed.org/Research/data/us/calc/) calculations to determine this amount.

Chapter 3

1. In 1998, two major league baseball players were in a tight race for who would be the first to break a 70-year old historic record in baseball (home runs in one season) that had much meaning in United States popular culture. One was Sammy Sosa, a Black Latino from the Dominican Republic who played baseball for a Chicago team, and the other was Mark McGuire, a white player from the United States. Talk radio and other media had commentary about who was "American" and what it would mean if Sosa (purportedly a "non-American") were to break the record first and win the contest. McGuire won.

2. The Brown Berets were a political party of Chicanos/as started in the 1960s, similar in philosophy and practice to the Black Panther Party.

3. A friend of mine from Sierra Leone pointed out that Africa's wealth is far more than financial (e.g., cultural, historical), and since that time, I have been clear with students about distinguishing types of wealth.

4. *Discretionary* stops refer to ones police can choose to make or not, such as when a driver changes lanes without signaling or drives less than five mph over the speed limit.

5. The data were from several counties but included only percentage of Latino/a motorists and percentage of Latinos/as stopped. I averaged the counties' figures and then created data that fit the actual percentages.

6. Students used the probability cubes to create a simulation in which 2.8% would be "Latino/a." Some groups combined cubes so they had 100 in total, of which three were "Latinos/as." Others found that 1 of 36 was very close to 2.8%.

7. There was no contradiction because the first part of my question only involved internal Chicago comparisons (and was true), while the second part, also true, involved Chicago data compared to national data.

8. I cut the numbers I gave the other class in half but maintained the actual percentages. I do not remember why I did that.

9. The TIF is *tax increment financing*, a Chicago development scheme.

Chapter 4

1. This is a simplification because the direct lines on a Mercator projection do not necessarily represent the shortest route between two places due to the Earth's spherical geometry. (See Kaiser & Wood, 2001, for details.)

2. The Mercator projection represents shapes accurately on a local level because the shape of both Mexico and Alaska are relatively accurate when viewed by themselves. However, the shape of North America (containing both) is *in*accurate because Alaska is proportionally much bigger that its real size due to the way the projection distorts size farther from the equator. An analogy is a picture of a face in which both chin and forehead are true to shape—but the forehead is three times bigger than real life. Both forehead and chin are true to shape by themselves, but the face as a whole is not.

3. Chicago's Local School Councils (LSC) are made up of six parents, two teachers, and two at-large community members (and one student in the high schools). LSCs hire principals, have some discretionary budgeting power, and design school improvement plans.

Chapter 5

1. CPS provided extensive professional development and on-site support for schools using CMP. Although I initially provided professional development in MiC to Rivera teachers in grades 4–8, I stopped in 1998 due to other commitments including teaching my own class. MiC was too difficult to sustain without ongoing support, especially when CPS ramped up its accountability demands and focus on test scores, and several teachers stopped using MiC because of this. Rivera's principal and I concurred that the school should shift to CMP because of the support.

2. Humberto joined the class in eighth grade. His English was less developed than the other students, and I believe that this hampered his understanding. I taught in English although usually had students work in groups and always in the language of their choice. I discussed this with him and his father several times, and he consistently maintained that language was not an issue, but I was not convinced. Nonetheless, he passed the class and the grade, attended a neighborhood high school, and graduated on time in 2003.

3. Gaussian elimination is a method to solve systems of multivariable equations by systematically eliminating one variable at a time.

4. Despite my explicit directions that the survey was to be anonymous, most students signed their names. Perhaps they assumed I would know their handwriting (which I did), maybe they did not care, or perhaps they wanted me to know what they had written.

Chapter 6

1. "Cookies" and "crumbs" refer to the world wealth simulation we did (chapter 3) in Omar's class. The students representing North America each had 14 cookies, while the four of us representing Africa shared one cookie and literally split the crumbs between us. That was a powerful image for students.

2. I requested permission from the Riverside Publishing Corporation to reproduce the image, but they refused. Coincidentally, Riverside also produces the Iowa Test of Basic Skills, the nemesis of Chicago students.

3. Ferguson's analysis of African American male students is quite specific and cannot easily extend to others. However, her notion of students attempting to develop their identities with integrity and personhood may be apropos to Rivera.

Chapter 8

1. I did not again teach my own class, although the new principal invited me, partially because the faculty was polarized after an exhausting and bitter battle to remove the temporary replacement, and I did not want to exacerbate tensions.

Chapter 9

1. However, schools in the United States in general sort out working-class youth of *all* races for the military, with most of the white students coming from rural schools.

2. Global cities "are central marketplaces of global finance, major sites for the production of innovations central to the informational economy, and places where global systems of production are organized and managed" (Lipman, 2004, p. 7).

3. Mayors Bilandic and Byrne served in the late 1970s and early 1980s after the senior Mayor Daley died in office. In 1983, Chicago elected its first African American mayor, Harold Washington, who also died in office in 1987.

References

Acuña, R. F. (1996). *Anything but Mexican: Chicanos in contemporary Los Angeles.* London: Verso.

Ahmad, E. (2001). *Terrorism: Theirs and ours.* New York: Seven Stories Press.

Allensworth, E. (2005). *Graduation and dropout trends in Chicago: A look at cohorts of students from 1991 to 2004.* Chicago: Consortium on Chicago School Research.

Anderson, G. L., Herr, K., & Nihlen, A. S. (1994). *Studying your own school: An educator's guide to qualitative practitioner research.* Thousand Oaks, CA: Corwin Press.

Anderson, J. (1988). *The education of Blacks in the south, 1860–1935.* Chapel Hill, NC: University of North Carolina Press.

Anderson, S. E. (1990). Worldmath curriculum: Fighting Eurocentrism in mathematics. *Journal for Negro Education, 59,* 348–359.

Anyon, J. (1980). Social class and the hidden curriculum of work. *Journal of Education, 162,* 67–92.

Apple, M. W. (1986). *Teachers and texts: A political economy of class and gender relations in education.* New York: Routledge & Kegan Paul.

Apple, M. W. (1992). Do the Standards go far enough? Power, policy, and practice in mathematics education. *Journal for Research in Mathematics Education, 23,* 412–431.

Apple, M. W. (2001). *Educating the "right" way: Markets, standards, God, and inequality.* New York: RoutledgeFalmer.

Apple, M. W. (2004). *Ideology and curriculum* (3rd ed.). New York: RoutledgeFalmer.

Bartolomé, L. I. (1994). Beyond the methods fetish: Toward a humanizing pedagogy. *Harvard Educational Review, 64,* 173–194.

Bigelow, B. (2002). Defeating despair. In B. Bigelow & B. Peterson (Eds.), *Rethinking globalization: Teaching for justice in an unjust world* (pp. 329–334). Milwaukee, WI: Rethinking Schools, Ltd.

Bigelow, B., Christensen, L., Karp, S., Miner, B., & Peterson, B. (Eds.). (1994). *Rethinking our classrooms: Teaching for equity and justice.* Milwaukee, WI: Rethinking Schools, Ltd.

Bigelow, B., & Peterson, B. (Eds.). (1998). *Rethinking Columbus.* Milwaukee, WI: Rethinking Schools, Ltd.

Bigelow, B., & Peterson, R. (Eds.). (2002). *Rethinking globalization: Teaching for justice in an unjust world.* Milwaukee, WI: Rethinking Schools, Ltd.

Blum, W. (2004). *Killing hope: U.S. military and CIA interventions since World War II.* (Rev. ed.). Monroe, ME: Common Courage Press.

Boaler, J. (1997). *Experiencing school mathematics: Teaching styles, sex, and setting.* Buckingham, UK: Open University Press.

Bond, H. M. (1934/1966). *The education of the Negro in the American social order.* New York: Octagon Books.

Brantlinger, A. (2005). The geometry of inequality. In E. Gutstein & B. Peterson (Eds.), *Rethinking mathematics: Teaching social justice by the numbers* (pp. 97–100). Milwaukee, WI: Rethinking Schools, Ltd.

Campbell, P. F. (1996). Empowering children and teachers in the elementary mathematics classroom of urban schools. *Urban Education, 30,* 449–475.

Campbell, P. F., & Shackford, C. (1990). *EUREKA! Program evaluation.* Groton, MA: Campbell-Kibler Associates.

Carey, D. A., Fennema, E., Carpenter, T. P., & Franke, M. L. (1995). Equity and mathematics education. In W. G. Secada, E. Fennema, & L. B. Adajian (Eds.), *New directions for equity in mathematics education* (pp. 93–125). Cambridge: Cambridge University Press.

Carlson, D. L. (2002, April). *Small victories: Narratives of hope in a neo-conservative age.* Paper presented at the Annual Meeting of the American Educational Research Association, New Orleans.

Carpenter, T. P., Fennema, E., Franke, M. F., Levi, L., & Empson, S. B. (1999). *Children's mathematics: Cognitively guided instruction.* Portsmouth, NH: Heinemann.

Cave, D. (2005, March 27). For Army recruiters, a hard toll from a hard sell. *New York Times.* Retrieved March 31, 2005, from http://www.nytimes.com

Chicago Public Schools (CPS) (2004). *Magnet school study.* Retrieved January 30, 2005, from http://www.cps.edu/AboutCPS/deseg_reports/CDC3_9_MagnetSchools.pdf

Chicago Public Schools (CPS). (2005). *School test score and demographic reports.* Retrieved March 31, 2005, from http://research.cps.k12.il.us/resweb/schoolqry

Christensen, L. (2000). *Reading, writing, and rising up: Teaching about social justice and the power of the written word.* Milwaukee, WI: Rethinking Schools, Ltd.

Civil, M. (2002). Everyday mathematics, mathematicians' mathematics, and school mathematics: Can we bring them together? In M. E. Brenner & J. N. Moschkovich (Eds.), *Everyday and academic mathematics in the classroom* (pp. 40–62). Reston, VA: National Council of Teachers of Mathematics.

Civil, M. (in press). Building on community knowledge: An avenue to equity in mathematics education. In N. S. Nasir & P. Cobb (Eds.), *Diversity, equity, and access to mathematical ideas.* New York: Teachers College Press.

Civil, M., Andrade, R., & González, N. (2002). *Linking home and school: A bridge to the many faces of mathematics.* UCSC-Center for Research on Education, Diversity & Excellence. Retrieved July 20, 2004, from http://www.crede.ucsc.edu/research/md/intro4_2.shtml

Civil, M., Bernier, E., & Quintos, B. (2003, April). *Parental involvement in mathematics: A focus on parents' voices.* Paper presented at the Annual Meeting of the American Educational Research Association, Chicago.

Conforti, J. M. (1992). The legitimation of inequality in American education. *The Urban Review, 24,* 227–238.

Crane, N. (2002). *Mercator: The man who mapped the planet.* New York: Henry Holt & Company.

Cummins, J. (1989). *Empowering minority students.* Sacramento, CA: California Association of Bilingual Education.

D'Ambrosio, U. (1985). Ethnomathematics and its place in the history and pedagogy of mathematics. *For the Learning of Mathematics, 5,* 41–48.

Darder, A. (1991). *Culture and power in the classroom: A critical foundation for bicultural education.* Westport, CT: Bergin & Garvey.

Darder, A. (1997). Creating the conditions for cultural democracy in the classroom. In A. Darder, R. D. Torres, & H. Gutiérrez (Eds.), *Latinos and education: A critical reader* (pp. 331–350). New York: Routledge.

Darder, A. (2002). *Reinventing Paulo Freire: A pedagogy of love.* Boulder, CO: Westview Press.

Darling-Hammond, L., French, J., & Garcia-López, S. P. (Eds.). (2002). *Learning to teach for social justice.* New York: Teachers College Press.

de Lange, J. (1987). No change without problems. In T. A. Romberg (Ed.), *Reform in school mathematics and authentic assessment* (pp. 87–172). Albany, NY: SUNY Press.

de Lange, J., & Romberg, T. A. (2004). Monitoring student progress. In T. A. Romberg (Ed.), *Standards-based mathematics assessment in middle school: Rethinking classroom practice* (pp. 5–21). New York: Teachers College Press.

Delgado Bernal, D. (1999). Chicana/o education from the Civil Rights era to the present. In J. F. Moreno (Ed.), *The elusive quest for equality: 150 years of Chicano/Chicana education* (pp. 77–108). Cambridge, MA: Harvard Educational Review.

Delgado Bernal, D. (2000). Historical struggles for educational equity: Setting the context for Chicana/o schooling today. In C. Tejeda, C. Martinez, & Z. Leonardo (Eds.), *Charting new terrains of Chicana(o)/Latina(o) education* (pp. 67–90). Cresskill, NJ: Hampton Press.

Dell'Angelo, T. (2004, July 12). South Side faces school shakeup. Residents skeptical of city's plan. *Chicago Tribune.* Retrieved March 31, 2005, from http://www.hydepark.org/education/2010.htm

Delpit, L. (1988). The silenced dialogue: Power and pedagogy in educating other people's children. *Harvard Educational Review, 58,* 280–298.

Donato, R. (1997). *The other struggle for equal schools: Mexican Americans during the Civil Rights era.* Albany, NY: SUNY Press.

Du Bois, W. E. B. (1935). Does the Negro need separate schools? *Journal of Negro Education, 4,* 328–335.

Ellsworth, E. (1989). Why doesn't this feel empowering? Working through the repressive myths of critical pedagogy. *Harvard Educational Review, 59,* 297–324.

Emerson, R. M., Fretz, R. I., & Shaw, L. L. (1995). *Writing ethnographic fieldnotes.* Chicago: University of Chicago Press.

FairTest. (2004a). *The ACT: Biased, inaccurate, coachable, and misused.* Retrieved August 4, 2004, from http://www.fairtest.org/facts/act.html

FairTest. (2004b). *University testing: 2002 SAT scores.* Retrieved August 4, 2004, from http://www.fairtest.org/univ/2002SAT%20Scores.html

Fecho, B. (2004). *"Is this English?": Race, language, and culture in the classroom.* New York: Teachers College Press.

Fendel, D., Resek, D., Alper, L., & Fraser, S. (1998). *Interactive mathematics program.* Berkeley, CA: Key Curriculum Press.

Ferguson, A. A. (2000). *Bad boys: Public schools in the making of black masculinity.* Ann Arbor, MI: University of Michigan Press.

Foster, M. (1994). Educating for competence in community and culture: Exploring the views of exemplary African-American teachers. In M. J. Shujaa (Ed.), *Too much schooling, too little education: A paradox of Black life in white societies* (pp. 221–244). Trenton, NJ: African World Press, Inc.

Foster, M. (1997). *Black teachers on teaching.* New York: The New Press.

Foucault, M. (1977). *Discipline and punish: The birth of the prison.* New York: Pantheon Books.

Frankenstein, M. (1987). Critical mathematics education: An application of Paulo Freire's epistemology. In I. Shor (Ed.), *Freire for the classroom: A sourcebook for liberatory teaching* (pp. 180–210). Portsmouth, NH: Boyton/Cook.

Frankenstein, M. (1990). Incorporating race, gender, and class issues into a critical mathematical literacy curriculum. *Journal of Negro Education, 59,* 336–359.

Frankenstein, M. (1995). Equity in mathematics education: Class in the world outside the class. In W. G. Secada, E. Fennema, & L. B. Adajian (Eds.), *New directions for equity in mathematics education* (pp. 165–190). Cambridge: Cambridge University Press.

Frankenstein, M. (1997). In addition to the mathematics: Including equity issues in the curriculum. In J. Trentacosta & M. Kenney (Eds.), *Multicultural and gender equity in the mathematics classroom* (pp. 10–22). Reston, VA: National Council of Teachers of Mathematics.

Frankenstein, M. (1998). Reading the world with math: Goals for a critical mathematical literacy curriculum. In E. Lee, D. Menkart, & M. Okazawa-Rey (Eds.), *Beyond heroes and holidays: A practical guide to K–12 anti-racist, multicultural education and staff development* (pp. 306–313). Washington, DC: Network of Educators on the Americas.

Frankenstein, M., & Powell, A. B. (1994). Toward liberatory mathematics: Paulo Freire's epistemology and ethnomathematics. In P. L. McLaren & C. Lankshear (Eds.), *Politics of liberation: Paths from Freire* (pp. 74–99). New York: Routledge.

Freire, P. (1970/1998). *Pedagogy of the oppressed* (M. B. Ramos, Trans.). New York: Continuum.

Freire, P. (1973). *Education for critical consciousness* (M. B. Ramos, Trans.). New York. The Seabury Press.

Freire, P. (1978). *Pedagogy in process: The letters to Guinea-Bissau* (C. St. John Hunter, Trans.). New York: Continuum.

Freire, P. (1993). *Pedagogy of the city* (D. Macedo, Trans.). New York: Continuum.

Freire, P. (1994). *Pedagogy of hope: Reliving* pedagogy of the oppressed (R. R. Barr, Trans.). New York: Continuum.

Freire, P. (1998). *Teachers as cultural workers: Letters to those who dare teach* (D. Macedo, D. Koike, & A. Oliveira, Trans.). Boulder, CO: Westview Press.

Freire, P., & Faundez, A. (1992). *Learning to question: A pedagogy of liberation* (T. Coates, Trans.). New York: Continuum.

Freire, P., & Macedo, D. (1987). *Literacy: Reading the word and the world.* Westport, CT: Bergin & Garvey.

Freudenthal, H. (1983). *Didactical phenomenology of mathematical structures.* Dordrecht, The Netherlands: Kluwer.

Freudenthal, H. (1991). *Revisiting mathematics education: China lectures.* Dordrecht, The Netherlands: Kluwer.

Galster, S. (2001). *Afghanistan: The making of U.S. policy, 1973–1990.* The National Security Archive. Retrieved April 28, 2005, from http://www.gwu.edu/~nsarchiv/NSAEBB/NSAEBB57/essay.html

Gandin, L. A. (2002). *Democratizing access, governance, and knowledge: The struggle for educational alternatives in Porto Alegre, Brazil.* Unpublished doctoral dissertation, University of Wisconsin, Madison.

Gandin, L. A., & Apple, M. W. (2003). Educating the state, democratizing knowledge: The Citizen School Project in Porto Alegre, Brazil. In *The state and the politics of knowledge* (pp. 193–219). New York, RoutledgeFalmer.

Gardner, H. (1983). *Frames of mind: The theory of multiple intelligences.* New York: Basic Books.

Gee, J. P. (1999). *An introduction to discourse analysis: Theory and method.* London: Routledge.

Getz, J. M. (1997). *Schools of their own: The education of Hispanos in New Mexico, 1850–1940.* Albuquerque, NM: University of New Mexico Press.

Giroux, H. A. (1983). *Theory and resistance in education: Toward a pedagogy for the opposition.* Westport, CT: Bergin & Garvey.

González, G. G. (1999). Segregation and the education of Mexican children, 1900–1940. In J. F. Moreno (Ed.), *The elusive quest for equality: 150 years of Chicano/Chicana education* (pp. 53–76). Cambridge, MA: Harvard Educational Review.

Graue, M. E., & Smith, S. Z. (1996). Parents and mathematics education reform: Voicing the authority of assessment. *Urban Education, 30,* 395–421.

Guajardo, M, A., & Guajardo, F. J. (2004). The impact of Brown on the brown of South Texas: A micropolitical perspective on the education of Mexican Americans in a south Texas community. *American Educational Research Journal, 41,* 501–526.

Guberman, S. R. (2004). A comparative study of children's out-of-school activities and arithmetical achievements. *Journal for Research in Mathematics Education, 34,* 117–150.

Gumbel, A. (2003, September 10). Pentagon targets Latinos and Mexicans to man the front lines in war on terror. *The Independent.* Retrieved March 31, 2005, from http://news.independent.co.uk/

Gutiérrez, R. (2001). Enabling the practice of mathematics teachers in context: Toward a new equity research agenda. *Mathematical Thinking and Learning, 4,* 145–187.

Gutiérrez, R. (2002). Beyond essentialism: The complexity of language in teaching mathematics to Latina/o students. *American Educational Research Journal, 39,* 1047–1088.

Gutiérrez, R. A. (2004). Ethnic Mexicans in historical and social science scholarship. In J. A. Banks & C. A. McGee Banks (Eds.), *Handbook of research on multicultural education* (2nd ed., pp. 261–287). San Francisco: Jossey-Bass.

Gutstein, E. (1998, April). *Lessons from adopting and adapting Mathematics in Context, a standards-based mathematics curriculum, in an urban, Latino, bilingual middle school.* Paper presented at the Annual Meeting of the American Educational Research Association, San Diego.

Gutstein, E. (2002). Math, SATs, and racial profiling. *Rethinking Schools, 16*(4), 18–19.

Gutstein, E. (2003a). Home buying while Brown or Black: Teaching mathematics for racial justice. *Rethinking Schools, 18*(1), 35–37.

Gutstein, E. (2003b, April). *Latino/a students' voices: The impact of high-stakes tests and the development of student agency.* Paper presented at the Annual Meeting of the American Educational Research Association, Chicago.

Gutstein, E. (2003c). Teaching and learning mathematics for social justice in an urban, Latino school. *Journal for Research in Mathematics Education, 34*, 37–73.

Gutstein, E. (2005). Real-world projects: Seeing math all around us. In E. Gutstein & B. Peterson (Eds.), *Rethinking mathematics: Teaching social justice by the numbers* (pp. 117–121). Milwaukee, WI: Rethinking Schools, Ltd.

Gutstein, E. (in press-a). "And that's just how it starts": Teaching mathematics to develop student agency. *Teachers College Record.*

Gutstein, E. (in press-b). Driving while Black or Brown: The mathematics of racial profiling. In J. Masingila (Ed.), *Teachers engaged in research: Inquiry into mathematics practice in grades 6–8.* Reston, VA: National Council of Teachers of Mathematics.

Gutstein, E. (in press-c). "So one question leads to another": Using mathematics to develop a pedagogy of questioning. In N. S. Nasir & P. Cobb (Eds.), *Diversity, equity, and access to mathematical ideas.* New York: Teachers College Press.

Gutstein, E. (in press-d). "The real world as we have seen it": Latino/a parents' voices on mathematics for social justice. *Mathematical Thinking and Learning.*

Gutstein, E., Barbosa, M., Calderón, A., Murillo, G., & Nevárez, L. (2003, April). *A Freirean approach to learning mathematics in an urban Latino/a middle school: Examining the long-term influence.* Paper presented at the Annual Meeting of the American Educational Research Association, Chicago.

Gutstein, E., Lipman, P., Hernández, P., & de los Reyes, R. (1997). Culturally relevant mathematics teaching in a Mexican American context. *Journal for Research in Mathematics Education, 28*, 709–737.

Gutstein, E., & Peterson, B. (Eds.). (2005). *Rethinking mathematics: Teaching social justice by the numbers.* Milwaukee, WI: Rethinking Schools, Ltd.

Hammersley, M., & Atkinson, P. (1983). *Ethnography: Principles in practice.* London: Tavistock Publications.

Harding, V. (1990). *Hope and history: Why we must share the story of the movement.* Maryknoll, NY: Orbis.

Harvey, D. (2003). *The new imperialism.* New York: Oxford University Press.

Haymes, S. N. (2002). Race, pedagogy, and Paulo Freire. In S. Fletcher (Ed.), *Annual Yearbook of the Philosophy of Education Society* (pp. 151–159). Champaign, IL: University of Illinois at Urbana-Champaign.

Hecker, D. E. (2001, November). Occupational employment projections to 2010. *Monthly Labor Review, 124*(11), 57–84.

Hiebert, J., Carpenter, T., Fennema, E., Fuson, K., Wearne, D., Murray, H. et al. (2003). *Making sense: Teaching and learning mathematics with understanding.* Portsmouth, NH: Heinemann.

Hill, H., & Ball, D. L. (2004). Learning mathematics for teaching: Results from California's mathematics professional development institutes. *Journal for Research in Mathematics Education, 35*, 330–335.

Hilliard, Asa, III. (1991). Do we have the will to educate all children? *Educational Leadership, 31*(1), 31–36.

Holt, Rinehart, & Winston (2004). *School district of Philadelphia realizes mathematics improvement with curriculum reforms aligned with Holt math materials.* Press Release. Retrieved March 15, 2005, from http://www.hrw.com/about/press/MICPhilly.htm

hooks, b. (1994). *Teaching to transgress: Education as the practice of freedom.* London: Falmer Press.

Human Relations Foundation/Jane Addams Policy Initiative. (2003). *Minding the gap: An assessment of racial disparity in metropolitan Chicago.* Chicago: Jane Addams Hull House Association.

Jablonka, E. (2003). Mathematical literacy. In A. Bishop, M. A. Clements, C. Keitel, J. Kilpatrick, & F. Leung (Eds.), *Second international handbook of mathematics education* (pp. 75–102). Dordrecht, The Netherlands: Kluwer.

Joseph, G. G. (1997). Foundations of Eurocentrism in mathematics. In A. B. Powell & M. Frankenstein (Eds.), *Ethnomathematics: Challenging Eurocentrism in mathematics education* (pp. 61–81). Albany, NY: SUNY Press.

Kaiser, W. L., & Wood, D. (2001). *Seeing through maps: The power of images to shape our world view.* Amherst, MA: ODT, Inc.

Karier, C. J. (1972). Testing for order and control in the corporate state. *Educational Theory, 22,* 159–180.

Khisty, L. L. (1995). Making inequality: Issues of language and meanings in mathematics teaching with Hispanic students. In W. G. Secada, E. Fennema, & L. B. Adajian (Eds.), *New directions for equity in mathematics education* (pp. 279–297). Cambridge: Cambridge University Press.

Kilian, M., & Horan, D. (2005, March 31). Enlistment drought spurs new strategies. *Chicago Tribune.* Retrieved March 31, 2005, from http://www.chicagotribune.com

King, M. L. (1986). *A last testament of hope: The essential writings and speeches of Martin Luther King, Jr.* (J. M. Washington, Ed.). New York: HarperCollins Publishers.

Knapp, M. S., & Woolverton, S. (2004). Social class and schooling. In J. A. Banks & C. A. McGee Banks (Eds.), *Handbook of research on multicultural education* (2nd ed., pp. 656–681). San Francisco: Jossey-Bass.

Kohl, H. (1991). *I won't learn from you: The role of assent in learning.* Minneapolis, MN: Milkweed.

Ladson-Billings, G. (1994). *The dreamkeepers: Successful teachers of African American children.* San Francisco: Jossey-Bass.

Ladson-Billings, G. (1995a). Making mathematics meaningful in multicultural contexts. In W. G. Secada, E. Fennema, & L. B. Adajian (Eds.), *New directions for equity in mathematics education* (pp. 126–145). Cambridge: Cambridge University Press.

Ladson-Billings, G. (1995b). Toward a theory of culturally relevant pedagogy. *American Educational Research Journal, 32,* 465–491.

Ladson-Billings, G. (1997). I know why this doesn't feel empowering: A critical race analysis of critical pedagogy. In P. Freire (Ed.), *Mentoring the mentor: A critical dialogue with Paulo Freire* (pp. 127–141). New York: Peter Lang Publishing.

Ladson-Billings, G. (2001). *Crossing over to Canaan: The journey of new teachers in diverse classrooms.* San Francisco: Jossey-Bass.

Ladson-Billings, G., & Tate, W. F. (1995). Toward a critical race theory of education. *Teachers College Record, 97,* 47–68.

Lankshear, C., & Lawler, M. (1987). *Literacy, schooling, and revolution.* Philadelphia: Falmer Press.

Lappan, G., Fey, J., Fitzgerald, W., Friel, S., & Phillips, E. (1997). *Connected mathematics.* Palo Alto, CA: Dale Seymour.

Lave, J. (1988). *Cognition in practice: Mind, mathematics, and culture in everyday life.* Cambridge: Cambridge University Press.

Lave, J., & Wenger, E. (1991). *Situated learning: Legitimate peripheral participation.* Cambridge: Cambridge University Press.

Lipman, P. (1998). *Race, class, and power in school restructuring.* Albany, NY: SUNY Press.

Lipman, P. (2002). Making the global city, making inequality: Political economy and cultural politics of Chicago school policy. *American Educational Research Journal, 39,* 379–419.

Lipman, P. (2004). *High stakes education: Inequality, globalization, and urban school reform.* New York: Routledge.

Lipman, P. (2005, April). *Public education and the remaking of urban/metroregion space: The case of Chicago and its metropolitan region.* Paper presented at the annual meeting of the American Educational Research Association, Montreal.

Lipman, P., & Gutstein, E. (2001). Undermining the struggle for equity: A case study of a Chicago Latino/a school. *Race, Gender, and Class, 8,* 57–80.

Lipman, P., & Gutstein, E. (2004). The politics and policies of cultural assimilation. In *High stakes education: Inequality, globalization, and urban school reform* (pp. 105–137). New York: Routledge.

Macedo, D. (1994). *Literacies of power: What Americans are not allowed to know.* Boulder, CO: Westview Press.

Mack, N. (1990). Learning fractions with understanding: Building on informal knowledge. *Journal for Research in Mathematics Education, 21,* 16–32.

MacLeod, J. (1995). *Ain't no makin' it: Aspirations and attainment in a low-income neighborhood.* Boulder, CO: Westview Press.

Manor, R. (2002, October 5). Mortgage OKs tougher for local blacks, Latinos. *Chicago Tribune,* pp. 1–2.

Martin, D. B. (2000). *Mathematics success and failure among African-American youth: The roles of sociohistorical context, community forces, school influence, and individual agency.* Mahwah, NJ: Erlbaum Associates.

Martin, D. B. (2004, April). *African-American parents speak on the struggle for mathematics literacy.* Paper presented at the Annual Meeting of the National Council of Teachers of Mathematics Research Presession, Philadelphia.

May, S. (Ed.). (1999). *Critical multiculturalism: Rethinking multicultural and antiracist education.* London: Falmer Press.

Mayfield, K., & Whitlow, B. (Eds.). (1983). *Use EQUALS to promote the participation of women in mathematics.* Berkeley, CA: Lawrence Hall of Science, University of California.

McLaren, P. (1998). Revolutionary pedagogy in post-revolutionary times: Rethinking the political economy of critical education. *Educational Theory, 48,* 431–463.

Michaels Development Company (MDC). (2005). *Legends South formerly known as Robert Taylor Homes.* Michaels Development Company. Retrieved March 31, 2005, from http://www.michaelsdevelopmentcompany.com/portfRobertTaylor.html

Mehta, C., Theodore, N., Mora, I., & Wade, J. (2002). *Chicago's undocumented immigrants: An analysis of wages, working conditions, and economic contributions.* Chicago: University of Illinois–Chicago, Center for Urban Economic Development.

Moll, L. C, & González, N. (2004). A funds-of-knowledge approach to multicultural education. In J. A. Banks & C. A. McGee Banks (Eds.), *Handbook of research on multicultural education* (2nd ed., pp. 699–715). San Francisco: Jossey-Bass.

Moody, B. (2004, July 23). Chicago public schools to get naval high school. Press release. *Navy Newstand.* Retrieved July 14, 2005, from http://www.news.navy.mil/search/display.asp?story_id=14385

Morrell, E. (2005, February 3). Doing critical social research with youth. Talk given at DePaul University, Chicago, IL.

Moschkovich, J. (2002). A situated and sociocultural perspective on bilingual mathematics learners. *Mathematical Thinking and Learning, 4,* 189–212.

Moses, R. P., & Cobb, C. E., Jr. (2001). *Radical equations: Math literacy and civil rights.* Boston: Beacon Press.

Mukhopadhyay, S. (1998). When Barbie goes to classrooms: Mathematics in creating a social discourse. In C. Keitel (Ed.), *Social justice and mathematics education* (pp. 150–161). Berlin: Freie Universitat.

Mukhopadhyay, S., & Greer, B. (2001). Modeling with purpose: Mathematics as a critical tool. In B. Atweh, H. Forgasz, & B. Nebres (Eds.), *Sociocultural research on mathematics education: An international perspective* (pp. 295–312). Mahwah, NJ: Erlbaum.

Murrell, P. C., Jr. (1997). Digging again the family wells: A Freirean literacy framework as emancipatory pedagogy for African-American children. In P. Freire (Ed.), *Mentoring the mentor: A critical dialogue with Paulo Freire* (pp. 19–55). New York: Peter Lang Publishing.

National Assessment of Educational Progress. (2004). *Gaps in average mathematics scale scores, by race/ethnicity, grades 4 and 8: 1990–2003.* Retrieved August 4, 2004, from http://nces.ed.gov/nationsreportcard/mathematics/results2003/scale-ethnic-compare.asp

National Center for Education Statistics. (2003). *Status and trends in the education of Hispanics.* Retrieved January 22, 2005, from http://nces.ed.gov/pubs2003/2003008.pdf

NCRMSE & FI (National Center for Research in Mathematical Sciences Education & Freudenthal Institute). (1997–1998). *Mathematics in context: A connected curriculum for grades 5–8.* Chicago: Encyclopedia Britannica Educational Corporation.

NCRMSE & FI (National Center for Research in Mathematical Sciences Education & Freudenthal Institute). (1998). *Teacher resource and implementation guide.* Chicago: Encyclopedia Britannica Educational Corporation.

National Council of Teachers of Mathematics. (1989). *Curriculum and evaluation standards for school mathematics.* Reston, VA: Author.

National Council of Teachers of Mathematics. (2000). *Principles and standards for school mathematics.* Reston, VA: Author.

No Child Left Behind Act of 2001. (2001). U.S. Public Law 107–110. 107th Congress, 1st session, January 8, 2002.

Nunes, T., Schliemann, A. A., & Carraher, D. W. (1993). *Street mathematics and school mathematics.* Cambridge: Cambridge University Press.

Oakes, J., Joseph, R., & Muir, K. (2004). Access and achievement in mathematics and science: Inequalities that endure and change. In J. A. Banks & C. A. McGee Banks (Eds.), *Handbook of research on multicultural education* (2nd ed., pp. 69–90). San Francisco: Jossey-Bass.

Oakes, J., Wells, A. S., Jones, M., & Datnow, A. (1997). Detracking: The social construction of ability, cultural politics, and resistance to reform. *Teachers College Record, 98*, 482–510.

O'Cadiz, M., Wong, P., Torres, C. (1998). *Education and democracy: Paulo Freire, social movements, and educational reform in São Paulo.* Boulder, CO: Westview Press.

ODT. (2001). *What's up south?* [World Map.] Amherst, MA: Author.

Oliver, M. L., & Shapiro, T. M. (1997). *Black wealth, white wealth: A new perspective on racial inequality.* New York: Routledge.

Ortiz-Franco, L. (1999). Chicanos have math in their blood: Pre-Columbian mathematics. In I. Shor & C. Pari (Eds.), *Education is politics: Critical teaching across differences, K–12* (pp. 215–225). Portsmouth, NH: Heinemann.

Ortiz-Franco, L., & Flores, W. V. (2001). Sociocultural considerations and Latino mathematics achievement: A critical review. In B. Atweh, H. Forgasz, & B. Nebres (Eds.), *Sociocultural research on mathematics education: An international perspective* (pp. 233–253). Mahwah, NJ: Erlbaum Associates.

Pang, V. O., Kiang, P. N., & Pak, Y. K. (2004). Asian Pacific American students: Challenging a biased educational system. In J. A. Banks & C. A. McGee Banks (Eds.), *Handbook of research on multicultural education* (2nd ed., pp. 542–563). San Francisco: Jossey-Bass.

Paral, R. (2002). Mexican immigrant workers and the U.S. economy: An increasingly vital role. *Immigration Policy Focus, 1*(2).

Parker, L., Deyhle, D., & Villenas, S. (Eds.). (1999). *Race is … race isn't: Critical race theory and qualitative studies in education.* Boulder, CO: Westview Press.

Perry, T. (1996). Situating Malcolm X in the African-American narrative tradition: Freedom for literacy and literacy for freedom. In T. Perry (Ed.), *Teaching Malcolm X* (pp. 1–21). New York: Routledge.

Perry, T. (2003). Up from the parched earth: Toward a theory of African-American achievement. In *Young, gifted, and black: Promoting high achievement among African-American students* (pp. 1–108). Boston: Beacon Press.

Peters, A. (1983). Peters projection world map. Cincinnati, OH: Friendship Press.

Peterson, B. (1995). Teaching math across the curriculum: A 5th grade teacher battles "number numbness." *Rethinking Schools, 10*(1), 1 & 4–5.

Peterson, B. (2003). Understanding large numbers. *Rethinking Schools, 18*(1), 33–34.

Pew Hispanic Center. (2003). *Hispanics in the military.* Washington, DC: Author.

Phillips, S., & Ebrahimi, H. (1993). Equation for success: Project SEED. In G. Cuevas & M. Driscoll (Eds.), *Reaching all students with mathematics* (pp. 59–74). Reston, VA: National Council of Teachers of Mathematics.

PNAC (Project for the New American Century). (2000). *Rebuilding America's defenses: Strategy, forces and resources for a new century.* Washington, DC: Author.

Provenzo, E. F. (Ed.). (2002). *Du Bois on education.* Walnut Creek, CA: Rowman & Littlefield.

Ramos, A. (Author). (1993). *The last angry brown hat.* [Play]. United States: Los Angeles.

Riggs, M. (Producer/Director). (1987). *Ethnic notions: Black people in white minds.* [Motion picture]. (Available from California Newsreel, 500 Third Street, Suite 505, San Francisco, CA 94107; http://www.newsreel.org).

Rist, R. (1970). Student social class and teacher expectations: The self-fulfilling prophecy in ghetto education. *Harvard Educational Review, 40*, 411–451.

Romberg T. A., & Shafer, M. C. (2003). Mathematics in Context: Preliminary evidence about student outcomes. In S. S. Senk & D. R. Thompson (Eds.), *Standards-based school mathematics curricula: What are they? What do students learn?* (pp. 225–250). Mahwah NJ: Erlbaum.

Rosenkranz, T. (2002). *2001 CPS test trend review: Iowa test of basic skills.* Chicago: Consortium on Chicago Schools Research.

Ruiz, L. I., & Racho, S. (1996). *Taking back the schools. Chicano: A history of the Mexican-American civil rights movement (Segment III).* [Documentary film]. (Available from Galán Incorporated Television and Film, 5524 Bee Caves Rd., Suite B-5, Austin, TX 78746; http://www.galaninc.com/site/archives/11).

Russo, A. (2003, June). Constructing a new school. *Catalyst Chicago.* Retrieved July 13, 2005, from http://www.catalyst-chicago.org/06-03/0603littlevillage.htm#

San Miguel, G. (1997). Roused from our slumbers. In A. Darder, R. D. Torres, & H. Gutiérrez (Eds.), *Latinos and education: A critical reader* (pp. 135–157). New York: Routledge.

Schlosser, E. (2002). *Fast food nation: What the all-American meal is doing to the world.* London: Penguin Books.

Secada, W. G. (1991a). Agenda setting, enlightened self-interest, and equity in mathematics education. *Peabody Journal of Education, 66,* 22–56.

Secada, W. G. (1991b). Diversity, equity, and cognitivist research. In E. Fennema, T. P. Carpenter, & S. J. Lamon (Eds.), *Integrating research on teaching and learning mathematics* (pp. 17–53). Albany, NY: SUNY Press.

Secada, W. G. (1992). Race, ethnicity, social class, language, and achievement in mathematics. In D. A. Grouws (Ed.), *Handbook of research on mathematics teaching and learning* (pp. 623–660). New York: Macmillan.

Secada, W. G. (1996). Urban students acquiring English and learning mathematics in the context of reform. *Urban Education, 30,* 422–448.

Secada, W. G. (Ed.). (1999–2002). *Changing the Faces of Mathematics (Vols. 1–6).* Reston, VA: National Council of Teachers of Mathematics.

Secada, W. G., Fennema, E., & Adajian, L. B. (Eds.). (1995). *New directions for equity in mathematics education.* Cambridge: Cambridge University Press.

Selden, S. (1999). *Inheriting shame: The story of eugenics and racism in America.* New York: Teachers College Press.

Setati, M. (in press). Learning and teaching mathematics in a primary multilingual classroom. *Journal for Research in Mathematics Education.*

Setati, M., & Adler, J. (2001). Between languages and discourses: Language practices in primary multilingual mathematics classrooms in South Africa. *Educational Studies in Mathematics, 43,* 243–269.

Shulman, L. S. (1986). Those who understand: Knowledge growth in teaching. *Educational Researcher, 15,* 4–14.

Siddle Walker, V. (1996). *Their highest potential: An African-American school community in the segregated south.* Chapel Hill, NC: University of North Carolina Press.

Silver, E. A., & Stein, M. K. (1996). THE QUASAR Project: The "revolution of the possible" in mathematics instructional reform in urban middle schools. *Urban Education, 30,* 476–521.

Skovsmose, O. (1994). *Toward a philosophy of critical mathematics education.* Boston: Kluwer Academic Publishers.

Skovsmose, O. (2004). *Critical mathematics education for the future.* Aalborg, Denmark: Aalborg University, Department of Education and Learning.

Skovsmose, O. (2005). *Traveling through education: Uncertainty, mathematics, responsibility.* Rotterdam, The Netherlands: Sense Publishers.

Skovsmose, O., & Valero, P. (2001). Breaking political neutrality. The critical engagement of mathematics education with democracy. In B. Atweh, H. Forgasz, & B. Nebres (Eds.), *Sociocultural aspects of mathematics education: An international research perspective* (pp. 37–56). Mahwah, NJ: Lawrence Erlbaum.

Skovsmose, O., & Valero, P. (2002). Democratic access to powerful mathematical ideas. In L. English (Ed.), *Handbook of international research in mathematics education* (pp. 383–407). Mahwah, NJ: Lawrence Erlbaum.

Sleeter, C. E., & Delgado Bernal, D. (2004). Critical pedagogy, critical race theory, and antiracist education: Implications for multicultural education. In J. A. Banks & C. A. McGee Banks (Eds.), *Handbook of research on multicultural education* (2nd ed., pp. 240–258). San Francisco: Jossey-Bass.

Sleeter, C. E., & McLaren, P. L. (Eds.). (1995). *Multicultural education, critical pedagogy, and the politics of difference.* Albany, NY: SUNY Press.

Spielberg, S. (Producer/Director). (1993). *Schindler's list.* [Motion picture]. United States: Universal Studios & Amblin Entertainment.

Spring, J. H. (1976). *The sorting machine: National educational policy since 1945.* New York: Longman.

Steele, L. (2004). Sweatshop accounting. *Rethinking Schools, 19*(1), 38–42.

Stevenson, M. (2003, May 9). U.S. Army recruiter crosses Mexico border. *Miami Herald.* Retrieved March 31, 2005, from http://www.latinamericanstudies.org/immigration/recruiter.htm

Streefland, L. (1993). Fractions: A realistic approach. In T. P. Carpenter, E. Fennema, & T. A. Romberg (Eds.), *Rational numbers: An integration of research* (pp. 289–325). Mahwah, NJ: Erlbaum.

Stubbs, A. (Ed.). (1978). *I write what I like/Steve Biko: A selection of his writings edited with a personal memoir by Aelred Stubbs.* London: Bowerdean Press.

Takaki, R. T. (1993). *A different mirror: A history of multicultural America.* Boston: Little, Brown, & Co.

Tate, W. F. (1994). Race, retrenchment, and the reform of school mathematics. *Phi Delta Kappan, 75,* 477–485.

Tate, W. F. (1995). Returning to the root: A culturally relevant approach to mathematics pedagogy. *Theory into Practice, 34,* 166–173.

Tate, W. F. (1996). Urban schools and mathematics reform: Implementing new standards. *Urban Education, 30,* 371–378.

Tate, W. F. (1997). Race-ethnicity, SES, gender, and language proficiency trends in mathematics achievement: An update. *Journal for Research in Mathematics Education, 28,* 652–679.

Tate, W. F. (1999). Conclusion. In L. Parker, D. Deyhle, & S. Villenas (Eds.), *Race is ... race isn't: Critical race theory and qualitative studies in education* (pp. 251–271). Boulder, CO: Westview Press.

Tate, W. F., & Rousseau, C. (2002). Access and opportunity: The political and social context of mathematics education. In L. English (Ed.), *International handbook of research in mathematics education* (pp. 271–300). Mahwah, NJ: Lawrence Erlbaum.

Tung, J. (1981). *The socialist road: Character of revolution in the U.S. and problems of socialism in the Soviet Union and China.* New York: César Cauce Publishers.

Turner, E. E., & Font Strawhun, B. T. (2005). "With math, it's like you have more defense." In E. Gutstein & B. Peterson (Eds.), *Rethinking mathematics: Teaching social justice by the numbers* (pp. 81–87). Milwaukee, WI: Rethinking Schools, Ltd.

Tyler, P. (2003, February 17). News analysis: A new power in the streets. *New York Times.* Retrieved March 31, 2005, from http://www.nytimes.com

Valdés, G. (1996). *Con respeto: Bridging the distances between culturally diverse families and schools.* New York: Teachers College Press.

Valenzuela, A. (Ed.). (2005). *Leaving children behind: How "Texas-style" accountability fails Latino youth.* Albany, NY: SUNY Press.

Walkerdine, V. (1998). *Counting girls out: Girls and mathematics.* London: Falmer Press.

Weiler, K. (1991.) Freire and a feminist pedagogy of difference. *Harvard Educational Review, 61,* 449–474.

Weis, L., & Fine, M. (1996). Narrating the 1980s and 1990s: Voices of poor and working-class White and African American men. *Anthropology & Education Quarterly, 27,* 493–516.

Wheelock, A. (1992). *Crossing the tracks: How untracking can save America's schools.* New York: The New Press.

Wolff, E. N. (1995). *Top heavy: The increasing inequality of wealth in American and what can be done about it.* New York: The New Press.

Woodson, C. G. (1933/1990). *The mis-education of the Negro.* Trenton, NJ: Africa World Press, Inc.

World Social Forum (WSF). (2005a). *Call from social movements.* Retrieved March 4, 2005, from http://www.forumsocialmundial.org.br/dinamic.php?pagina=decl_mov_soc_2005_in

World Social Forum (WSF). (2005b). *World Social Forum 2005 memorial.* Retrieved March 4, 2005, from http://www.forumsocialmundial.org.br/main.php?id_menu=14_5&cd_language=2

Zinn, H. (2003). *A people's history of the United States: 1492–present.* New York: HarperCollins.

Appendix 1: Real-World Projects

Note: Here are seven projects essentially in the form that I gave them to students, except for the "racial profiling" project, which is the teacher's version. They were all group projects and were all preceded and followed by whole-class discussions about both the mathematics and the issues in the projects. Please feel free to contact me with questions, suggestions, critiques, and/or feedback at gutstein@uic.edu

Project 1: Morningside Neighborhood Project
[Note: Street names are pseudonyms.]

We are going to study the current struggles in Morningside. Right now, Morningside is an important neighborhood in the city for many reasons —we will look at Morningside and these issues using mathematics as a tool to understand (and change) our world.

Real Estate Development in Morningside

Real estate developers buy land, sometimes with buildings, to build new housing. Sometimes they tear down the old buildings, sometimes they fix them up. They then sell the new (or fixed up) buildings.

   1. Why do you think real-estate developers buy buildings and fix them up?

Currently, several real estate developers are working in Morningside. The following article explains some things happening at the east edge of

Morningside. What direction is east? Can you point to it? What are the other directions? Point to them also.

Find the Sears Tower on Map #1, then find the corner of Manville and Schlichter where the park in the article is located. The *scale* in the map is 1 mile = 12 centimeters.

2. What does the sentence about the scale of the map mean?

3. About how far is it from the Sears Tower to the park? Explain how you found the answer.

4. If you can drive about 25 miles per hour in a car on city streets, about how long will it take you to drive from the new lofts at the park to the Sears Tower? Explain how you found the answer.

5. Does your answer to problem #5 help you understand why Falken Associates wants to build lofts at 45th and Diversey? Why do you think they want to build lofts there?

6. Find both the park and the corner of 53rd and Walmet on Map #2. Use a ruler and the scale of Map #1 to figure out the scale of Map #2. Explain HOW you did this.

7. About how far is it from the park to 53rd and Walmet? Explain how you found the answer.

8. Write a paragraph saying why or why not you think the city should allow Falken to buy the land where the park is.

Project 2: Will Development Bury the *Barrio*?

As you all know, real estate developers are looking at Morningside as a new place to develop property. In this project, we will read an article from the weekly *Gazette*, entitled, "Will Development Bury the *Barrio*?" and then answer lots of questions.

Make sure that you *thoroughly* explain how you solved each problem, including showing *all* your work (if you used a calculator, explain *exactly* what you did).

On page 20, the article says "one commercial property in the heart of Morningside was on the market for $299,000 a year ago; now it's going for $369,000 with no improvements."

1. What is the percentage increase in the price?

2. If the same rate of increase continues for the next 2 years, what will be the price in the year 2000?

The Rehaven Development Co. is building 752 homes just south of Morningside. The houses will cost an average of $198,000; the least expensive will be $125,000 and the most expensive, $350,000. Twenty percent are supposed to be "affordable," so those are probably the $125,000 homes. Use this information for the following questions.

3. Assume that the article got the average price wrong (but other information correct) and also assume houses cost either $125,000 (20% of the total) or $350,000. What would the average price of a house be?

4. Now forget those assumptions you just made for problem #3 and assume the article is totally correct. House prices are between $125,000 and $350,000; 752 will be built, and the average price will be $198,000. For this problem, assume that there are two other house prices between the high and low figures—you can make up those amounts. Figure out how many houses of each of the four house prices will be built (remember 752 in all) so that the average of all the houses is $198,000.

5. To buy a $125,000 house, the article says that a family of four needs to make $47,000 a year, or 80% of the median income in the metropolitan area. How much is the median income in the metropolitan area for family of four?

6. If a family needs an income of $47,000 to buy a $125,000 house, how much is needed to buy a $350,000 house?

7. According to the article, the annual median family income for a family of four in Morningside is $22,000. How expensive a house could that family afford?

8. According to development supporters, up to 4,000 new jobs will be created in Morningside, and the Rehaven expansion will create an additional 400. Opponents say there's no guarantee those jobs will go to Morningside residents, and that Rehaven guaranteed that 20% of the jobs will go to Latinos/as from the

whole city. Using the figure of 20% of the jobs going to Latinos/as, how many jobs will go to Latinos/as and about how many to Latinos/as from Morningside?

9. Write a 1–2 page paper that explains your view about the development in Morningside. Do you think development will bury the barrio? Why or why not? You must use mathematics to support your arguments—this is a KEY part of this essay! Use information from the article and from other sources (parents, teachers, the media, etc.) to support your views. This needs to be a well-written essay, like for Language Arts! What do you think should be done and what do you think you, as a young person, can do about it?

Project 3: World Wealth Simulation

Use the data on the attached sheet to answer the following questions.

1. Which continent has the most wealth per person, on average? How much (in dollars)? Which continent has the least wealth per person, on average? How much (in dollars)?

2. (You can use either cookies, easier! or $$ for these questions, please carry them out to one decimal place.) Complete the table below where each entry means the ratio of the average wealth of a person in the "column" continent to the average wealth of a person in the "row" continent.

Wealth Ratio	Africa	Asia	Europe	N. America	Oceania/Aust.	S. America
Africa	—					
Asia		—				
Europe			—			
N. America				—		
Oceania/Australia					—	
S. America						—

3. What are some possible reasons for the unequal wealth distribution? Do you think it was always like that? Why or why not?

4. What did you think/know about this situation before this and what did you learn from this activity? How did you use mathematics to understand the situation (be specific!)?

5. After doing the activity, what are your questions and what more do you want/need to know?

6. What do you think/feel about the situation now?

World Wealth Data

Continent	Population (in millions) 2000	Percent of Population	Wealth % (GNP in billions of dollars)	Percentage
Africa	794		495.4	
Asia	3,672		7,172.6	
North America	314		8,933.6	
Sth/Cntrl America	519		1,430.7	
Europe	727		9,606.3	
Oceania/Australia	31		442.4	
Total	6, 057	100.0%	28,081	100.0%

Number of people in classroom _____   Total Number of Cookies _____

Continent	Pop. %	# of People in Class	Wealth %	# Cookies
Africa				
Asia				
North America				
South America				
Europe				
Oceania/Australia				
Total	~100.0%		~100.0	

World population figures are from the United Nations Population Division (www.un.org/esa/population). GNP figures are from the World Bank (www.worldbank.org/depweb/english/modules/economic/gnp). For this chart, one-third of Russia's GNP was attributed to Asia and two-thirds to Europe. *Note:* North America data does *not* include Mexico! [Adapted from Bigelow, B. & Peterson, B. (Eds.). (2002).]

Project 4: Analyzing Map Projections—What Do They Really Show?

In this project, you will investigate two different world maps, the *Mercator* Projection and the *Peters* Projection, and answer some questions about how these maps show the world.

Part 1

Creating maps takes mathematics. Every map (a two-dimensional object) of the world (a three-dimensional object) distorts reality in some way. Imagine peeling an orange without tearing it and then laying the peel totally flat. You can't! So it becomes clear that mapmakers must make some decisions about how to represent the world in two dimensions. Again, we see that mathematics affects how we understand the world around us.

The main point of this project is to compare the distortions in the Mercator Projection Map and the Peters projection. The Mercator was created in 1569 in Germany during the rise of European colonial expansion. It has been a popular map in the United States for quite some time, especially in schools, although that has been changing in recent years. But it is the map in all our classrooms at Rivera.

You will examine several countries in different parts of the world to see how Mercator visually represents areas and if it distorts their sizes. You can look at countries at the same latitude as well as those in different latitudes. For every country you pick, make sure that you have a good estimate of its area based on the scale of the map. Mexico will be our standard unit of measure, and its size is about 760,000 square miles.

Make sure you compare and record your estimates of the areas of the following pairs of places: (1) Mexico and Alaska; (2) Greenland and Africa; (3) India and Scandinavia (which, for these purposes, is Sweden, Norway, and Finland).

Find the equator on the Mercator map. Figure out two different ways to mathematically describe the effect on the viewer that the placement of the equator has.

As always, explain *exactly* how you did the math to find your estimates.

Part 2

  1. When you finish Part 1, get a world almanac and write down the real area of each region/country, and the difference.

2. On the Peters Projection (yours or the big one), examine the size of Mexico and Alaska, and Greenland and Africa. Using estimation, does the Peters Map accurately show the sizes of the countries/regions (by now you know Mexico is slightly bigger than Alaska and Africa is over 14 times bigger than Greenland!)

3. In your groups, discuss and then turn in, in writing, your answers to these questions:

a. Which map do you feel is more accurate and why? (Remember we all agreed that a map should accurately represent directions, longitude, latitude, shape, and sizes.)

b. How does moving the equator down in the Mercator affect how we see the North (mainly North America, Europe, including the former Soviet Union, Greenland), as opposed to how we see the South (mainly Africa, Asia, Central/South America, Australia)—who lives mainly in the north versus who lives mainly in the south (in terms of race)?

c. Which map are you more used to?

d. After doing this project, which map do you prefer and why?

Part 3: Individual Writeup

1. What did you learn in this project, about using math, about maps, about understanding the world?

2. Knowing we were all raised on the Mercator Map, how does that make you feel?

3. Why do you think we (including teachers) were always given the Mercator maps?

4. What questions does this raise in your mind and what more do you want to know?

5. In your opinion, is this in any way connected to anything else we've studied over the last two years?

Project 5: Driving While Black/Driving While Brown—DWB/DWB: A Mathematics Project About Racial Profiling

[Note: This is the Teacher's version.]

The purpose of this project is to investigate *racial profiling*, or Driving While Black or Driving While Brown (DWB/DWB). African Americans and Latinos/as have complained, filed suit, and organized against what they believe are racist police practices—being stopped, searched, harassed, and arrested because they "fit" a racial profile—they are African American (Black) or Latino/a (Brown). But is this true? How do we know? And can mathematics be a useful tool in helping us answer this question?

Part I. Review Basic Probability Ideas

To understand racial profiling, students need to understand several concepts: *randomness, experiment, simulation, sample size, experimental* and *theoretical probability,* and *the law of law numbers* (i.e., the more experiments you run, the closer you come to theoretical probabilities). One way to begin discussing these ideas is to have pairs of students toss a coin 100 times (the *experiment*) and record results, then combine the class data and have the whole class together examine how the combined data comes closer to a 50–50 split than do the individual pairs (the *law of large numbers*).

Part II. Find Chicago's Racial Breakdown

Give each group of students a small bag with colored cubes to match the racial breakdown of your area. I used 9 black (African Americans), 9 tan (whites), 6 reds (Latinos/as), and 1 yellow (Asians/Native Americans) to approximate Chicago racial proportions. Do not tell students the total number of cubes or how many of each color. Students pick one cube without looking, record its color, and replace the cube. They record the results of each 10 picks in the chart below (tally marks work well). Each line in the chart below is the *cumulative total* of picks. Tell students that they are *conducting an experiment* (picking/replacing 100 times), *collecting data* (recording each pick), and *analyzing data* (determining from their simulation, how many there are of each color and the total, and what are the Chicago racial/ethnic percents).

Make sure students record the fraction and percentage of each race/ethnicity for every 10 picks in the chart.

Questions for each group. Emphasize *thorough* written explanations for all questions.

> 1. Without opening up the bag, how many cubes of each color do you think are in it? Why?

# of picks	White #	White fract.	White %	AfAm #	AfAm fract.	AfAm %	Latino #	Latino fract.	Latino %	Asian #	Asian fract.	Asian %
10												
20												
30												
40												
50												
60												
70												
80												
90												
100												
Total												

2. What happened as you picked more times, and what you think will happen if you pick 1,000 times?

Part III. Investigating DWB/DWB

Here are sample Illinois data based on police reports from 1987–1997. Racial profiling data for any locality can usually be found through web searches. In an area of about 1,000,000 motorists, approximately 28,000 were Latinos/as. Over a certain period of time, state police made 14,750 *discretionary* traffic stops (e.g., if a driver changes lanes without signaling, or drives 1–5 mph over the speed limit, police *may* stop her or him but do not have to). Of these stops, 3,100 were of Latino/a drivers. Have students use what they learned in Part II and set up their own simulation of the situation using cubes (they may need more cubes, but you can let them figure this out. In my class, they either used 3 different colored cubes of 100, or 1 of 36—this part is very difficult!). Have them pick and replace, record the data, and calculate the results of simulating 100 "discretionary" stops.

More group questions:

3. What percentage of the motorists in Part III were Latino/a?

4. What percentage of the discretionary traffic stops were Latino/a?

5. How did you set up the simulation for problem #3 (how many "Latino/a" cubes and how many total)? Why did you choose those numbers?

6. How many Latinos/as were picked out of 100 picks, and what percentage is that?

7. Do your results from your simulation experiment (#6) support the claim of racial profiling? Why or why not?

Combine individual groups' results and analyze as a whole class.

8. Individual writeup:

a. What did you learn from this activity?

b. How did mathematics help you do this?

c. Do you think racial profiling is a problem, and if so, what do you think should be done about it?

d. What questions does this project raise in your mind?

End with whole-class discussion.

Project 6: The Cost of the B-2 Bomber—Where Do Our Tax Dollars Go?

Wednesday was the first anniversary of the World Trade Center bombing. During class, you raised many questions about why it happened, how could it happen here, and what's coming next. I told you about how our government helped pay for the war in Afghanistan against the Soviet Union in the 1980s, how the CIA then considered Osama Bin Laden a friend, and how much it cost—the estimates are up to five billion dollars (that's $5,000,000,000). When I told you that, someone said, "that's our tax dollars." Absolutely, the taxes paid by people in the United States.

After you went back to doing math, Sonia told me that her brother was in the Navy. I asked why and she said, "because he didn't really know what he wanted to do." I asked her if he had a "free ride" (all expenses paid) to four years in college, would he be in the Navy, and she said no. But there isn't the money in our society for him to have a free ride to college—right?

In the 1990s, the U.S. military developed a new bomber, the B-2. It was the most expensive airplane ever developed. According to the Air Force B-2 Program Office (1998), the total cost for developing and building 21 planes (including "test planes") was $44,754.0 (in millions of dollars). That is $44,754,000,000 for 21 planes. A scholarship to an out-of-state, four-year, university like the University of Wisconsin–Madison (UW), including dorm room, food, books, tuition, and fees, is about $27,000 per year.

(By the way, the United States spends more on its military budget than the next 15 countries combined spend on theirs.)

Explain in *detail* how you solved *every* problem.

1. How much did it cost to develop each B-2 bomber?

2. How much does it cost for the full four years at UW?

3. Last June, about 250 students graduated from Simón Bolivar high school. Could the cost of one B-2 bomber give those graduates a free ride to the UW for four years?

4. For the cost of one B-2 bomber, how many years of graduating Bolivar classes (assuming the same size each year) could get free rides at UW?

5. There are 83 regular CPS high schools. Could one B-2 bomber pay for the full graduating class of 2008 (your year) to have a full, four-year ride at UW? (Assume each high school graduates 250 seniors on average ... the actual number is lower).

6. On another sheet of paper, each person has to answer the following, in good, complete sentences:

a. What do you think/feel about this situation?

b. Do you think anything should be done about this situation? If not, why not, and if so, what should be done about it?

c. Does using mathematics in this way help you understand more about the world? Is this a good use of mathematics?

d. Do you like doing mathematics projects like this? Why or why not?

Project 7: Mortgage Loans—Is Racism a Factor?

Recently, the *Chicago Tribune* published an article, "Mortgage OKs Tougher for Local Blacks, Latinos," which we will read, that has a section, *Institutional racism cited for disparity*. According to a researcher for a community organization, institutional racism is to blame for the difficulty African Americans and Latinos have in getting mortgages in Chicago (and elsewhere). But according to a spokesperson from Bank One, it is unlikely that racism was causing banks to refuse loans to Latinos and African

Americans because, after all, banks are in the business of making money from their loans.

Who is correct? Is racism a factor? Are African Americans and Latinos really having a harder time getting loans in Chicago (and elsewhere in the United States)? And if they are, does racism have anything to do with it? And how would you know the answers to these questions or what else might you have to know?

You MUST provide data from the article to justify your explanations and explain your mathematics!

1. Is it easier to get a mortgage in Chicago (for you, a Latino/a) than in the rest of the United States?

2. In paragraph 1, they say that Latinos and Blacks in Chicago are more likely to be turned down for mortgages than Whites. In paragraph 2, they say that Latinos, Blacks, and Whites have an easier time getting mortgages in Chicago than elsewhere. Isn't this a contradiction? How can both paragraphs be true?

3. We do not know how many Latinos or Whites were denied loans in the Chicago area in 2001. But suppose 1,500 Latinos were denied loans in the Chicago area. Using that estimate and data from the article, find how many Latinos did get home loans last year in the Chicago area.

4. Explain, in your own words, what disparity ratio means in the article.

5. Is the disparity ratio between Latinos and Whites greater in Chicago or nationally?

6. The Bank One representative argues that racism is not a factor because banks "want to make loans." Using data from the article/chart, list two questions you would ask him that would challenge that position.

7. Pretend, for a moment, that your group works for Bank One. What could you say to defend the article's statement: "it is unlikely that racism was causing lenders to refuse loans to Black and Latinos here [Chicago]." In other words, come up with some other explanations, besides racism, to explain why there is a disparity ratio in the Chicago area.

8. In the report cited in the article, there is the following text:

"The disparities in rejection ratios remain even if we compare applicants of the same income. Upper income African Americans [Latinos] (earning more than 120% of the median income) were denied 5.23 [3.02] times more often than upper income whites. Upper-middle income African Americans [Latinos] (earning between 100%–120% of the median income) were denied 5.22 [2.61] more often than upper-middle income whites. Moderate-income African Americans [Latinos] were rejected 4.51 [2.18] times more often than moderate-income whites while low-income African Americas [Latinos] were rejected 3.26 [1.87] times more often than low-income whites."

a. The Chicago metropolitan area annual median income is $70,500 (family of four). What is the income range of "upper income" families in Chicago?

b. Moderate-income families are defined to have incomes between $35,250 and $56,400. What percentages are those of the median Chicago family income?

c. Low-income family income is less than 50% of the median. What income range is that?

d. Create two graphs, one for African Americans, one for Latinos (you can combine them on the same graph) that shows the rejection rates for the four different income groups listed. Make sure your graphs are completely labeled, clear, accurate.

e. From the text above, do you think it's easier for a low-income Latino to get a mortgage compared to a low-income White, or for an upper-income Latino to get a mortgage compared to an upper-income White?

f. What reasons can you come up with to explain your answer to question 8e?

9. Write a good essay answering the following question (you must use data from the article or the quote above to make your argument): Is racism a factor in getting mortgages in the Chicago area?

10. What did you learn from this project, and how did you use math to earn it?

Largest Disparities in Black/White Rejection Rates*

Metropolitan Area	White Rate	Black Rate	Disparity Ratio
Milwaukee	5.70	32.01	5.61
Chicago	6.32	31.66	5.01
Cleveland	8.34	33.87	4.06
Gary	9.34	34.09	3.65
Newark, NJ	7.72	26.88	3.48
Memphis	10.50	36.23	3.45
Hartford, CT	6.98	24.06	3.45
Kansas City, MO	9.89	33.27	3.36
Bridgeport, CT	9.32	30.96	3.32
Philadelphia	7.25	24.00	3.32
U.S. Average	17.17	39.73	2.31

*Rates are percent of applicants denied a home mortgage.

Appendix 2: Methodology

This was a practitioner-research investigation (Anderson, Herr, & Nihlen, 1994) in which I used semi-ethnographic methods including participant-observation, open-ended surveys, focus-group and individual interviews of students and parents (audiotaped and transcribed), and textual analysis of documents (Hammersley & Atkinson, 1983). My data include class work and homework, unit tests, mathematics projects, standardized tests scores, and high school admission tests results. I kept a practitioner journal in which I periodically recorded reflections and observations on classroom climate, culture, and discussions; students' mathematics work and dispositions; and my interactions with students and their families. I periodically collected sets of weekly journal assignments (41 from my two-year class) that included students' reflections on their mathematical learning and thoughts about issues we studied or discussed. A research assistant took field notes of classes for one semester during the fall of 2002. I gave students several anonymous surveys about attitudes and dispositions toward mathematics, and the classes and curriculum. I collected all the real-world projects (except one) including mathematics and written work; the latter ranged from students' responses to open-ended questions to full essays and dealt with their views, interpretations, and feelings on particular issues we studied.

My informal conversations with students, families, teachers, and community members, both inside and outside of school, inform my analysis. As of this writing, my students are in various places: Some are in high school, college, gangs, prison, or the military, while some are working and others have dropped out. I maintain contact with many and with some parents as well, and I currently work on an educational project in the community. I continue to reflect on and learn from ongoing conversations with students and parents about the classes and the meaning and influence on their lives.

I triangulated my data from the multiple sources. I analyzed the data using open and focused coding (Emerson, Fretz, & Shaw, 1995) and iteratively looked for patterns and relationships that emerged and guided further analysis. Throughout my teaching and analysis, I was conscious that I was both researcher and teacher and had the power to grade and discipline students, write high school recommendation letters, etc. It was possible that students, in their journals, other writing, and speaking, wrote and said things that they thought I wanted to hear. I tried to minimize this by decoupling grades from students' writings and explicitly creating space for multiple perspectives, but nonetheless, students' views may have been influenced by our relationship (see chapter 6).

I conducted the ten parent interviews either in English (one) or a combination of English and Spanish with translation help from native Spanish-speaking, bilingual university students. I speak some Spanish but am far from fluent. I audiotaped the interviews and a bilingual research assistant transcribed them. The portions in Spanish were translated into English by a bilingual, native Spanish speaker (Mexican) or by a bilingual research assistant or me with verification by a native Spanish speaker. All interviewees had the initial questions beforehand, in Spanish.

It is always problematic to speak for others, especially when there are language, culture, race, gender, and social class distances as in this situation. Our world views are shaped by our relations to others and to power in society, and the best we may be able to do is to struggle to be as conscious as possible of that and as open to critique, challenge, and change as we can be. I am very aware of my position with respect to Rivera families and students and discuss the power dynamics throughout the book. I use students' and parents' own words at length for them to speak for themselves as much as possible, because their words convey their meanings in ways that my interpretations cannot capture (Weis & Fine, 1996). I have used students' words as they wrote them and only corrected minor grammatical issues. And, as best as I could, I tried to check my analyses with students and parents themselves. Given these caveats, I acknowledge that my interpretations are partial and necessarily limited by my own location and that there are always multiple perspectives.

Index